WITHDRAWN

D0085294

CELLULOID WARS

Sergeant Marschall of the 7th Cavalry returning from battle near the "Street Without Joy" in Vietnam. For many men combat is the single greatest experience of their lives. Millions of others have shared that experience vicariously in darkened theaters. Courtesy of John Marschall, Jr. Photo Enhancement by Stephen Mozara, Jr.

CALVIN T. RYAN LIBRARY
U. OF NEBRASKA AT KEARNEY

CELLULOID WARS

A Guide to Film and the American Experience of War

Frank J. Wetta
and Stephen J. Curley

Research Guides in Military Studies, Number 5
Roger J. Spiller, Series Adviser

GREENWOOD PRESS
New York • Westport, Connecticut • London

Library of Congress Cataloging-in-Publication Data

Wetta, Frank Joseph.
　Celluloid wars : a guide to film and the American experience of
war / Frank J. Wetta and Stephen J. Curley.
　　p. cm. – (Research guides in military studies, ISSN 0899-0166 ;
no. 5)
　Includes bibliographical references and indexes.
　ISBN 0-313-26099-0 (alk. paper)
　1. War films – United States – History and criticism.　2. United
States in motion pictures.　3. War films – United States – Catalogs.
4. War films – United States – Bibliography.　I. Curley, Stephen J.
II. Title.　III. Series.
PN1995.9.W3W48　1992
791.43'658 – dc20　　　92-8210

British Library Cataloguing in Publication Data is available.

Copyright © 1992 by Frank J. Wetta and Stephen J. Curley

All rights reserved. No portion of this book may be
reproduced, by any process or technique, without the
express written consent of the publisher.

Library of Congress Catalog Card Number: 92-8210
ISBN: 0-313-26099-0
ISSN: 0899-0166

First published in 1992

Greenwood Press, 88 Post Road West, Westport, CT 06881
An imprint of Greenwood Publishing Group, Inc.

Printed in the United States of America

The paper used in this book complies with the
Permanent Paper Standard issued by the National
Information Standards Organization (Z39.48-1984).

10 9 8 7 6 5 4 3 2 1

To our families

Jean, Kristen, and Jason Wetta
and
Betty, Bridget, Kathleen, and Matthew Curley

Contents

A Photo-essay begins on page 24.

Illustrations

Foreword

The influence of film upon twentieth century life cannot be overstated. As a movement in mass art, the rise of motion pictures is unique. No other art form has so pervaded public consciousness. No other art makes such insistent claims upon our attentions, our tastes and our sensibilities. Nor do we demand-- perhaps even expect--so much from any other artistic expression.

Film and modern life work upon each other in a complex and intimate symbiosis. We have come to take this intimacy between life and films very much for granted: we are no longer surprised when films alone create mass cultural trends and sustain them for a highly public moment. Films are a perfectly appropriate engine for cultural change in a disposable society.

Perhaps because films have so profoundly and widely affected modern life, scholars have found it difficult to make sense of them as a whole, as contributors to intellectual history, as cultural artifacts in their own right, shaping as well as reflecting their times. The shelves of film history are full of books pretending to be films. Photos have taken primacy over text, which now seems wholly incidental to the purpose of the book. It is as if their authors assume that anyone interested in film is likely to be impatient of any message not conveyed by image. The intervals between books on the order of Lillian Ross' *Picture*, for example, are substantial, and are growing.

Ross' *Picture* is a book about a film about a book about war, a biography of sorts, depicting John Huston's struggle to make a film based on Stephen Crane's Civil War classic *The Red Badge of Courage*. Huston has every intention of making a film true to Crane's original conception, but Huston's studio bosses are dubious about the commercial value of what looks to be dangerously close to an "art film." Powerful distributors fear the film will be a "flop d'estime." The fine tension between art and the market shapes how the film will look when it reaches the public screens. But while Huston and his masters disagree over his vision of the film, no one argues that when it comes to movies, war sells. Why this is so, and what the answer means for our understanding of the durability and box-office power of war films, Frank J. Wetta and Stephen J. Curley, the co-authors of *Celluloid Wars*, explain in the chapters that follow.

Not only have Wetta and Curley catalogued in some detail the influence of war upon the history of filmmaking, but they have also examined the influence of films upon war making--a question that is altogether more problematical. Once, the notion that the behavior of armies and their soldiers would be affected by what they had seen on a motion picture screen would have been laughable. War was too serious a business to be susceptible to images from idle entertainments, no matter how technically adept or historically factual. Art in any form--much less this newest form--was supposed altogether too precious to survive translation from the pleasant surroundings of a darkened theater to the mayhem of a battlefield.

And yet there is testimony, in at least one case very grim testimony, that just such translation did occur. When Lieutenant William Calley, who was eventually convicted for his role in the Vietnam War's My Lai massacre, explained that he and his comrades meant to "go to Vietnam and become Audie Murphys," the reader understands that Calley's picture of Murphy was taken from Murphy's own film autobiography *To Hell and Back*, and not from any penetrating study of Murphy's heroic career in World War II. We understand, too, that here we are seeing an effect of film played out in unintended ways.

No one is ever likely to calculate the number of war memoirists who date their interest in the military life from the first time they saw soldiering portrayed on the screen, but the number must be very large indeed. One's impression is that the number of soldiers whose identity is in some way founded upon war movies is increasing as the line between fantasy and reality blurs in both books and motion pictures. I have known career military officers who, in a strange sort of burlesque, seem to be acting out their impression of George C. Scott's portrayal of the lead role in *Patton*, knowing all the while that they were doing it, and knowing that others knew it as well. What is stranger, the performance seemed to be regarded as an acceptable pose to strike.

In his classic memoir of the Vietnam War, *Dispatches*, Michael Herr frames nicely the suspicion that we have been too accepting of war movies as paradigms for war in fact. Having just arrived in Vietnam, Herr makes his way into the field, anxious above all to "cover the war." He is eventually handed over to a grizzled infantry sergeant, who takes a look at this journalist fresh from the 'States and delivers a searing judgment: "This ain't the fucking movies over here, you know."

No artistic pose was likely to overturn this sergeant's cynicism. Just as Calley had arrived in the war zone with a celluloid standard of conduct, so had Herr. Both men were entirely innocent of the disjunctures between what they had seen on the screen and what they were about to see in war. The gulf between expectations and reality was too great to be bridged by any form of art, for art's great power lies in its suggestibility, not in its ability to depict life as it is. At their best, war movies are only vague approximations of reality; at their worst, they are merely cartoons.

Those who wish to understand war films for what they are should be able to form some intellectual basis for their standards of judgment. Professors Wetta and Curley have written and compiled this research guide for that purpose. Students of film history will find here an introduction to an important genre, one that continues to exercise a certain influence over the art of film in general. Those interested in military history, increasingly required to take serious account of war films much as they might any other sort of cultural evidence, now have in hand a valuable guide composed by two scholars who have tested their extensive knowledge and insights in the classroom for a number of years. *Celluloid Wars* fills an important place, therefore, both in the literature of film history and military history.

Roger J. Spiller
U.S. Army Command and General Staff College
Fort Leavenworth, Kansas

Preface

Through most of this century, our lives have flashed before us at twenty-four frames a second. The flickering images of what we have come to call "the movies" are our opinions of ourselves as individuals, as a people, as a race. The movies offer abundant, artistically mediated, historical evidence.

In particular, movies have been an integral part of the American experience. They combine myth, folklore, and political and social messages in ways that both reflect and direct America's world view. Americans are a warlike people, their nation born, sustained, and expanded in conflict. War is not an aberration but a fundamental element in the country's history. War films, then, have much to say about the American character. In *Patton* (1970), General Patton (George C. Scott) sets the record straight: "Men, all this stuff you heard about America not wanting to fight...is a lot of horse dung. Americans, traditionally, love to fight. All real Americans love the sting of battle." War films are unique historical documents and can be as valuable in their own way as the more traditional sources historians use to reconstruct the past--letters, diaries, memoirs, government documents, manuscripts or published records.

This guide, therefore, takes popular culture seriously. John Wayne, for example, is seen to embody a whole litany of private and public virtues as Sergeant Stryker in *Sands of Iwo Jima* or Captain Brittles in *She Wore a Yellow Ribbon*. In addition, war films reflect the insularity of Americans: "Of how many populations in the world," wrote Edward Grossman, "can it be said that many more of the people go to the movies than know what war is like?" (32). If combat is the single great experience of the common man, millions of others who were never in

combat have shared that experience vicariously in darkened
theaters or in the comfort of their living rooms. Have images of
combat often been distorted? After all, it is the duty of the
historian to interpret sources. Some filmmakers have consciously
used the medium to send political messages about war. Yet films
are historical documents even if the original intention of a
filmmaker was simply to entertain.

Entertainment, of course, reminds us that film is subject to
aesthetic, as well as historical, analysis. The war film is an
evolving art form. It has been slighted by some critics as
superficial or derivative, but it has also been capable of producing
some of the most popular and critically acclaimed movies ever
made. Few top-one-hundred lists would fail to include films like
The Birth of a Nation, *All Quiet on the Western Front*, *Patton*,
Gone with the Wind, *Casablanca*, and others that derive their
action--combat, resistance, imprisonment, escape, psychological
struggle, etc.--from war.

Because war films--like other genre and nongenre films--are
essentially polygonal in nature, this guide addresses the various
historical, aesthetic, social, and cultural questions that can be
asked of them. What is the subject of the film? Are there
several subjects? To what historical events does it allude? What
important themes are dealt with? What is the plot of the film?
Are there important subplots? Who are the various characters and
what do they represent? What ideas does the film deal with?
What techniques do the filmmakers use--docudrama, realism, satire,
fantasy? What are the historical and cultural aspects of the film?
How does the film use lighting, music, or dialogue to convey its
meaning? What moral or ethical issues are raised? What motivates
characters? What does the film say about sex, race, class,
ethnicity, stereotypes, or other issues? What are the conscious or
unconscious messages in the film? How does the film generate
meaning? What signs, symbols, and icons does it use? What
formulas and conventions does it depart from or adhere to?

Especially since the mid 1970s, increased scholarly attention has
been paid to the war film as a genre. Serious moviegoers, trying
to understand the complex issues involved in films about
American wars, need a flexible reference guide. Because this book
was written to answer that need, its plan of organization reflects
the kind of use to which it will be put.

The first two chapters are discursive essays about the artistic
and historical significance of film. Chapter 1, "'Uncle Toby's War':
War Films and Aesthetic Experience," offers some definition of
war films as a genre and then discusses in detail four critical

approaches to war films. Each approach emphasizes a different aspect of war films: their subject, their audience, their filmmakers, or their techniques. Chapter 2, "'Been to See the Elephant': Film and Combat Experience," explores some interrelationships between fictional war films and actual combat experience. Just as filmmakers have claimed that their films reconstruct the experience of actual combat, soldiers have said they behaved in battle like actors in the movies. A photographic essay compares movie stills with pictures from actual wars.

Chapters 3 through 14, the heart of this reference guide, contain lists of war films, arranged alphabetically by the individual American wars they depict: "Early American Wars" (Colonial wars, Revolutionary War, War of 1812); "Wars with Mexico" (Texas Revolution, Mexican War); "American Civil War"; "Indian Wars" (1622-1890); "New Imperial Wars" (Spanish-American War, Philippine and Moro insurrections); "The Great War" (World War I); "World War II, Wartime Films" (films released during wartime); "World War II, Postwar Films" (films released afterward); "Korean War"; "Vietnam War"; "Banana Wars and Interventions" (military actions in Third-world countries); and "Nuclear Warfare" (actual and imagined). Each chapter opens with a chronology that includes references to films that relate either directly or allegorically to specific historical events. Then a brief commentary emphasizes themes and key films in their historical context. The filmographies are generous but selective. Some wars, like the conflicts with Britain, Mexico, and Spain, have been the subject of relatively few films; in such cases we found it appropriate to list virtually all the sound movies made about those wars. Filmographies for other wars are more selective; our choice emphasizes the more significant films, the more widely available films, and "talkies." In the case of the Second World War, the number of films produced is so great that, for the convenience of the reader, we have separated them into wartime and postwar productions. In all cases, filmographies focus on English-language feature films that are American made or have been widely seen in America.

We have chosen to arrange films alphabetically by war rather than by production date, or in a single unclassified alphabetical list. The usefulness of this system of classification is clear to anyone who has tried to study war films. A single alphabetical list is uninformative, and simple chronology is easily obtainable from any number of sources--production dates are among the easiest things to discover about a film. But chronology often hides more than it reveals. While it may suggest something about the historical context of a film's production, it says little about the content of that film. Consider, for instance, this hypothetical question: how was the combat soldier treated in films about the Korean War? A chronological list of all films shows us merely what films were produced after the start of the Korean War; even if the list were limited to war films, we still would have to isolate films about the Korean War. The organization of this book makes the question easy to handle: films on the Korean War are listed separately.

This is how to use the filmographies. Each film is listed, in its section, alphabetically by title. Names of the film's director, producer, screenwriter, and principal actors follow. Next come the name of the distributing company, the year of release, and running time. Asterisks after the film's title indicate our judgment of the historical or aesthetic importance of this film. The rating system suggests which films would likely be of interest to students or fans of the war film:

****	Of interest to all
***	Of interest to most
**	Of interest to some
*	Of interest to few

Films that receive high ranking are not necessarily those of outstanding artistic or entertainment value. The ranking also includes movies judged to be of special interest or historical or political significance because of theme, message, approach, subject or other relevant criteria. *Tearing Down the Spanish Flag* and *The Green Berets*, for example, were awarded four stars because the former was America's first war film and the latter preached an important, if largely discredited, political message. The entry includes running time in minutes (m) for all films except silents (whose running time is suggested by the number of reels). A notation indicates whether the film is color or black-and-white (b/w). The names of the director (Dir.) and main actors (With...) are followed by the releasing company (see appendix for abbreviations) and the year of release. Films that receive four asterisks are annotated. Here is a sample entry from the filmography:

> *Platoon.***** 120m, color. Dir. Oliver Stone. With Tom Berenger, Willem Dafoe, Charlie Sheen, Forest Whitaker, Francesco Quinn, John C. McGinley, Richard Edson, Kevin Dillon, Reggie Johnson, Keith David, Dale Dye, Oliver Stone. Orion, 1986.
>
> The definitive Vietnam film. Oscars for picture, director, editing, and sound. An innocent recruit (Sheen) is caught between evil (Berenger) and good

(Dafoe) sergeants. The film's atmosphere is palpable
and the details of a grunt's life are frighteningly
realistic. Best scene: breath stopping exploration of a
Vietcong tunnel. Footnote: Stone, writer and director,
based it on his own experiences in Vietnam.

The book also offers two annotated bibliographies. Chapter 15,
"War Film Bibliography," lists about one hundred of the most
important books and articles written about war films. (An earlier
version of this chapter appeared in *Journal of Popular Film &
Television* 18.2 [Summer 1990]: 72-79.) This list excludes
specialized studies of a single film or filmmaker in order to focus
on works of wider interest to the genre of the war film. Chapter
16, "General Reference to Film," lists works chosen for their
overall usefulness in doing research about any type of film, but
focuses on those works of particular interest to students of war
films.

Under references to books are film bibliographies; guides to
anthologized reviews and criticism; handbooks, histories,
encyclopedias, biographies, and monographs on individual films.
Under references to periodicals are periodical indexes and a list of
the more important journals. Annotations in both Chapters 15 and
16 comment on the coverage of the work and often include
suggestions for using the work to find information about war
films. Each entry is alphabetized in standard library style by the
last name of the first author (or the title of an anonymous
work). The work's title is followed by the place of publication,
publisher's name, date of publication, and number of pages. The
annotation, written in paragraph form, follows. Here is a sample
entry from the war film bibliography:

Basinger, Jeanine. *The World War Two Combat Film:
Anatomy of a Genre.* New York: Columbia UP,
1988. 373pp.

Presents "a history of World War II combat films,
tracing their origin and evolution and indicating important
information about the system that produced them, the
individuals that created them, and the technological
developments that changed them" (introd.). Claims that the
WWII combat movie established the pattern for all combat
movies and influenced the entire concept of the war film.
Especially valuable for its fully annotated 54-page
chronological filmography of WWII and Korean combat films
from *A Yank on the Burma Road* (1942) to *The Final
Countdown* (1980). One of the better studies.

The appendices offer two lists for war-film enthusiasts. The
first ranks the top ten films about any American war; the second

lists the best films for each American war treated in this book. The appendix also contains abbreviations used for film-releasing companies. Information in this book is made easily accessible through three indexes: the main index to the text (exclusive of the filmographies); an index to film titles listed in the filmographies; and an index to directors listed in the filmographies.

The past two decades have witnessed a burgeoning industry in the publication of scholarly books about various aspects of film--production, influence, art, sociology, history, direction, and the like. This phenomenon has been fueled by the advent of video-cassettes and home video-recorders, which has made it relatively simple for almost anyone to find and view films at will. We believe that serious interest in war films will only increase. We hope that our reference guide will suggest fruitful directions for further study and be useful for war-film students as well as casual viewers.

Grossman, Edward. "Bloody Popcorn." *Harper's* Dec. 1970: 32-40.

Acknowledgements

For assistance in preparing this guide, we would like to thank Texas A&M University at Galveston, Galveston College, Tamar Fielder, Kristin Williams, Teresa Rios, Tracey Row, Betty Thompson, Michelle Nelson, Elliott Bray, and Roger Spiller. In particular, we thank Joseph G. Dawson, Texas A&M University, College Station, for his many valuable suggestions for improving the manuscript.

For assistance in locating photographs and film stills, we thank Terry Geesken of the Museum of Modern Art, Film Stills Archive; Jerry Kearns, Library of Congress; Charles R. Shrader, historian and Lieutenant Colonel, U.S.A. (Ret.); Peter Maslowski, University of Nebraska, Lincoln; and Michael Kochman, Paramount Pictures.

Frank J. Wetta
Galveston College

Stephen J. Curley
Texas A&M University at Galveston

1

"Uncle Toby's War": War Films and Aesthetic Experience

> "We may not yet recognize the tradition, but it
> [the war film] is essentially, I think, not a drama
> but a certain kind of native ritual dance."
> *--James Agee*

Strictly speaking, children have never played war. They have played *image of war*. In other words, they have geared their imitative activities to what they have been allowed to understand about how war is conducted. Unless they have had the misfortune to live in a combat zone, this meant that their picture of war has always been at second remove. When lads in twelfth-century France slapped at each other with sticks, they were imitating what their fathers, returned from the crusades, had told them about great broadsword fights against the Saladin's forces. In eighteenth-century England, they pointed sticks at each other and yelled "bang!" imitating what their uncles, returned from the Seven Years' War, told them about trading musket fire with Spaniards. The style of their imitation depended to a large extent on the stories carried home by soldiers. It has been this way for ages: the image of war is inherited by oral tradition. Telling the story helps the soldier understand his part in the emotionally muddled gathering that is war. (For instance, in Laurence Sterne's novel *Tristram Shandy*, Tristram's Uncle Toby languishes for four years with a groin wound and incommunicable war memories. After he recreates miniature fortifications of the Battle of Namur in his back yard, he can communicate his experience to others and resume his life.) Listening helps initiate the child into one of the central mysteries of the heroic-horrific adult world.

Photography changed this ritual dramatically. A Mathew Brady photograph of a twisted body half-buried in Pennsylvania mud, in a profound sense, is worth a thousand words of oral tradition. This single moment, the undeniably vivid and factual image of war, is forever frozen on a daguerreotype plate. Now both the soldier and child have ocular evidence against which they may test the accuracy of oral tradition. Making the photograph move-- literally, making *movies*--is the next step; it unsticks that moment, dilating it to ten minutes, half an hour, two hours. *The Birth of a Nation* (1915) showed all of us--war veteran and child alike--a rag-tag group of soldiers hunkering down behind an embankment of scattered sandbags. A flag pole sticks out of the mouth of a silent cannon as a soldier drags his fallen comrade behind the works; the rest of the soldiers on the line are too preoccupied to notice. This *moving* picture, worth a million words, gives us a new script for our war game. "It was like that," the movie shows us; and we can go home, make authentic flourishes with our war-stick, and kill and die as the actors had on the silver screen. We could now imitate not only what we had heard, but what we had seen. No matter how accurate the screen image is, it cuts a hard groove in our minds. We imitate actors imitating soldiers.

War films have had much to do and much to answer for. They have had to explain on-going wars to folks back home; they have had to raise morale for fighting boys overseas (a super- critical audience keenly aware of inauthentic weaponry, uniforms, behavior, battleground, or slang); and they have had to reinterpret and reconstruct wars long past. They have had to answer to the charge that they have glorified war and oversimplified its issues. The Duke of Wellington is reported to have said that the Battle of Waterloo was won on the playing fields of Eton; it has also been suggested that the Vietnam War was lost in the Hollywood jingoism of World War II films. Col. David Hackworth, the most decorated living veteran of Vietnam, described the American troops assembled in the Middle East awaiting the start of the six-week Operation Desert Storm: "Hollywood completely colors their way of seeing war" (Allen).

The following pages describe various aspects of how Hollywood sees war. They may be read as a basic introduction to the genre, as a viewer's guide, or as an outline for scholarly research. Our discussion falls into four broad categories, suggested by M.H. Abrams in *The Mirror and the Lamp* (1953). Abrams said that all theories about a work of art (he was speaking primarily of poetry and fiction) tend to emphasize one of these coordinates:

the *universe*, or the subject of the work; the *audience*, or those for whom the work is made; the *artist*, or the maker of the work; and the *work itself*, or the artifact made. These coordinates signify the purposes and aspects of a single phenomenon. In terms of cinema, the war film may have a mimetic purpose (it imitates war on the screen); a pragmatic purpose (it entertains or instructs its audience); an expressive purpose (it reveals the efforts of its collaborators or auteur); and an objective purpose (it exists as a work of art with its own techniques).

COORDINATE	ASPECT	PURPOSE
Universe	*War*	*Mimetic*
Audience	*Audience*	*Pragmatic*
Artist	*Filmmaker*	*Expressive*
Work	*War Film*	*Objective*

These categories are not constants, but variables; they may overlap considerably. Nonetheless, as this discussion will show, they are useful ways for thinking about war films.

THE MIMETIC APPROACH

War films are about war--that is their subject. One of the most popular approaches to a war film is to discuss how it deals with its subject, how it imitates the state of war that it depicts. Plato conceived of our everyday world of sense impressions as a shadow or mirror of ultimate reality, of unchangeable *Ideas*. All art, he said, is one further remove from that reality; it *imitates* reality. The Greek word *mimesis* (literally, imitation) has long been used by scholars to talk about this function of art. Discussing the imitative function of war films leads us to issues like the experience of combat, realism, historical accuracy, reenactment vs. recreation, characterization, and cultural reflection.

Realism vs. Fantasy

Recent war films have dwelled noticeably on sensational slow-motion physical violence. Some films like *The Deer Hunter* (1978) focus in such excruciating detail upon the special effects of exploding artillery shells, dismembered flesh, protruding bones and gushing blood that war films are sometimes indistinguishable from slasher films. Realism may have been pushed to its furthest extreme here. The ancient Greeks, convinced that sensational action distracted an audience from the main idea of a play, arranged things so that violence took place off-stage. Many modern war films seem to prefer the opposite tack: they exclude ideas so an audience won't be distracted from the expensive and gory special effects.

Behind all talk of realism lies this central question: does a film accurately portray the soldier's experience? The example of *Deer Hunter* offers a fascinating study in the limits of realism. Its graphic closeups of blood and guts are intensely realistic, yet its central incident--the playing of Russian Roulette for torture or profit--is historically unrealistic. It did not take place in the Vietnam War. However, the fantasy of ritualized suicide reveals something profoundly accurate about the horrific experience of that war. Similarly, a grotesque fantasy like *Apocalypse Now* (1978) is paradoxically more accurate about larger truths than the false heroics of *The Green Berets* (1968). James Agee made the point eloquently in his response to critics who found *Bataan* (1943) unrealistic. The film's story, he said, is

> as perfectly artificial, and as strongly rooted also in nature, as a good ballet or, in another aspect, Italian opera, which like the pulp story has a large believing, yet critical audience. It seems to me irrelevant to criticism on any other grounds so long as it ventures on to no other grounds.... We may not yet recognize the tradition, but it is essentially, I think, not a drama but a certain kind of native ritual dance. As such its image of war is not only naive, coarse-grained, primitive; it is also honest, accomplished in terms of its aesthetic, and true (45).

In other words, the war film can get at some profoundly human truths, not in spite of, but because of its artificiality.

Perfectly artificial fantasy in one sense is evident in the recent spate of films about returning to Vietnam to rectify the botched job. Historically the Vietnam War failed, but in the fantasy of the Rambo films (e.g., *First Blood*, 1982), a single hero succeeds. A recent study (Studlar and Desser) finds this popular evolution to film fantasy predictable. It occurred also in films made after World War II in Japan and Germany: the social trauma of a badly conducted war cries out for the comforting fantasy of mythmaking. Sullied flesh can be happily transformed into rippling muscle on superwarriors who display heroic courage and endurance in the face of superior forces. Thus, simultaneously, Hollywood gives us wartime atrocities in *Casualties of War* (1989) and wartime adventures in *Rambo*--the box office favors fantasy and encourages paradox.

Reenactment

An interesting issue concerns the purpose of imitation. Are war films supposed to reenact or reconstruct wartime experience? The most accurate reenactment of war may not be the Hollywood film but the documentary. Reviewer Manny Farber wrote that the best war films made during World War II were documentaries, not fictional narratives. Especially when we come to the action of combat, we find a hunger for authenticity so great that many fictionalized accounts of war incorporate actual combat footage. In wartime, exciting on-the-spot footage is in demand and there for the taking. But afterwards, actual footage becomes less desirable: it may draw unwanted attention to itself as the clumsy product of outdated film technology. However, movies like *Tora! Tora! Tora!* (1970) used 40-year-old footage for the sense of authenticity; in turn, its expensive battle reenactments have been sold to other filmmakers as stock footage. When the war recedes into the pages of history, some filmmakers decide to reenact actual battles, use actual weapons, costume their actors with replica uniforms. This painstaking attention to antiquarian detail often involves hiring, as extras, war-reenactment groups like those associated with the Sons of Confederate Veterans. What these groups do in front of local tourists to commemorate the anniversaries of battles can also be done in front of a movie camera. However, even here, dramatic license may alter history. An amusing example was dramatized on the screen in *Sweet Liberty* (1986) in which a group of frustrated reenacters thwart a movie director's instructions to change the conduct and outcome of an actual Revolutionary War battle.

Characterization

War films lend themselves to vivid characterizations and caricatures. Discussions of characterization sometimes sound like sociological treatises. Combat films, especially, like to play out their situations with one from each kind of ethnic group: the towheaded kid from the Midwest, the fast-talking wiseguy from Brooklyn, the athletic black from Detroit, the cowboy from Texas, the WASP officer, etc. These men, accidentally thrown together in desperate circumstances, must forget their individual differences and unite to form a fighting unit if they are to survive.

Often their survival depends heavily upon the direction given them by a hero--what myth analyzer Joseph Campbell calls the man of a thousand faces. The hero may be a man among men, a Sergeant Stryker ready, willing, and able to sacrifice himself as he leads his men to victory in *Sands of Iwo Jima*. As such the hero may bring to the group his special talent (extraordinary courage, knowledge of explosives, marksmanship, or leadership), which will prove essential to their survival. Or he may be a modern anti-hero as in *Catch-22* (1970): just before a bombing raid, when all the other pilots return a cheery thumbs-up to their leader, Yossarian signals back with a middle-finger up. He's looking for his chance to break off from the group, to row off into the distance away from war's insanity. However, most often those who are self-centered are typecast as villains, for their very selfishness (greed, cowardice, betrayal) undercuts the effectiveness of group effort.

Depending on a number of circumstances, allies may be portrayed as helpful or cowardly; enemies, as permanent or temporary. Shifting post-war concerns have often modified wartime stereotypes. For instance Russians, once glorified in films made during the Second World War when they were America's ally in action (see *The North Star*, 1943), were vilified in postwar films when they had replaced Germans as the enemy. On the other hand, almost all Germans were demonic Nazis in wartime films, but postwar or Cold-War films like *The Desert Fox* (1951) distinguish between good and bad Germans and tended to give more screen time to the good ones.

Culture: Reflector or Manipulator

Do films reflect their culture or shape it? Does a film say more about the war it is portraying--the Civil War or the Great War--or more about the period in which it was produced? *M*A*S*H* (1970) is ostensibly about the Korean conflict: members of a mobile Army surgical hospital care for the wounded as they come off the front lines in Korea, and inbetween surgeries they do what they can to maintain their sanity. The novel *M*A*S*H*, by Richard Hooker, on which the movie is based, clearly portrays the doctor-draftees as campus cutups straight from college fraternity houses of the early 1950s. In Robert Altman's cinematic version, the crewcuts are longhairs, the slang is hippie, and the attitudes are straight out of the anti-war movement of the early 1970s. In other words, *M*A*S*H* has more to say about the Vietnam than the Korean experience. (The spin-off television series is even more anachronistic: here the surgeon Hawkeye is further transformed from a 1970s hippie womanizer to a 1980s angst-ridden feminist.)

The movie *M*A*S*H* was not shown on Army posts. A board of military censors said it would undermine the faith of the enlisted man in the competence and dedication of Army doctors. But every enlisted man knew the real reason for the blackout was that the movie was anti-military, a rallying point for those discontented with the Vietnam War. Its subversive undercutting of conventional affirmation for war and war heroes both reflected the times and encouraged additional anti-military sentiment.

THE PRAGMATIC APPROACH

The Latin poet Horace said that an artist's aim is either to teach (*prodesse*) or to delight (*delectare*). Certainly much that has been written about film addresses the effect that films have on an audience. MGM studio mogul Louis B. Mayer claimed that movies were pure entertainment, period; people paid money to escape from their problems, to wallow in sentimentality, to see Andy Hardy-type fantasies. He didn't have much use for message-laden European art films (or as the saying goes: if you want to send a message, send a telegram). Director John Huston, on the other hand, believed movies could educate their audiences. That is one of the reasons why Mayer and Huston had a falling out over their joint venture *The Red Badge of Courage* (1951). The full story is told in Lillian Ross's book *Picture*. But while they disagreed about what kind of effect movies are supposed to have on an audience, they agreed that movies are made to elicit some kind of audience response.

Audience response to a war film is complex. Although it may make us uncomfortable to admit that the violent action of war on the screen is entertaining, there obviously can be a connection between box office success and special-effect explosions and slow-motion deaths. Just as obviously, film audiences learn a great deal about the nature of war in general and about the war depicted in particular. Discussion of audience response, or the pragmatic purpose of filmmaking, deal with the genre of war films, political propaganda, the delight of spectacle, and the lessons of history.

Genre: Searching for a Definition

If we think of a film as something made to affect its audience
in a certain way, then we must consider the special properties of
the genre, or category, to which it belongs. Critics distinguish
between genre and non-genre films. Non-genre films are original
treatments of a subject; genre films have a familiar look and feel.
The names of common genres come readily to mind: western,
disaster film, romantic comedy, screwball comedy, musical, crime
story, survival film, war film, and the like. Genre films have a
great deal in common with each other. Westerns have, for a
number of cultural reasons, gotten most of the attention, but the
war film is distinctive enough for the term *war films* to be used
as a subject heading for classifying books by the Library of
Congress.

However, there is disagreement about which films ought to be
included in the genre. Purists, like Jeanine Basinger (1986),
restrict the genre to the combat film which portrays actual armed
conflict between uniformed soldiers: no actual fighting, no war
film. The advantage of narrow definition, of course, is precise
analysis. Looking at a limited number of films with many
commonalities can turn up some interesting results, such as
Kathryn Kane's (1982) suggestive taxonomy of theme, character,
setting, and plot elements in the World War II combat film. The
disadvantage is that narrow definition may force us to exclude
from consideration films that most people think of as war films--
among them some of the best films in the genre. Considering the
war film without admitting discussion of *Casablanca* (1942), for
example, seems myopic. Most would agree with Stanley Solomon
(1976) that "the actual depiction of battle does not seem crucial
to the war film" (242). Some, like Brock Garland (1987), broaden
still further the definition of what constitutes a war film: his list
includes the science fiction film *Aliens* (1986) because like many
an earthbound combat film it portrays an isolated group, organized
to fight for its survival against enemy forces.

Any extended discussion of genre also reveals the problem
inherent with any neat classification in a messy world. As Robert
Pirsig says in his novel *Zen and the Art of Motorcycle
Maintenance*, classification is an intellectual scalpel that can be
wielded to divide the whole into other quite different component
parts. A war film may also belong to other overlapping genres.
To Be or Not To Be (1942) may also be treated as a comedy;
Dr. Strangelove (1964), a fantasy; *Gone With the Wind* (1939), a

so-called woman's film; *Oh, What a Lovely War!* (1969), a musical; *Fort Apache* (1948), a western. And any war film can also be considered part of a sub-genre (e.g., a service film, an Air-Force film, a WWII-air-in-the-Pacific film).

The Genre of the War Film

The war film is identifiable as a genre because individual war films share certain common elements. Thomas Sobchack points to formula plots as the distinctive aspect: "the most popular plot involves a group of men, individuals thrown together from disparate backgrounds, who must be welded together to become a well-oiled fighting machine" (110). Barry Keith Grant calls the achievement of a "common goal" the "essential concern of the war film," and he too relies on the metaphor of *welding* to define the genre: "individuals must be welded together into a unit, a platoon, in which each works for the good of all and a clear, mutually accepted hierarchy is established" (11).

Thematically, much attention has been paid to how the Hollywood western dramatizes movements between the polar opposites of civilization and the wilderness. Similarly, the war film dramatizes the polar opposites of order and chaos. Order may be seen in the individual's faith in the abiding value of love and loyalty, in a platoon's disciplined response to being under attack, in a nation's hunger for re-establishing the lasting harmony of peace. Chaos is the opposite: personal betrayal, wartime atrocities, and the forces of evil extending the war.

Genre war films contain conventional episodes with predictable outcomes. When a boyish-looking G.I., worried just before the big battle, shows a picture of his girlfriend to Sarge, we know that the boy won't make it back alive. And when a soldier's best buddy is killed, we know that the soldier will overcome his fright to lead the successful charge against the enemy machine-gun nest.

And genre war films are loaded with standard war-film iconography. Certain actors--Gary Cooper, John Wayne, Audie Murphy, William Bendix, Sylvester Stallone--lend their standard characterizations to any war film, regardless of the war depicted. Audiences respond predictably to the doughboy helmets that signify America's unpreparedness at the start of World War II; to uniforms decorated excessively with the medals of pomposity; to the evil look of Nazi accoutrements--the luger, the earflap helmet, the SS death's head insignia; to the theaters of war--the desert rock formations of the Indian wars, the snow-covered hills of Korea, the steamy jungles of Vietnam. Each of these iconographic elements has meaning attached to it because of our repeated associations with it in film after film.

The non-genre or anti-genre war film, by contrast, deliberately undercuts our expectations, runs counter to our previous viewing experiences, unsettles us with its unpredictablity. But in some sense, the originality of plot, theme, convention, or iconography is set up by our familiarity with the way things usually work in the genre. In other words, the cinematic definition of a genre war film is our touchstone for originality. A filmmaker, knowing full well that we expect to see the hero fight fair, can decide to subvert that expectation and thus draw puzzled attention to the significance of what just happened. Yet even the most original of war films still owes some debt to the genre established by other war films.

Pro-war and Anti-war Propaganda

Perhaps the most controversial observation that can be made about a war film concerns its use as propaganda. There is considerable disagreement about the wisdom of classifying film as either pro-war or anti-war. For one thing, there's no disputing taste: audiences may not agree with critics (for instance, see our lists of top films in Appendices A and B). A famous anecdote told by literary critic Leslie Fiedler concerns his viewing of *The Birth of a Nation* (1915) in Soviet Russia in the company of some high-level communist party officials. Although he fully expected the communists to follow the party line and criticize the racist-capitalist views espoused by the film, they instead fell under the spell of the film and cheered the Ku Klux Klan on to rescue the bourgeois white Southerners from the proletariat ex-slaves.

Is *Patton* (1970) pro-war or anti-war? It was hailed by the left-wing press as the latter: surely, they said, there was no mistaking the barbarousness of war and the ruthlessness--near madness--of the man who loved it so much that he slapped a shell-shocked soldier. Yet the movie was hailed by U.S. President Richard Nixon and right-wing columnists for its honest depiction of the necessity of decisiveness in war and its brilliant portrayal of heroism. Some say Nixon's fascination with the movie influenced his handling of the Vietnam War; there is evidence that he showed the film often to his advisors, identified himself with Patton, and watched the film just before ordering the bombing of Cambodia. The debate about propaganda is further complicated by statements made by filmmakers. John Huston, whose documentary about shell-shocked soldiers *Let There Be Light* (1945) was suppressed until 1980, says: "If I ever make a picture that's pro-war, I hope they take me out and shoot me" (Auster and Quart xi). Yet he cast the All-American Boy-Soldier hero Audie Murphy as star of *Red Badge of Courage*. Admittedly war films, "sometimes exaggerated, overplayed, or underplayed real-life situations," writes actor Tim Holt, but "Not all of the fighting was done with guns. The fantasies of film were an important morale factor" (Jones and McClure 15).

Entertainment or Education

Is the purpose of war film to entertain or to educate about the moral and political war? Both. War films are action adventures, the purest kind of escapism. We thrill at the sight of a handsome actor like Van Johnson bombing the enemy in *Thirty Seconds Over Tokyo* (1944). We watch with fascination studio-simulated explosions, sinkings, downings, and acrobatic deaths. We cheer the good guys and hiss at the bad guys in *Guadalcanal Diary* (1943), the first movie to portray an actual World War II American victory. We cry with a Revolutionary War wife (Claudette Colbert) as she watches her husband (Henry Fonda) march off optimistically to battle and crawl back injured in *Drums Along the Mohawk* (1939).

Yet war movies also teach us. Certainly, no one would dispute that we learn historical detail from docu-dramas like *Tora! Tora! Tora!* and *The Longest Day*. Even the 90-day wonder films of World War II "increased the public's awareness of what was going on...[and] emotionalized the war situation. This led to an exposure of the nature of the enemy and his assaulting ideology" (Lewis 21). Perhaps in the final analysis, fiction is the greater teacher. A profound truth about Nazis is vividly conveyed by the famous Ernst Lubitsch's light touch in *To Be or Not To Be* (1943); historical detail would only get in the way of the lesson.

History or Art

War films, perhaps more than most genres, are tied to specific historical events, and consequently critics look carefully at the issue of historical accuracy in war films. But such accuracy may or may not have anything to do with the quality of a film. Certainly, John Ford's attention to the historical period is integral to the artistic success of his films about the cavalry and Indian wars. But in the hands of a lesser director, like John Wayne in *Green Berets*, the detailed attention to uniforms and military slang is evidence for a lack of attention to artistic details. Some films that take great liberties with history have been artistic successes. Producer Irving Thalberg said "It is sometimes very hard to stage things with historical accuracy when you have to do so with a certain amount of dramatic emphasis" (qtd. in Isenberg 32).

As the movie industry was developing, actual armed conflict was being filmed. "The movies were obviously the ideal medium for conveying the excitement of battle scenes, and movie audiences had previously been conditioned to such scenes by the dramatic footage of the Mexican revolution, which had been shown in the newsreels," writes Garth Jowett. But in 1914, actual footage of the European war was harder to come by. "What film could be smuggled from the European front lines was eagerly snapped up, while 'faked' material was quite common" (Jowett 66). In one sense, the historical truth of documentary footage whetted our appetite for the artistic truth of fictional footage. Today's moviegoer is conditioned to suspend disbelief and learn history from artful representations; the surreptitiously *faked* documentary has given way to the overtly fictionalized modern docu-drama that splices together historical footage and reconstructions.

THE EXPRESSIVE APPROACH

The war film may be described in terms of the vision of filmmakers who conceive of and arrange the screen image. This essentially romantic (in the sense of the nineteenth century cultural movement) approach emphasizes what the creators express of themselves in film. "Genius," said British essayist Thomas Carlyle, "has privileges of its own." One of the obvious privileges of genius is to stamp its signature on a work of art. The personal forces that go into the creation of a film are influenced by *auteur* theory, collaboration, the film industry, and censorship.

Auteur Theory and the War Film

One of the most exciting and controversial aspects of film study is what critics call *auteur* theory. Just as a novel has its author, a symphony its composer, a painting its artist, so too the

film has its director, or its *auteur*. The term comes from French
filmmaker and critic Francois Truffaut who in a 1954 essay "Une
certaine tendance du cinema francais" (published in the influential
Cahiers du Cinema), called for a new cinema founded on the
genius of auteurs like Orson Welles, Jean Renoir, and Alfred
Hitchcock. Andrew Sarris, who popularized Truffaut's cause in
America, characterized the *auteur* as a technically competent
filmmaker who stamps his or her films with personally identifiable
motifs or themes (for example, Hitchcock's cameo appearances in
his own films and his focus on guilt). Whatever its shortcomings,
auteur theory helped innovative directors emerge from the faceless
bureaucracy of the studio system and influence the development of
the cinema.

Some great directors have put the stamp of their personal
vision on war films. Robert Aldrich's penchant for savagery and
anarchy is seen in *Attack!* (1956), *The Dirty Dozen* (1967), and
Too Late the Hero (1970). John Ford's romantic sensitivity and
attention to physical detail mark *They Were Expendable* (1945)
and his cavalry epics like *She Wore a Yellow Ribbon* (1949).
Howard Hawks studies the male ego in *The Dawn Patrol* (1930),
Sergeant York (1941), and *Air Force* (1943). But not everyone
subscribes to the single-vision *auteur* theory.

Collaborations

Some critics object that because film is a collaborative art, not
the product of a single mind, it will never be the product of one
auteur. Directors, after all, are part of a team that may include
studio, producer, editor, actors, composer, cinematographer, and
screenwriter. Examples of collaboration abound. Warner Brothers
influenced Raoul Walsh's hard-nosed war adventures *What Price
Glory?* (1926), *Objective Burma!* (1945), and *The Naked and the
Dead* (1958). Producer Darryl F. Zanuck, working with different
directors, made possible the two similar, giant war docu-dramas:
The Longest Day (1962) with director Ken Annakin and *Tora!
Tora! Tora!* (1970) with directors Richard Fleischer, Toshio
Masuda, and Kinji Fukasaku. Editor Dede Allen teamed up with
director Arthur Penn on a number of movies, including the
Indian war fantasy *Little Big Man* (1970). John Ford's decisions
were strongly influenced by the peculiar talents of the actors in
his famous stock company--Ward Bond, Victor McLaglen, and John
Wayne. Composer Dimitri Tiomkin scored 1940s war documentaries
both for Frank Capra and John Huston. Cameraman Russell
Harlan collaborated with director Lewis Milestone on *A Walk in*

the Sun (1945). Writer-producer Beirne Jun Lay worked with directors on a number of air warfare films like *Twelve O'Clock High* (1949) and *Above and Beyond* (1953). In sum, the term *auteur* has been broadened to include anyone, or any team, who has left an identifiable mark on film.

The Film Industry and the War Film

Understanding the film industry from which these so-called *auteurs* emerged helps us understand forces that shaped war films. Films must be appreciated as a business as well as an art form. This was recognized from the beginning: financing an expensive extravaganza like *The Birth of A Nation* required a great deal of capital. So businessman Harry E. Aitken "sold" it and other motion pictures as one would sell commodities in a futures market. He sold shares in a product that did not yet exist but one which he promised to deliver at a certain date. Aitken's practice was institutionalized and wedded to a kind of genteel blackmail by Adolph Zukor, head of the first big film company, Paramount Pictures. Through the practice of "block-booking," Zukor pressured theater owners to buy sight-unseen an entire year's output of Paramount's films. They had little choice if they wanted to exhibit any of the popular Paramount films. Samuel Goldwyn and Louis B. Mayer, of Metro-Goldwyn-Mayer, took Zukor's practice a step further by purchasing a string of theaters and thus exercising a virtual monopoly over production, distribution, and exhibition. Independent theater owners, to protect themselves from being driven out of business by Paramount and MGM, formed the First National Exhibitors Circuit: they contracted with big name stars (Charlie Chaplin was their first) to make movies exclusively for their theaters. Then the film artists staked out their own territory: United Artists Corporation, founded in 1919 by D. W. Griffith, Charlie Chaplin, Mary Pickford, and Douglas Fairbanks, enabled actors or producers to unite as business partners while working on a particular film.

In some ways the process came full circle. What Aitken had done--assemble financial backing for a film--the actors, director, or producer could do too. With time, the industry giants fell. In 1948, a trust-busting decision forced studios to relinquish their strangle hold on distributors and exhibitors; in the 1950s, television cut into the studios' profits and weakened them still more. By the 1960s, studios had become little more than financial brokers. In fact, the modern studio is modeled much on the pattern of United Artists--it owns no production lot, no stable of actors, no permanent technical staff, no string of theaters. It is a kind of marketing distributor for the independent productions brought to it. One often hears that a movie is simply *released* rather than *made* by a certain studio.

Censorship and Control

Censorship--conscious or unconscious--also influences the kind of war films an audience is permitted to see. Censorship may influence what filmmakers select or edit out: for instance, a screenwriter or director can pretend the horrific does not exist as they pay homage to the heroic aspects of combat. The Hollywood studio system tended to produce *clean* battle scenes over and over again during the Second World War. Paul Fussell, in his 1989 book *Wartime*, makes the point that film steered clear of dismemberment and decapitation (common results of actual battles) and made it look as if upper-arm wounds were the only injuries suffered. Clearly, what was good for morale was good for the movies. The Office of War Information made sure that films boosted the war effort: the war-film American G.I. almost without exception learned how to fight effectively for the right; the enemy suffered from severe personality defects that undermined his effectiveness. Thus though Americans might suffer temporary setbacks, they would surely fight on until they won the war.

Perhaps an even stronger censorship is exercised by market pressures. When box office receipts for war films fall, as they typically do, after wartime, a film may be withheld from distribution or halted in production. That is one way the market controls what we see. For instance, the unpopularity of the Vietnam War meant that for a very long time moneyed interests were unwilling to back a war movie about the Vietnam experience. It was not until the financial success of Rambo-type fantasies about superhuman G.I.'s returning to rescue M.I.A.'s and forgotten P.O.W.'s, that Vietnam became a permissible topic for film. Special-interest groups also become a force for censorship when they threaten boycotts if a film is made or released; profit-conscious backers may withdraw their support from the targeted film and be much less willing to associate themselves with other potentially controversial films in the future.

One form of censorship, peculiar to the war film, is caused by the granting or withholding of military assistance. Any film that uses combat scenes profits from material assistance offered by the

Department of Defense (DoD). Army-supplied planes, tanks, artillery, and shooting locations save filmmakers big money. But not everyone who asks shall receive. John Wayne sought and got assistance for *Green Berets*; Francis Ford Coppola sought and was denied assistance for *Apocalypse Now*. The DoD supports only those films portraying U.S. military forces favorably. Until the Vietnam War helped fuel anti-military sentiment in the U.S., requests were rarely turned down. After Vietnam, the assistance granted has been much more selective. Those who seek assistance must first submit a script to the DoD. Then they must revise objectionable parts. In Coppola's case, the Army objected to the portrayal of an Army officer as a government-sanctioned assassin; Coppola refused to alter his script. So he had to settle for what he could afford to buy: he used as props military surplus equipment that had never been deployed in Vietnam. Most other filmmakers, hungry for what is essentially a subsidy of their films, have succumbed to pressure and altered their scripts to suit the military.

THE OBJECTIVE APPROACH

A fourth approach to the war film is aesthetic, in terms of film itself. The motto over the head of the MGM lion "Ars gratia artis," literally "Art for art's sake," emphasizes this aspect. A war film, a ribbon of exposed celluloid artfully spliced together, has its techniques. In approaching the film as object, we look at the filming process, the screen image, composition, the use of time, editing, and sound.

The Filming Process

A war film is the product of a complex process. John Wayne, for example, first purchased the rights to film Robin Moore's 1965 novel *The Green Berets*. He put together financing and packaging, an $8-million deal naming him as director in collaboration with television director Ray Kellogg. Wayne wrote letters to the Department of Defense asking for their "cooperation," the code word for free material assistance that would otherwise have taken a prohibitive amount of money to buy. The Army looked over the script and found it worth supporting for propaganda purposes--although the script did criticize the way the war was being handled, on the whole it presented a favorable view of America's involvement. The script echoed World War II films about loners who, after they witness American heroism or enemy atrocities, join the fighting team. In the film *The Green Berets* (1968), a career officer (Wayne) convinces a skeptical journalist (David Janssen) that America must use its might to oppose the savage Viet Cong.

During the film's pre-production phase, Wayne cast the roles: Wayne himself (the big-name star for many war films), his son Patrick Wayne, Jim Hutton, Janssen, Raymond St. Jacques, Bruce Cabot, and Jack Soo. The U.S. Army supplied two technical advisors (one a Green Beret who had already served in Vietnam), a cast of extras, military equipment, uniforms, guns, ammunition, and the location--the jungle-like base for advanced guerrilla training at Fort Benning, Georgia. Walter Simonds, the art director, supervised construction of a replica Viet Cong base (which was later donated to the Army).

During the film's production phase, depending on a combination of what the shooting schedule said and what the weather permitted, scenes were filmed as efficiently as possible. This meant, as it does for most movies, that scenes were shot out of chronological sequence. There were scripts to follow, but shooting scripts were often discarded in favor of ad libbing. Actors deferred to the judgment of actual Green Beret soldiers on the set who made sure the technical and colloquial language of this war was used accurately.

During the post-production phase, rough footage was cut and reassembled, sound was mixed in, and screen credits were added. The final copy of the film was given to Warner Bros.-Seven Arts to be released in the spring of 1968 (Madsen 10). In sum the film did everything a successful war film ought to do. It was a careful effort with stars to draw an audience, expensive special effects, and extensive military cooperation. Yet it fell flat (for a John Wayne film) at the box office and was judged a critical flop. Among criticisms aimed at the film were its military jingoism and its inauthentic look and feel (the jungle looked like Georgia and, at the film's conclusion, the sun appeared to set in the East).

Tone

Tone is the film's total effect, the result of the combination of many small details. Any film made today rests on the shoulders of all its predecessors. What we have come to accept as a good war film incorporates techniques that have evolved over the years.

Renoir called his treatment of World War I *La Grande Illusion* (1937); in some sense, all war films create grand illusions of life through screen images.

In *Patton* (1970), for example, tone is everything. The tone of the famous opening shot is vibrant and riveting. The background is a huge, brilliantly colored American flag. This flat, symbolic backdrop serves as a foil for the round, blustering character of Patton (George C. Scott), who emerges as its personification. His eccentric uniform--blue and orange sashes, leather riding crop, gold and silver medals, and gun belt--his gravelly voiced jocular obscenities, and his military bearing, focus our attention. By contrast the tone of the film's conclusion is quiet and subdued. A now-aged general, bowed by politics, fades into insignificance in his drab overcoat as he and his dog waddle away into the depths of a colorless winter backdrop. The slow-exposure filmstock of the opening sequence captures the exact color of the threads on his battle ribbons, the glint off the ivory handled pistol in his holster. The fast-exposure filmstock used for the Battle of the Bulge reveals grainy images of a gray war, illuminated only by the yellow flash of tank cannon.

Composition

Composition, or the use of the camera, is also evocative. In *Tora! Tora! Tora!* (1970), for example, long panoramic shots angled down from the perspective of Japanese pilots over Pearl Harbor alternate with hectic closeups of individual American soldiers on the ground. The composition enhances the notion of contrasting Japanese control and American helplessness. The choice of camera shot interprets the meaning of a scene: at one point the camera lingers over the frustratingly slow fingers of the Japanese emissary, typing the warning message that will be delivered too late to be useful. The fixed-position camera in that scene conveys excruciating stasis; the mobile camera that follows an intelligence officer (E.G. Marshall) as he runs seeking help in vain from empty office to empty office in the Pentagon conveys a different kind of frustration. And when the camera lens zooms in to take an extreme close-up of Admiral Isoroku Yamamoto, the mastermind of the attack, it underlines the truth of his final pronouncement, the fear that this attack has awakened a "sleeping giant and filled him with terrible resolve."

Time

Screen time gives the heightened illusion of actual time; individual films illustrate the range of effects. *The Longest Day* (1962) in 169 minutes recounts the actual events of two days, 5-6 June 1944. *The Battle of the Bulge* (1965) in 162 minutes dramatizes a simplified version of a multi-day encounter; it splices reality as if it were film, reshuffling and recombining so that one character in one skirmish portrays what actually happened to a number of characters in many skirmishes. Jumpcuts take us from a German tank to the inside of an American bunker; some events are obviously happening simultaneously (sometimes shown with split-screen or parallel editing). In *The Deer Hunter* (1978), when director Michael Cimino--who won an Academy Award for editing--spends almost half his film on a wedding ceremony and reception, time seems permanent and reassuring. We watch a ritual that reinforces the tradition that bonds generation to generation. Then suddenly he jumpcuts from the comradery of a Northeast winter into a horror of a Vietnamese summer: the groom and his ushers have traded their tuxedos for jungle fatigues and are fighting for survival. Tradition is threatened. Flashbacks create a sense of the psychological instability of time in *Passage to Marseille* [sic] (1944). Time seems to fold back on itself: 4) the exiled French bomber pilot (Humphrey Bogart) in 1944 becomes 3) the castaway rescued at sea while France's Maginot Line gives way to German onslaught, 2) the political prisoner on Devil's Island, and 1) the crusading French newspaperman convicted on charges trumped-up by fascists. Every moment is flashback. Then time period by time period, director Michael Curtiz flashes forward to the doomed "present." In film, screen time is often distorted to represent the psychological trauma of dreams, fantasies, memories, or madness. Screen time also pauses at select moments. For instance, the first 45 days at sea aboard the U-Boat in the magnificent German-made *Das Boot* (1981) slip by almost imperceptibly: a snippet of a conversation one day, a song another day--they are all that reminds us that time passes. But when the submarine sits on the bottom off Gibraltar, time stops: individual rivets pop from the pressure, the engines quit, breathing becomes labored and audible, every second is a perceptible burden.

Editing

After the footage is shot it is put together, or edited. *The Killing Fields* (1984) shows how editing can reveal meaning. The opening credits are followed by text that introduces the action in Cambodia as a "side show war" and takes us to an exact day, 7 August 1973. This description tells us that what we are about to see is intended to be exact history and puts it in perspective. Calm conversation is punctuated by the abrupt violence of an exploding grenade tossed by passing motorcylcists. During evacuation, the whir of helicopter blades and the frantic scrambling of would-be passengers shouting in one scene is juxtaposed to the eerie calm that follows: the choppers gone, everything is silent and leisurely. The civilized *New York Times* office of newspaperman Sidney Schanberg (Sam Waterston) cuts to the hellish mud-pit labor camp where his former translator Dith Pran (Haing S Ngor) sucks wounds on cattle to stay alive. The repetition of capture-and-escape scenes; Pran's contrasting relationships with the ambitious Schanberg and a warm-hearted Khmer Rouge father; Schanberg's failed rescue of Pran mirrored by Pran's failed rescue of the Khmer Rouge father's son; the metaphor of the burial-pit field that Pran finds himself in; the alternating shots of Pran and Schanberg during their reunion at the refugee camp--all these are enhanced by careful editing of shots. Sometimes editing can also be part of the filming process as when an uncut shot is set up to reveal mise-en-scene juxtapositions. Director Roland Joffe uses an effective mise-en-scene shot when the camera shows in the foreground Pran begging for the lives of newsmen, huddled anxiously in the background.

Sound

Sound is also a complex interpretive tool in the hands of a competent filmmaker. In *The Red Badge of Courage* (1951), sound underlines meaning. For example, the human voice is used on two planes. The voice-over narration by actor James Whitmore comes from the text of Stephen Crane's novel: it makes clear what certain scenes are supposed to mean. Interestingly enough the narrator was added by MGM vice president Dore Schary after director John Huston finished the movie; MGM was fearful that otherwise the audience would respond unfavorably (as they had at preview screenings when some laughed at what was supposed to be a solemn death scene and walked out). Human voice is also used effectively on screen to emphasize the ordinariness of the human condition, even within the extraordinary circumstances of war. It is deliberately emphasized in dialogue: frightened soldiers brag to allay their fears; a cheerful soldier (Andy Devine) babbles on incessantly; a general tells the same tepid joke about eating hardtack to several units before battle. The nervous buzz of pre-battle conversation explodes into the shouts and gunfire of battle, which in turn give way to the tweet of birds reasserting nature's continuation at battle's end: we wonder how things could once again sound so normal. The wild yell of charging rebels is juxtaposed to the quiet, hesitant conversation of a cowered, captured rebel who admits he never spoke to anyone from Ohio before.

The sound effects of war--rifle shots, exploding bombs, a dramatic musical score--have also become a staple of the war film. The bigger the bang, the more exciting the battle. Explosions, of course, dramatize the cataclysmic nature of war. They separate us from the ordinary. Music, to which we respond like Pavlov's dogs to a dinner bell, carries us emotionally through particularly important scenes. Perhaps the most famous use of music in a war film comes to us--surprisingly--from the silent era in King Vidor's *The Big Parade* (1925) in which soldiers synchronously march and die in step to the distant drum of some universal unheard rhythm. In the era of soundtracks, insistent atonal music (like Philip Glass's score for *Hamburger Hill*, 1987) makes us feel pre-battle tensions. Rousing martial music pumps our adrenalin during battles. Slow, plaintive melodies make us weep over the dead. Of special note are the musical motifs which end a war film. Sentimental renditions of patriotic music tend to reaffirm the values of what the soldiers are fighting for. At the end of *Red Badge*, for example, the problems of the movie are neatly and permanently resolved by the rousing warhorse "Battle Hymn of the Republic." But at the end of *The Deer Hunter* (1978), when the characters join in singing a halting tear-choked version of "God Bless America," we have the sense of no resolution at all.

Abrams, M.H. *The Mirror and the Lamp*. New York: Oxford UP, 1953.

Agee, James. *Agee on Film: Reviews and Comments by James Agee*. Vol. 1. New York: Grosset and Dunlap, 1967. 2 vols.

Allen, Henry. "Movies Color Soldier's View of War: In the Desert, Glory Is Just a Shot Away." *Houston Chronicle* 6 Jan. 1991: A18.

Auster, Albert, and Leonard Quart. *How the War was Remembered: Hollywood and Vietnam*. New York: Praeger, 1988.

Basinger, Jeanine. *The World War II Combat Film: Anatomy of a Genre*. New York: Columbia UP, 1986.

Campbell, Joseph. *The Hero With a Thousand Faces*. Princeton, NJ: Princeton UP, 1968.

Crane, Stephen. *The Red Badge of Courage: An Episode of the American Civil War*. 1895. New York: Harper, 1957.

Farber, Manny. "Movies in Wartime." *New Republic* 3 Jan. 1944: 16-20.

Fussell, Paul. *Wartime: Understanding and Behavior in the Second World War*. New York: Oxford UP, 1989.

Garland, Brock. *War Movies: The Complete Viewer's Guide*. New York: Facts on File, 1987.

Grant, Barry Keith, ed. *Film Genre Reader*. Austin: U of Texas P, 1986.

Hooker, Richard. *M*A*S*H*. New York: Pocket, 1969.

Isenberg, Michael T. *War on Film: The American Cinema and World War I*. London: Associated UP, 1981.

Jones, Ken D., and Arthur F. McClure. *Hollywood at War: The American Motion Picture and World War II*. New York: Barnes, 1973.

Jowett, Garth. *Film: The Democratic Art*. Boston: Little, 1976.

Kane, Kathryn. *Visions of War: Hollywood Combat Films of World War II*. Ann Arbor: U of Michigan P, 1982.

Lewis, Jacob. "World War II and the American Film." *Cinema Journal* 7 (Winter 1967-68): 1-21.

Madsen, Alex. "Vietnam and the Movies." *Cinema* 4 (Spring 1968): 10-13.

Pirsig, Robert. *Zen and the Art of Motorcycle Maintenance*. New York: Bantam, 1975.

Ross, Lillian. *Picture*. New York: Rinehart, 1952.

Sarris, Andrew. "Notes on the Auteur Theory in 1962." rpt. Gerald Mast and Marshall Cohen, eds. *Film Theory and Criticism: Introductory Readings*. New York: Oxford UP, 1974. 500-15.

Sobchack, Thomas. "Genre Film: A Classical Experience." *Film Genre Reader*. Ed. Barry Grant. Austin: U of Texas P, 1986. 102-13.

Solomon, Stanley J. *Beyond Formula: American Film Genres*. New York: Harcourt, 1976.

Sterne, Laurence. *The Life and Opinions of Tristram Shandy*. 1759-67. New York: Oxford UP, 1983.

Studlar, Gaylyn, and David Desser. "Never Having to Say You're Sorry: *Rambo*'s Rewriting of the Vietnam War." *Film Quarterly* 42.1 (Fall 1988): 9-16.

The wounded wait at Savage's Station following the Battle of Cold Harbor (1864) during the Civil War. Courtesy of the Library of Congress.

24

Sometimes films capture the look and mood of real war. Here, in *Gone With the Wind* (1939), Scarlett O'Hara (Vivien Leigh) walks among the wounded at the railroad station in Atlanta. Courtesy of the Museum of Modern Art/Film Stills Archive. ©1939 Turner Entertainment Co. All Rights Reserved.

Sergeant Alvin York contemplates Sergeant Alvin York, portrayed by Gary Cooper in *Sergeant York* (1941). Courtesy of the Museum of Modern Art/Film Stills Archive. ©1941 Turner Entertainment Co. All Rights Reserved.

"We live in the trenches out there. We fight. We try not to be killed, but sometimes we are—that's all," says Paul Baumer (Lew Ayres), in *All Quiet on the Western Front* (1930), about the experience of combat. Courtesy of the Museum of Modern Art/Film Stills Archive. Copyright © by Universal Pictures, a Division of Universal City Studios, Inc. Courtesy of MCA Publishing Rights, a Division of MCA Inc.

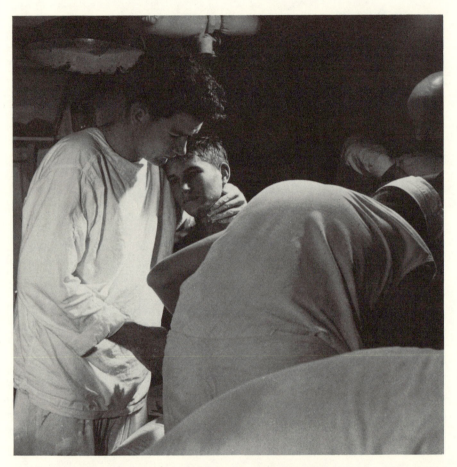

Held by a medic, Private J. B. Slagle, U.S.A., is treated for wounds on board the hospital ship *Solace* after the fighting at Okinawa (April 1945). Courtesy of National Archives, photo no. 80-G-413963.

"I would think of John Wayne and the brave men who raised the flag on Iwo Jima that day. I would think of them and cry," wrote Ron Kovic about *Sands of Iwo Jima* (1949). The film *Born on the Fourth of July* (1989) is based on Kovic's autobiography. Courtesy of the Museum of Modern Art/Film Stills Archive. Still from *Sands of Iwo Jima* courtesy of Republic Pictures Corporation.

The anxiety of combat shows on the faces of troopers of the 101st Airbourne on patrol in Vietnam. Courtesy of U.S. Army Military History Institute, Carlisle Barracks.

A sergeant (Anthony Berrie) of the 101st Airbourne holds a wounded comrade (Dylan McDermott) in *Hamburger Hill* (1987), a film based on the Battle of Hill 937 in Vietnam. Courtesy of Paramount Pictures. *Hamburger Hill* Copyright © 1991 by Paramount Pictures. All Rights Reserved.

2

"Been to See the Elephant":
Film and Combat Experience

"The life of man upon earth is a battlefield."
Job 7:1

"People go to the *movies* instead of *moving*! Hollywood
characters are supposed to have all the adventures for everybody
in America, while everybody in America sits in a dark room and
watches them have them!" exclaims Tom in Tennessee Williams'
play *The Glass Menagerie* (1944-45). "Yes, until there's a war.
That's when adventure becomes available to the masses!
Everyone's dish, not only Gable's! Then the people in the dark
room come out of the dark to have some adventures themselves--
goody, goody! It's our turn now, to go the South Sea Island--to
make a safari--to be exotic, far-off!"
    Like Tom we are trapped in our own mundane worlds of the
warehouse, night-school course, and rear apartment--the common
routine of life. Most of us never leave the dark room for the
South Sea's adventure--not even in wartime. Ironically, despite the
number of great and little wars of the twentieth century, few
have ever seen a battle, experienced the violent communal effort
of combat, or been possessed by the mad urge to destroy that
frequently overcomes men in battle. Our experience of war comes
mainly from watching movies--and many of us believe that we
understand the nature of war and the experience of combat
because we have watched movies about war and men in combat.
This chapter, an essay on the relation of film to the experience
of combat, reflects the relationship between fiction and reality.
Walt Whitman observed that the true experience of the soldier is
essentially beyond the comprehension of outsiders (viewers in

the dark room). The "interior history" of war--"its practicality, minutiae of deeds and passions, will never be even suggested." Who, he asked, could really understand the "incredible dauntlessness, habits, practices, tastes, language,... fierce friendships,... appetites, rankness, and animality, and a hundred unnamed lights and shades of camp?" Even this poet who had witnessed so much of war firsthand felt inadequate except to provide only "a few stray glimpses into that life, and into those lurid interiors" (Whitman 779).

Nevertheless, we rely upon poets, writers, and filmmakers to see for us, and we are especially edified when they approach this topic with honesty and intelligence. In this sense, motion pictures are important sources for historical understanding.

THE PAST AND HISTORY

In a thoughtful essay on the nature of historical understanding, J.H. Plumb drew a distinction between the *past (self-satisfying myth)* and *history (what really happened)*. "Man, from the earliest days of recorded time," he pointed out, "has used the *past* in a variety of ways: to explain the origins and purposes of human life, to sanctify institutions of government, to give validity to class structure, to provide moral example, to vivify cultural and educational processes, to interpret the future, to invest both the individual life or a nation's with a sense of destiny." *History*, on the other hand, is the attempt to observe events of former times with "detachment and insight and intellectual comprehension" (11).

Even *history*, however, is not the real thing; it is a reconstruction not a recreation of events, a perception of what really happened, always imperfect, incomplete, and fragmentary. The events of former times exist only in the surviving evidence, brought to life through our imagination. Unlike the physical scientists, historians or filmmakers-as-historians cannot return to the subject in any immediate way; the evidence is always incomplete at best, the memories imperfect. They simply cannot go back into time and retrieve or recreate events. The historian "must collect, interpret, and then explain his evidence by methods which are not greatly different from those techniques employed by the detective" (Winks viii).

Ocular Evidence

Traditionally, evidence examined by historians is found in written documents: letters, diaries, autobiographies, memoirs, newspapers, government records, and the like. But scholars can look to nontraditional sources as well: the architecture of industrial America, for example, or the oral testimony of participants in events both great and small, and the elements of popular culture, including advertisements, songs, folklore, fashion, popular literature, and motion pictures. Garth Jowett has called attention to the great significance of the latter as indicators of American life and history in his definitive social history of the movies.

War films in particular occupy a special place in the corpus of unorthodox evidence because they reflect an experience fundamental to the development of American society. The "average American cannot move without bumping into the country's military past"-- from the very structure of American government (federal-state relations) to the mundane articles of everyday life--greenbacks, wristwatches, or computers (Perret 563). And, we need to add, wars have given the motion picture much of its subject matter.

When war films attempt to portray events from the American military experience they frequently reflect the *past* as defined by Plumb: they have sanctified the institutions of government and the obligations we owe it (*Sergeant York*, 1941), they have provided moral example (*Bataan*, 1943), and they have invested their audiences with a sense of destiny (*Drums Along the Mohawk*, 1939) or racial pride (*Glory*, 1989). On the other hand, war films have also tried to reconstruct events as they really happened with detachment (*Tora! Tora! Tora!* 1970), insight (*A Walk in the Sun*, 1946), and intellectual comprehension (*Platoon*, 1988). Frequently war films bring together myth (the *past*) and reality (*history*) as in John Ford's classic cavalry trilogy, *Fort Apache*, (1948), *She Wore a Yellow Ribbon*, (1949) and *Rio Grande* (1950).

All films--those of serious intent (*The Deer Hunter*, 1978) or mere adventure stories (*The Dirty Dozen*, 1967)--carry messages about American society in general, and the American experience of war in particular. Historians can use films much as they use other kinds of sources.

Motion pictures have been called "the most highly developed and most engrossing of the popular arts." Their "pervasive and disturbing power" reflect the "direct correspondences between the movies and life" (Warshow 24-25). Because of this power and connection to the experiences of real life, movies offer us a unique source for understanding the forms and content of American society. Art imitates life; life imitates art. Movies shape and reflect the things we do, the styles of our behavior, our values and attitudes. "We had arrived late in the afternoon [a soldier said about his first day in Vietnam] and it was getting dark. After they gave us our bunks, they let us off for the evening. I went walking and saw this outdoor screen and movie. So I went closer to see what the movie was. It was John Wayne in *The Green Berets"* (qtd. in Santoli 104).

Michael T. Isenberg, in his comprehensive survey of American-made films about the First World War, lamented that this rich lode of evidence contained in war films remains largely unexamined because of the inaccessibility of many old films and the lack of an accepted methodology for interpretation. In addition, there exists a certain prejudice among scholars with regard to film as a legitimate source for historical inquiry. "To date, the historian of ideas has been concerned primarily with the thought of social and intellectual elites." He often disdains popular culture as unworthy of serious consideration (25-33).

Myth and Illusion

But popular myths engendered by Hollywood have much to offer in understanding both the American *past* and American *history.* "Myths may often distort or conceal, but these stories are nevertheless always true in the sense that they express deeply held beliefs" (Hellmann ix). For instance, John Wayne's *The Green Berets* (1968) showed "Americans their preferred self-image: a small band of rugged yet pure-hearted individualists, on a frontier landscape, aiding pastoral natives [the South Vietnamese] against...wild savages [the North Vietnamese and the Viet Cong] emerging from the anarchic forest" (Hellmann 92). It was America's Manifest Destiny at war.

Thus films often present myth and romance in bold, vivid images accessible to a vast audience.

Consider John Keegan's reflection on one of the great scenes in military history. He wrote of the English stand at Agincourt in terms of mythic, movie imagery. Laurence Olivier's production of Shakespeare's *Henry V* (1944) became the mirror in which the British people saw themselves. The image of that battle in the film is "a composition of strong verticals and horizontals and a conflict of rich dark reds and Lincoln greens against fishscale grays and arctic blues." It is "Olivier in battle armour; it is an episode to quicken the interest of any schoolboy bored by a history lesson, a set-piece demonstration of English moral superiority and cherished ingredient of a fading national myth." But, Keegan concluded, we ought to compare this technicolor myth (the *past*) with real war and the hard natural light which exposes the hidden *history* of "slaughter-yard behavior and outright atrocity" (78).

Americans, too, have their own technicolor myths. *She Wore a Yellow Ribbon* (1949) is an example. Bosley Crowther called John Ford's film "a vivid illustration, a composite of all the legends of the frontier cavalrymen." The movie "blazed with bold and dashing courage, unabashed sentiment, the grandeur of rear-guard heroism." The sound tract reported "the rattle and clang of saber sheaths, and the trump and agitation of wheeling horses hoofs." Crowther concluded, "I challenge any viewer to resist a bit of a tingle down the spine even now when he sees those mounted troopers ride out from the frontier fort" (71).

Images of war and warriors may be purposely stylized and romanticized. In *Henry V* (1944) Olivier, who both directed and starred in the film, places his actors within sets copied from two-dimensional medieval art--paintings come alive. Similarly, when John Ford put his company of actors within the panorama of Monument Valley, Frederic Remington's paintings come alive. The myth of the American West is summed up neatly in the spoken commentary at the conclusion to Ford's *Fort Apache* (1948): "So here they are--the dog-faced soldiers, the regulars, the fifty cents-a-day professionals, riding the outposts of a nation. From Reno to Fort Apache, from Sheridan to Stark, they were all the same, men in dirty-shirt blue, and only a cold page in the history books to mark their passage. But wherever they rode, and whatever they fought for--that place became the United States" (qtd. in Anderson 125).

In this and his other movies, director John Ford "is the keeper of a folk memory compounded of the ideals of America's founding fathers, the legends of the past, the aspirations of her immigrant peoples" (qtd. in O'Connor 115). His westerns and war movies have something valuable to say about our sense of the American past.

Thus films can be about illusion and mythical subjects and at the same time say something important about the experience of war in particular and the experience of a nation in general. Myths, after all, are not lies. Myths reveal the essence of a people's ideals, virtues, values, aspirations, and self-image. John Wayne was given a posthumous congressional gold medal not because he was a real cavalryman or real Marine hero, but rather because he came to personify in his films American national values. Here reality and illusion became one. Wayne was a real hero to people and a mythical figure to emulate. "It is astonishing how often American GIs in Vietnam approvingly referred to John Wayne, not as a movie star, but as a model and a standard" (Baritz 37). Yet, if this is the *past* of our immigration, what about *history*? George MacDonald Fraser, historian and writer of lively well-researched historical fiction, argued that films can capture correctly the essence of things in profoundly meaningful ways:

> There is popular belief that where history is concerned, Hollywood always gets it wrong--and sometimes it does. What is overlooked is the astonishing amount of history Hollywood has got right, and the immense unacknowledged debt which we owe to the commercial cinema as an illuminator of the story of mankind. This although films have sometimes blundered and distorted and falsified, have botched great themes and belittled great men and women, have trivialized and caricatured and cheapened, have piled anachronism on solecism on downright lie--still, at their best, they have given a picture of the ages more vivid and memorable than anything in Tacitus or Gibbon or Macaulay, and to an infinitely wider audience. (xi-xii)

But some critics are a great deal more skeptical about the benefits: "if the history as presented by the movies turns out to be a muddy blur of fantasy and fact, the consequences cannot be good" (Bernstein).

REALISM

Filmmakers have long aspired to be historians. If they are careless historians, it is not always from a want of caring. The attempt to reconstruct events with serious intent began with the very origins of Hollywood itself. D.W. Griffith--an aspiring historian-as-filmmaker if ever there was one--predicted, "We will be able to teach history in the future through the film medium. Realism will be the key element in the historical film" (qtd. in Cook 80) Griffith modeled many scenes on Mathew Brady's photographs and even employed Civil War veterans as advisors in filming *Birth of a Nation* (1915; abbreviated sound version, 1930). To reconstruct the clash of armies, he combined "extreme long shots of the battlefields with medium and close shots of bloody hand-to-hand fighting to evoke the chaotic violence of combat itself." Griffith reconstructed the siege of Petersburg, the burning of Atlanta, and Sherman's march with such skill that their "intensity is still compelling, despite six decades of technological refinement" (Cook 80). Griffith, of course, put these reconstructed events in the context of mythmaking--an almost perfect mix of romance and realism--the moonlight and magnolia myth of the Old South and the Southern view of the Civil War covered with a veneer of near documentary quality.

The Seething Hell

Can films also reconstruct what Walt Whitman called "the seething hell and the black infernal background of war"? (778). What about the stupidity, ugliness, exhaustion, mutilation, meaningless deaths, and simple endurance typical of the human experience of actual war? The success of such efforts depends on attention to detail--weapons, language, mood, form and conduct. All of this is difficult to achieve. "Battle scenes in films often make people who have been in battles restless," Sir John Hackett wrote. "On screen there are particular conventions to be observed. Men blown up by high explosives in real war, for example, are often torn apart quite hideously, in films, there is a big bang and bodies, intact, fly through the air with the greatest of ease [as in *The Devil's Brigade*, 1968]. If shot...they fall like children in a game, to lie motionless. The most harrowing thing in real battles is that they usually *don't* lie still" (qtd. in Holmes 67).

Paul Fussell also noted the discrepancy. During World War II *Collier's* and *Life* as well as the movies would never show "what was termed, in the Vietnam War, traumatic amputation: everyone has all his limbs, his hands and feet and digits, not to mention expressions of courage and cheer" (269-270). The dying did not writhe in distress. They simply seemed to fall asleep as if they were very, very tired. Or death might be a glorious gesture, as James Cagney portrayed it in *The Fighting 69th* (1940), of noble sacrifice.

Restricted by the censors or by good taste no films until the post-Vietnam era have shown the realities, the confusion, the profanity, the raw emotions, or the graphic physical trauma of combat in sharp focus.

This is not to say that earlier filmmakers have not tried to convey at least something of the tragedy of the wounded and the despair of the dying. Despite their limitations, they could evoke the right mood, look, and emotions, if not the vivid facts or language of battle. The famous scene where Scarlett O'Hara walks among the casualties in *Gone With the Wind* (1939) is both powerful and authentic. Of *Thirty Seconds over Tokyo* (1944), James Agee commented, "There are...some shots facing, even emphasizing, the ugliness, humiliation, and pity of losing a leg, which are precisely the honest sort one had learned never to expect in American war films." Agee hoped that feature films would capture, if only for a moment, the true agony of combat shown in a Paramount newsreel: "a heart rending picture of a wounded Marine crawling toward help with the scuttling motions of a damaged insect" (152).

John Ford's *The Lost Patrol* (1934) revealed "the emptiness, puzzlement and disorganization of the battlefield" (Holmes 67). The battle scenes in *The Red Badge of Courage* (1951) include "impressively realistic" details: "the platoon waiting for the Confederate advance, stopping it by rifle-fire, exulting, and then realizing that the brutes are coming in again." There are "some lovely military moments--the General cracking the same joke to different units, [Union soldier Henry] Flemings's long-range conversation with an unseen Confederate sentry, the badinage among the soldiers" (Fraser 185). The film evokes the private circumstances of battle realistically. Henry's constant introspection reflects honestly the anxieties of the common soldier: "Each man would (like Henry) be thrown back on his own ability to plug on, loading and firing doggedly with his own cocoon of *emotions*" (Griffith 89).

Paul Baumer, the disillusioned young German soldier played by Lew Ayres in *All Quiet on the Western Front* (1930), reflected the mood of the common man caught helplessly in the slow grinding down of the First World War: "We live in the trenches out there. We fight. We try not to be killed, but sometimes we are--that's all."

A Walk in the Sun (1946) also set the right tone in its depiction of a day in the life of fifty-three men of the Texas Division during the botched Salerno campaign of 1943. The march to, and then the attack on, a German-held farm house becomes the world of the combat infantryman in miniature. There are few false moments here, but rather an evocation of the experience of war through the rhythm of movement and intimate dialogue. When a farmer-turned-soldier comments that the soil there is no good, his buddy replies, "Maybe too many soldiers walked on it. They've been walking on it for a long time."

Battleground (1949), another film that is honest in its motive and accurate in its gritty recreation of men in battle, is "not a film about ideas; rather it's about the *look* of combat,... the exhausted faces of the soldiers as they struggle without food, waiting for supplies to be parachuted to them, the lack of sleep, and the tension, fear and physical discomfort that keep the dogfaces' nerves on edge" (National Board 38). In this case, director William Wellman went to great effort to reconstruct the siege of the 101st Airborne troopers at Bastogne between December 20 and 26, 1944, during the German advance in the Ardennes forest. "Throughout the film there is an awareness of the actual conditions of combat life, and a masked reference to some of the language used in battle: 'Leave your cots and grab your socks,' an inspired paraphrase" (Basinger 159).

Contemporary war films are not so squeamish. What was once only implied is now shown in gruesome detail. This, we note parenthetically, is not unique to war movies. Explicit sex, violence, and obscene language are characteristic of modern cinema. Although such scenes and dialogue are defended on the grounds that they are honest reflections of human emotions and the reality of experience, there is a thin line between simple honesty and the base desire to simply shock the audience by ugly detail.

Nevertheless, *Platoon* (1986), *Hamburger Hill* (1989), and *Born on the Fourth of July* (1990) do not hold back and do indeed show the horrors of war. These films bring to the screen a certain terrible honesty or immediacy that reveals rather than repels. Recent films also do not mask the obscene language of the soldier. In *Heartbreak Ridge* (1986) Clint Eastwood, as a tough Marine gunnery sergeant, engages in an "orgy of baroque obscenity" with "scatological obsession" (Kael 246-47). Likewise, the marines in *Full Metal Jacket* (1987) "talk in a profane military slang that can't always be deciphered but makes its point: that clean English can't express how they feel" (Kael 327).

Celluloid Soldiers

If *Battleground* whitewashed routine military profanity, it went to great lengths to achieve the image of real war. Its actors were trained in the tactics of firing positions, scouting, patrolling, grenade throwing, bayonet fighting, and crawling. During filming it was forbidden to launder the uniforms. The studio even put actors through Hollywood's version of bootcamp (Rubin 35):

0900-0950	Calisthenics
0950-1000	Ten minute break
1000-1050	Firing positions, prone, sitting, kneeling
1050-1100	Break
1100-1200	Scouting, patrolling, creeping, crawling
1200-1300	Lunch
1300-1350	Grenade throwing, bayonet fighting
1350-1400	Break
1400-1450	Orientation film and lecture

Such were the efforts to reconstruct the experience of combat. In a more recent example, *Glory* (1989) takes great liberty with the story of black men who made up the 54th Massachusetts Regiment (actually free men of color, not ex-slaves) during the Civil War, but also takes pains to ensure the accuracy of infantry uniforms, weapons, and tactics in its battle sequences by casting Civil War reenactors as extras. In *The Bridge* (1959), a West German film, the story of a unit of sixteen-year-old German schoolboys defending a small town in the last days of World War II, battle sequences, "photographed in brilliant sunshine and accompanied by one of the few sound tracks ever to capture fully the distinctive metallic crash of rifle and cannon fire, are frighteningly real" (Dolan 82).

Directors Oliver Stone (*Platoon*, 1986), Brian DePalma (*Casualties of War*, 1990), and Patrick Duncan (*84 Charlie Mopic*, 1990) contracted with Warriors Inc., a "performer training" company, headed by tough former Marine Dale Dye and his partner Russ Thurman. For the cast of *Platoon*, Dye ordered a fourteen-day bootcamp that bears comparison with that for *Battleground*:

> 06:30, jungle orientation hike, introduction to close-order drill.... 07:30, intro to rappelling, ropes, gloves, snap links required at site.... 08:30, the jungle environment, classes in the field.... 12:00, ambush and counter-ambush, blank ammo required.... intro to medic activities, recovering WIAs/KIAs.... 21:00, taps, deploy night activities, 1st squad on perimeter security.

Thurman made it clear to the actors in *84 Charlie Mopic* that war movies had a moral obligation to real fighters. "I'm the gunny [gunnery sergeant] and I spent 21 years in the Marine Corps," he shouted. "I don't particularly care for actors, especially those like you who think that they have the right to portray Marines, sailors or soldiers. You think that just because you look good, smell good and talk good to impress a director that you can come out here and play one of my brothers in combat? No way. For one thing, you're going to represent 58,000 guys on the Wall in Washington DC. Now that we got some reference points, gentlemen, we're going to go on a little wimp walk, maybe 10 miles." The result was transformation of California surfer "boys into what often on screen passes for first-class fighting men" (Norman).

Such films studiously avoid the false heroics of the false romance of battle--what Wilfred Owen (931), in his poem "*Dulce et Decorum Est*" about the Great War, called "the old Lie." Films that are honest about the experience of combat (*Pork Chop Hill*, 1960, for example) understand the essential difference between what might be called the anticipation and the actuality of the situation.

On a larger scale, filmmakers have attempted to present the big picture, to reconstruct gigantic operations. *The Longest Day* (1962) refought the Normandy invasion--Omaha Beach, Utah Beach, the Ranger assault on Pointe du Hoc, the French commando attack on Quistreham, the paratroop drop on Ste Mere Eglise, and the glider attack on the Orne River bridge. Here the emphasis periodically shifts from the strategic decision-making of generals to the small-unit operations of privates and NCOs. *Tora! Tora! Tora!* (1970) took a similar approach to reconstruct in exacting detail the American defeat at Pearl Harbor.

These panoramic docudramas, however, generally fail as drama-- one critic called *The Longest Day* "emotionally unaffecting" (Halliwell 525) and *Tora! Tora! Tora!* an "immense...calcified war spectacle" (899). "Photogenic historical epics" can reconstruct, instruct, or entertain, but fail to evoke strong emotions or to involve us in the world of the common soldier in the way smaller movies let us share, as *A Walk in the Sun* or *Hamburger Hill* do, in the "social realism" of combat--"its feeling of verisimilitude for the discomfort, ants, heat, and mud--of the jungle and the brush: the fatigue of patrols, the boredom and sense of release,... the terror of ambushes, and the chaos and cacophony" of combat. Or the "murderous immediacy of the world" of the men in the ranks (Auster and Quart 132).

SECRET ATTRACTIONS

In his brilliant and influential study *The Face of Battle*, John Keegan confessed, "I have not been in a battle, not near one, nor heard one from afar, nor seen the aftermath." But, "I have read about battles,... have talked about battles and...have watched battles in progress, on the television screen. I have seen a good deal of other, earlier battles of this century on newsreel, some of them convincingly authentic, as well as much dramatized feature film" (13).

The Vicarious Experience

The vicarious experience is all the vast majority of us know of battle. We see a great deal of war on television or in the movie theater; hardly any of us ever enter the world of the combat soldier. By 1943, only 375,000 World War II American soldiers were assigned to fighting units, and of these only a very few served in rifle companies--the soldiers who lived and died on the razor's edge of battle. By 1945, 11 million men were in the army, yet only 700,000 (6 percent) in the combat infantry (Fussell 283). And even those in the infantry are likely never to engage the enemy in combat.

A Department of Defense consultant puts it this way: "It is important to remember that in modern combat, the vast majority of troops do not engage in combat. In the U.S. Army in World War II, no more than 25 percent of those who served ever came under enemy fire. The infantrymen, the real fighters, comprise less than 10 percent of armed-forces strength" (Dunnigan 215). This disproportionately distributed burden of actual combat has been called "one of the great ironies of the American war effort" (Stokesbury 380).

What was true for the 1940's remained true for the 1960's. In Vietnam only 30 percent of those who served were combat soldiers, but the number who saw action may have been closer to 14 percent (Keegan and Holmes 49). Thus, for most American soldiers, "Vietnam was no more dangerous or disconcerting than any overseas assignment. Working in administrative and support units, they put in long hours in comparative safety" (Millett and Maslowski 553).

"I Was John Wayne"

The great majority of those who have served in the armed forces have little more personal understanding of the battlefield, the killing zone, than those of us who see images of war in the safety of movie theaters. Still, most of us believe we know something of the experience of combat and the way men should behave in such situations. William Manchester observed that few of his fellow Marines had read *A Farewell to Arms* or *All Quiet on the Western Front*, but almost all had seen "B movies about bloodshed," and "if a platoon leader had watched Douglas Fairbanks, Jr., Errol Flynn, Victor McLaglen, John Wayne, or Gary Cooper, he was likely to follow his role model" (Manchester 83).

During the filming of *The Outsider* (1961), the story of Ira Hayes (the American Indian who helped raise the flag atop Mount Suribachi), director Delbert Mann inquired of some young Marine recruits at Camp Pendelton the reasons for their enlistment. Half of them said that they had been inspired by John Wayne movies. Wayne had become "the archetypal role-model for young Marines for the next twenty years" (Holmes 68).

Josiah Bunting, author of *The Lionheads*, a novel based on his experiences as an Army combat veteran of Vietnam, said that real officers (especially the lieutenant-colonels) modeled their behavior on what they had seen in movie houses: "this whole area of machismo.... The influence of John Waynism, if you want to call it that, on these people was terribly profound." So it was with the lesser ranks as well. "We thought we will go to Vietnam," platoon leader William Calley testified at his court-martial, "and be Audie Murphys, I was John Wayne" (qtd. in Holmes 68).

Ron Kovic, author of *Born on the Fourth of July*, a bitter recollection of Vietnam, stated that after he and his playmates saw *The Sands of Iwo Jima* (1949), they played wargames in the woods or mulitated little plastic soldiers in little battles. Such boyhood experiences inspired him to seek martial glory by joining the Marines. "Castiglia and I saw *Sands of Iwo Jima* together," Kovic recalled. "The Marine Corps hymn was playing in the background as we sat glued to our seats, humming the hymn together and watching Sergeant Stryker, played by John Wayne, charge up the hill and get killed just before he reached the top. And then they showed the men raising the flag on Iwo Jima with the Marines' hymn still playing, and Castiglia and I cried in our seats. I loved the song so much, and every time I heard it I would think of John Wayne and the brave men who raised the flag on Iwo Jima that day. I would think of them and cry." And "I'll never forget Audie Murphy in *To Hell and Back* at the end he jumps on top of a flaming tank...and grabs the machine gun.... He was so brave I had chills running up and down my back, and wishing it were me up there" (Kovic 43).

Vietnam veteran Philip Caputo, author of *A Rumor of War*, recalled a similar sense of identification: "I saw myself charging up some distant beachhead, like John Wayne in *Sands of Iwo Jima*, and then coming home a suntanned warrior with medals on my chest" (Caputo 6). Thomas Baird, another Vietnam veteran, said that World War II movies formed frames of reference before, during, and after his experience. *A Walk in the Sun*, he remembers "more than any other, would rerun in my mind years later as I crossed rice paddy dikes in Vietnam moving toward a local farmer's house or tree line." Once, falling into a ditch, he came up crying: "This ain't a war movie! This ain't a John Wayne movie!" (Baird 11). Nevertheless his memories and fantasies of the films of World War II--for example, *Guadalcanal Diary* (1943) or *Gung Ho!* (1943)--seemed to merge and interpret what he was experiencing in actual combat. Years later, he lauded the movies' therapeutic value: "The best of the Vietnam films act on us this way: they awaken our memories forcing us to deal with our remorse for the things we did" (16). Like many others, combat veterans or not, Baird could not avoid the pervasive influence of films. They gave shape and meaning to his thoughts and actions. William Manchester remembered an old comrade of the Pacific War, Lefty Zapp, who "joined the Marines on impulse after seeing John Payne, Randolph Scott, and Maureen O'Hara in *To the Shores of Tripoli* (1942), a gung-ho movie that conned a lot of guys into boot camp" (237).

Watching movies about war and playing with toy soldiers--a kind of home movie--are among the ways we learn to believe and behave. Little lead and plastic soldiers are "idealized models of reality, fragments of cultural aspirations brightly painted and gracefully posed. And it was the relationship of the toy warrior to the real warrior that made the toy soldier infinitely interesting, for there were always interesting questions to be asked." These little soldiers of the living-room battlefield, like their counterparts in war movies, "taught virtues of leadership, discipline, strategy, bravery and patriotism. They prepared a man for war" (Schine 60-61).

Movies give inspiration and form to our ideals and meaning to our experience. "The movies...offered structures of thought and feeling to an almost inconceivable quantity of people, and we live on their legacy in ways we have hardly begun to recognize." We simply cannot escape their influence (Wood 193).

There is, indeed, a certain irony in that John Wayne, whose films had given form and meaning to the actions of so many men, had never been a soldier, let alone seen combat. For Wayne, it was always a sensitive point. "Every man thinks meanly of himself for not having been a soldier," said Dr. Samuel

Johnson. He claimed for the soldierly profession "the dignity of danger. Mankind reverence those who have got over fear, which is so general a weakness" (qtd. in Boswell 926). Perhaps we would all be soldiers, someone said, if it were not for the bullets. All want to be heroes--just like the actors in the movies-- but no one wants to die. So the vicarious experience of movie- going holds an appeal that transcends reality. The distinction between the real and the unreal becomes blurred in the dark room. Movies are better than real life.

"Been to See the Elephant"

It is true, but a very hard thing to say: war has its appeal both in actuality and in fantasy. Returning combat veterans used to have a phrase for their experience of combat: they said they had "been to see the elephant." Like one of Barnum's sideshow freaks, it is exotic, bizarre, and exciting. Other veterans have referred to the experience as "The Big Parade" (used as the title for King Vidor's 1925 film about the Great War). J. Glenn Gray, a philosopher and veteran of the Second World War, identified three "secret attractions of war." They are "the delight in seeing, the delight in comradeship, the delight in destruction. Some fighters know one appeal and not others, some experience all three, and some may, of course, feel others I do not know. These three had reality for me, and I have found them throughout the literature of war" (Gray 28-29).

We can observe the same elements in film as well. Roger Shatzkin identified the common experience of "pleasure derived from watching things (in movies) burned, flooded, exploded, and smashed from the safety of a theater" (Shatzkin 140). Gray called it a "mindless curiosity, a primordial urge," that gives life its spice. We enjoy scenes of battle first-hand or on film for the very same reasons that we slow down to observe an auto accident on the freeway or leave our homes at night to watch a house fire down the block. We are oddly attracted by what ought to repel us. "How many men in each generation," he asked, "have been drawn into the twilight of confused and murderous battle 'to see what it is like'?" (Gray 28). In *A Walk in the Sun* (1946), Sterling Holloway, playing a young inexperienced soldier, is killed as he returns to beachhead at Salerno just to see what is happening. Gray found a safer place: "Last evening I sat on a rock outside the town and watched a modern battle, an artillery duel [and] the panorama was so far-reaching that I could see both the explosion of the guns and where their speedy messengers struck.... [It] was an interesting, stirring sight" (Gray 33). There are other exciting examples in film: the climax to *The Guns of Navarone* (1961) in which the face of a mountain cliff explodes, or the emergence from the fog of the Normandy invasion fleet as seen from the perspective of a German bunker in *The Longest Day* (1962). For the California surfer boy in *Apocalypse Now* (1978), war is a spectacle "better than Disneyland."

Pauline Kael fretted over her fascination with an image in *Hamburger Hill* (1987): "Is it a shell bursting? It has no right to be so incredibly beautiful" (354). John Wayne envisioned his production of *The Alamo* (1960) "as a hymn to courage and human spirit on both sides, and art-directed it accordingly." The result was a war movie noted for "the sumptuous visual beauty of its compositions, lighting and set design" (National Board 6). Men are seductively drawn to battle by the prospect of such excitement and horrible beauty.

"Fierce Friendships"

A second appeal lies in the bonds men form in battle. Roger Spiller, historian at the Combat Studies Institute of the United States Army Command and General Staff College, wrote of the comradery: "Within the world of combat, a peculiar and highly specialized society is created, one where rules, rituals, codes of conduct and behavior, standards of success and failure are in force" (Spiller 27). Consider too the comment of Richard Holmes of the Royal Military Academy at Sandhurst: "Few regard war as anything other than an evil, unavoidable in some circumstances, but an evil none the less: yet at the same time they do not regret their own participation in it. The majority feel that their experience of war links them to others who share it, as firmly as it separates them from those who do not" (Holmes 395). The links are very strong: "Those men on the line were my family, my home. They were closer to me than I can say, closer than any friends had been or ever would be" (Manchester 451). Again, J. Glenn Gray: "Many veterans who are honest with themselves will admit, I believe, that the experience of communal effort in battle...has been the high point in their lives. Despite the horror, the weariness, the grime, and the hatred, participation with others in the chances of battle had an unforgettable side, which they would not want to have missed" (44). Most of us, in fact, miss it entirely: the communal experience of battle is unavailable even for those trained for war. Combat veterans belong to a select fraternity to which few are admitted. We viewers in a dark room share in it as best we can at second remove, in film.

Among those films that seem to get to the essence of this peculiar communal experience are *A Walk in the Sun* (1945), *Battleground* (1949), and *The Big Red One* (1979), although every film that focuses on small unit action cannot help but touch the subject.

A Walk in the Sun follows the old formula of the "melting-pot" platoon (one Texan, one Jew, one farmboy, etc.) as a symbol of American society, but this movie avoids false heroics and seeks realism through understatement and subdued action and its intimate focus on the group. In terms of communal experience, the film is astute in "catching men in an experience that, unlinked to any former occurrence in their lives and detached from any normal human endeavor, will remain forever in their memories as an experience of light and shadow; danger and safety; warmth and cold; friendships and enemies" (Basinger 148-149).

Battleground tells the story of another small band of brothers--I Company, 3d Platoon, 2d Squad of the 101st Airborne--besieged at Bastogne during the Battle of the Bulge. One cannot view this movie without a feeling that this is truly what combat is like. "It is the realism of the small thing that makes the veteran recognize and remember his situation" (Basinger 170). It is that precise focus on the tiny details of the community of the killing zone that allows the uninitiated to begin, in a small way, to understand the comradeship that bonds men together in battle and to see the experience, despite its horror, as appealing.

Sam Fuller, director and scriptwriter, put his communal memories on film in *The Big Red One*. The movie follows five men through the European war. They form in the course of the war a little group closed to all outsiders--including raw recruits who fill up the ranks of the men around them and then are killed off one by one. Whatever came to Fuller's life afterward, could it ever have been as meaningful as the experience of comradeship in war? In one sense, what makes Robert Aldrich's *Attack!* (1956) and Oliver Stone's *Platoon* (1986) so disturbing is precisely the absence of this compensating brotherhood for the beleaguered soldiers.

"Napalm in the Morning"

The third enticement is the urge to destroy. "Men who have lived in the zone of combat long enough to be veterans are sometimes possessed by a fury that makes them capable of anything." They are often overcome by "the mad excitement of destroying" (Gray 51-52). And some "from the very first actually enjoyed combat" (Kennett 89).

We can see it in the face of Steve McQueen as Buzz Rickson, the mad commander of a Flying Fortress in *The War Lover* (1963). And in McQueen's portrayal of the "human war machine" in *Hell is for Heroes* (1962) (Basinger 316). We see it too in the black-comic exaggeration of Major Kong (Slim Pickins) the apocalyptic pilot of a B-52 in *Dr. Strangelove* (1964) who welcomes the final holocaust. "Well, boys," he exclaims to his crew, "I guess this is it: nuclear combat, toe to toe with the Rooskies!"

The attack on the seacoast village in *Apocalypse Now* is another surrealistic "depiction of 'the horror, the madness, the *sensuousness*' of war, amplified by the visceral you-are-there sensation of its huge 70 mm screen tableaux and Dolby Sound" (Adair 151, emphasis added). Robert Duvall is Kilgore (the name, an obvious pun), commander of the helicopter assault force. He broadcasts "The Flight of the Valkyries" as his machines swoop down upon the targets. "I love the smell of napalm in the morning," he announces with gleeful bloodlust.

But what is to be the reaction of the audience to such scenes and sentiments? To turn away in disgust? No. "Few of us are unaffected by the vicarious pleasure offered by the representation of large-scale destruction." Whatever the intentions of director Francis Ford Coppola, "each more horrible scene tends to be more spectacular and thus ever more exciting in visual-aural effects. Can the viewer really enlarge a sense of moral horror against the visceral impact of better and better pyrotechnic displays?" (Hagen 244).

In fact, we want more, drawn as we are (as combat veterans sometimes are) into the phantasmagoria of the event. Darryl F. Zanuck admitted that he had failed with *The Longest Day*: "If people could see the brutality and inhumanity of war, I reasoned they would be filled with such revulsion that they would never permit their leaders to send them back to the battlefield. I was wrong" (qtd. in Rubin 45-46). Spectacle can divert the viewer's attention from the mundane human tragedy that can overcome men in real battle.

"We must kill them," the insane Colonel Kurtz (Marlon Brando) states in *Apocalypse Now*. "We must incinerate them--pig after pig, cow after cow, village after village." A young soldier wrote during his tour of duty in Vietnam that "now more than ever I am determined to do everything possible to wipe these rotten bastards off the face of the earth. I have a long time here, and heaven help any one of them, man, woman, child, that crosses my path. Total and complete destruction is the only way to treat these animals" (qtd. in Keegan and Holmes 159). Col. Kurtz summed up the urge: "Out there with these natives, there must be a temptation to be God, because there's a conflict in every human heart between the rational and irrational, between good and evil.... Sometimes the dark side will overcome the better angels of our nature."

POPCORN VETERANS

The strange enticements of battle, then, lure men into what becomes for many the single great experience of their lives. To see, to share, to destroy--it leaves an indelible mark upon men's lives and, perhaps, upon their souls as well. Robert Stile, a veteran of the American Civil War, called his experience "the only great thing in my life" (qtd. in Griffith 312). "The war was a high for my dad," gunnery sergeant Dale Dye recalled. "He came home to a humdrum, mundane existence. He used to sit around with some of his war buddies reliving the glory days" (qtd. in Norman). Another said of his own past and history: "Thinking about Vietnam once in a while, in a crazy kind of way, I wish that just for an hour I could be there. And then be transported back. Maybe just to be there so I'd wish I was back here again" (qtd. in Holmes 403). In *The Best Years of Our Lives* (1946) a post-war soda jerk (Dana Andrews) wanders amid endless rows of mothballed bombers and relives his combat experiences as a pilot. He believes the best years of his life are all back in the war.

King Henry V--in both Laurence Olivier's (1944) and Michael Branagh's (1989) cinematic translation of Shakespeare's *Henry V*-- urges his soldiers to
> imitate the action of the tiger;
> Stiffen the sinews, summon up the blood,
> Disguise fair nature with hard-favour'd rage.

Henry V knew how to paint war attractively, motivate his little army, and make sure that those who survive the assault of the French men-at-arms would remember the field at Agincourt. The king promises his men exclusive comradeship: "We few, we happy few, we band of brothers." We will, he said, "remember with advantages" (50) what we have done, whereas those unlucky many who stay behind

> Shall think themselves accurs'd they were not here;
> And hold their manhoods cheap whiles any speaks.

In his 1989 film, director-actor Michael Branagh attempted an anti-war version of the battle, but could not dampen the enthusiasm aroused by this famous "Band of Brothers" speech. Even slow-motion filming of murderous action on the field--the mud and blood of the slaughter yard--could not stifle the excitement of combat for the moviegoer. The enticements offered by the king are simply too powerful to resist.

George C. Scott as the titular hero in *Patton* (1970) makes the point in his appeal to the men of his armored command. Although less poetic than Henry V's, Patton's speech is hardly less forceful:

> There's one thing you men will be able to say when you get home and you may all thank God for it. Thirty years from now when you are sitting around the fireside with your grandson on your knee and he asks what you did in the Great World War II, you won't have to say, "Well, I shoveled shit in Louisiana."

We veterans of the celluloid wars munch our popcorn and nod our assent.

Adair, Gilbert. *Hollywood's Vietnam: From "The Green Berets" to "Apocalypse Now"*. New York: Proteus, 1981.

Agee, James. *Agee on Film: Reviews and Comments by James Agee*. Vol. 1. New York: Grosset and Dunlap, 1967. 2 vols.

Anderson, Linsay. *About John Ford....* New York: McGraw, 1981.

Auster, Albert, and Leonard Quart. *How the War was Remembered: Hollywood and Vietnam*. New York: Praeger, 1988.

Baird, Thomas. "Man and Boy Confront the Images of War." *New York Times* 27 May 1990: H11+.

Baritz, Loren. *Backfire: A History of How American Culture Led Us into Vietnam and Made Us Fight the Way We Did.* New York: Ballantine, 1985.

Basinger, Jeanine. *The World War II Combat Film: Anatomy of a Genre*. New York: Columbia UP, 1986.

Bernstein, Richard. "Can Movies Teach History?" *New York Times* 26 Nov. 1989, sec. 2: 1.

Boswell, James. *Life of Johnson*. London: Oxford UP, 1966.

Bunting, Josiah. *The Lionheads: A Novel*. New York: Braziller, 1972.

Caputo, Philip. *A Rumor of War*. New York: Holt, 1977.

Cook, David A. *A History of Narrative Film*. New York: Norton, 1981.

Crowther, Bosley. *Reruns: Fifty Memorable Films*. New York: Putnam's, 1978.

Dolan, Edward F., Jr. *Hollywood Goes to War*. New York: Gallery, 1985.

Dunnigan, James F. *How to Make War: A Comprehensive Guide to Modern Warfare*. New York: Quill, 1983.

Fraser, George MacDonald. *The Hollywood History of the World, from "One Million B.C." to "Apocalypse Now."* New York: Beech Tree, 1988.

Fussell, Paul. *Wartime: Understanding and Behavior in the Second World War*. New York: Oxford UP, 1989.

Gray, J. Glenn. *The Warriors: Reflections on Men in Battle*. New York: Harper, 1967.

Griffith, Paddy. *Civil War Infantry Tactics*. New Haven: Yale UP, 1987.

Hagen, William M. "*Apocalypse Now* (1979): Joseph Conrad and the Television War." *Hollywood as Historian: American Film in a Cultural Context*. Ed. Peter Robbins, Lexington: U of Kentucky P, 1983. 230-45.

Halliwell, Leslie. *Halliwell's Film Guide*. 2nd ed. New York: Scribner's, 1979.

Hellmann, John. *American Myth and the Legacy of Vietnam*. New York: Columbia UP, 1986.

Holmes, Richard. *Acts of War: The Behavior of Men in Battle*. New York: Free, 1985.

Isenberg, Michael T. *War on Film: The American Cinema and World War I*. London: Associated UP, 1981.

Jowett, Garth. *Film: The Democratic Art*. Boston: Little, 1976.

Kael, Pauline. *Hooked*. New York: Dutton, 1989.

Keegan, John. *The Face of Battle*. 1976. Middlesex: Penguin, 1983.

Keegan, John, and Richard Holmes. *Soldiers: A History of Men in Battle*. New York: Viking, 1986.

Kennett, Lee. *G.I.: The American Soldier in World War II*. New York: Scribner's, 1987.

Kovic, Ron. *Born on the Fourth of July*. New York, McGraw, 1976.

Manchester, William. *Goodbye Darkness: A Memoir of the Pacific War*. New York: Dell, 1980.

Metcalfe, Philip. *1933*. New York: Harper, 1988.

Millett, Allan R., and Peter Maslowski. *For the Common Defense: A Military History of the United States of America*. New York: Free, 1984.

National Board of Review of Motion Pictures and the Editors of *Films in Review. 500 Best American Films to Buy, Rent or Videotape*. New York: Pocket, 1985.

Norman, Michael. "Drillmasters' Seminar: the Art of War." *New York Times* 4 Feb. 1990: H17+.

O'Connor, John E. "A Reaffirmation of American Ideals: *Drums Along the Mohawk* (1939)." *American History / American Film: Interpreting the Hollywood Image*. 1979. Ed. John E. O'Connor and Martin A. Jackson. New York: Ungar, 1980. 97-119.

Owen, Wilfred. "*Dulce et Decorum Est*." *The Norton Introduction to Literature*. Ed. Carl E. Bain, Jerome Beaty, and J. Paul Hunter. 5th ed. New York: Norton, 1991.

Perret, Geoffrey. *A Country Made by War*. New York: Random, 1989.

Plumb, J.H. *The Death of the Past*. Boston: Houghton, 1971.

Rubin, Steven Jay. *Combat Films, American Realism: 1945-1970*. Jefferson, McFarland, 1981.

Santoli, Al. *Everything We Had: An Oral History of the Vietnam War by Thirty-three American Soldiers Who Fought It*. New York: Ballantine, 1981.

Schine, C. "Floor Wars." *New York Times Magazine* 13 Aug. 1989: 60-61.

Shatzkin, Roger. "Disaster Epics: Cashing in on Vicarious Experience." *Film in Society*. Ed. Arthur Asa Berger. New Brunswick: Transaction, 1980. 137-42.

Spiller, Roger. "Isen's Run: Human Dimensions of Warfare in the 20th Century." *Military Review* (May 1988): 16-31.

Stokesbury, James L. *A Short History of World War II*. New York: Morrow, 1980.

Warshow, Robert. *The Immediate Experience: Movies, Comics, Theatre & Other Aspects of Popular Culture*. New York: Doubleday, 1964.

Whitman, Walt. *Complete Poetry and Collected Prose*. New York: Library of America, 1982.

Williams, Tennessee. *The Glass Menagerie. The Norton Introduction to Literature*. 3rd ed. Ed. Carl E. Bain et al. New York: Norton, 1981. 1238-96.

Winks, Robin. *The Historian as Detective: Essays on Evidence* New York: Harper, 1969.

Wood, Michael. *America in the Movies*. New York: Basic, 1975.

3

Early American Wars

CHRONOLOGY

Colonial Wars (1689-1763):

The American wars of the 17th through mid-18th centuries were an extension of the struggle among Britain, France, and Spain involving European issues and control of the North American continent. In essence, the four wars listed below are New World extensions of one great world war for empire:

King William's War, 1689-1697

Queen Anne's War, 1702-1713

King George's War, 1744-1748

The French and Indian War, 1754-1763. (See also Chapter 6, "Indian Wars.") Britain emerges as the victor and France is ousted from North America. The British American colonies now have little reason to remain subservient to British strategic and economic interests (see *The Last of the Mohicans*, 1936; *The Iroquois Trail*, 1950; *Fort Ti*, 1953).

Revolutionary War (1775-1783):

1775-1776. Rioting and fighting turn from a confused attempt to redress grievances to a war for separation from the British imperial system.

9 April 1775. Minutemen and British fight at Lexington and Concord (see *Cardigan,* 1922; *Johnny Tremain,* 1957; *April Morning,* 1987).

17 June 1775. Battle of Bunker (actually Breed's) Hill is fought (see *Revolution,* 1985).

4 July 1776. Americans declare independence (see *1776,* 1972).

1777-1778. The British defeat at Saratoga convinces the French to come in openly on the American side to disrupt the British empire. A colonial uprising is now becoming a world war.

Winter of 1777-1778. The American army endures a harsh period at its encampment at Valley Forge.

February 1778. France and America sign a treaty of alliance.

1778-1783. A British attempt to shift the fighting to the Southern colonies ends in failure.

September-October 1781. A British army under General Cornwallis is trapped by a French-American force on the Yorktown peninsula and made to surrender.

1781-1783. Fighting continues, but the British will to victory has been broken. London searches for a way out. The war ends with British recognition of American independence.

Trouble With Barbary Pirates (1805-1812):

North African sea raiders from the Barbary coast--Morocco, Algeria, Tunisia and Tripoli--prey upon American shipping in the Mediterranean. President Jefferson uses naval and marine forces and a little ransom to deal with the problem (see *Barbary Pirate,* 1949; *Tripoli,* 1950).

Conflict With France and Britain (1798-1815):

America attempts to stay neutral during the French Revolution and Napoleon's imperial wars but is drawn into conflict with France (The Quasi-War, 1798-1800) and the British Empire (War of 1812). Issues are the violation of American maritime rights and the desire among certain Western politicians to use the opportunity to seize Canada for America.

1812-1814. The American invasion of Canada fails, but the United States scores impressive naval victories.

1814-1815. With the defeat of Napoleon, the British take the opportunity to launch offensives. They seize Washington, DC, and burn public buildings but later withdraw (see *Magnificent Doll*, 1946). Another invasion at the mouth of the Mississippi River is defeated by Andrew Jackson south of New Orleans (see *The Buccaneer*, 1938; 1958). The war ends with the *status quo antebellum*, but Jackson's victory led many to believe the war had been won.

COMMENTARY

America has been at war with alarming regularity since its inception. The nation gained and preserved its independence against foes both foreign and domestic--Indians, North Africans, the French, and the British. Surely screenwriters can find spectacle, adventure, emotion, and violence here (as in scenes from *The Buccaneer*, 1958, dramatizing the British charge against Jackson's riflemen and artillery at New Orleans).

Yet this period has been little mined by filmmakers. Perhaps they have been deterred by what are perceived as arcane issues. More likely, the advent of film technology came too late for the Revolutionary War to be of much interest. When D.W. Griffith began working for Biograph Studios in 1908, he was closer in time to the Civil War than we are to the Second World War. Civil War veterans were everywhere; Revolutionary War veterans were long dead. In 1915 when Griffith made *The Birth of a Nation*--about the Civil and not the Revolutionary War--attention was turning to a new war in Europe. (Griffith did, however, dramatize the major phases of the Revolutionary War and the establishment of the Republic in *America*, 1924.)

Early American wars with recognizable names--the French and Indian War, the Revolution, and the War of 1812--have primarily been used as backdrops for costume dramas. Yet filmmakers have done better when they concentrated less on satin and powdered wigs than on individual human dramas. The most notable film depicting this early period is *Drums Along the Mohawk* (1939), John Ford's first color film. It focuses on the details of colonial life: clearing land, militia drills, Indian raids, domestic farewell scenes, the timeless drama of marriage and birth. Pioneers enduring hardship and defeating Indian attacks symbolize the mission and destiny of the American people. At the film's end, they are presented with a new flag marking the transition from colony to nation. Made on the eve of the Second World War, this film uses the colonial period for a "reaffirmation of American ideals" (O'Connor 97).

O'Connor, John E. "A Reaffirmation of American Ideals: *Drums Along the Mohawk* (1939)." *American History / American Film: Interpreting the Hollywood Image.* Ed. John E. O'Connor and Martin A. Jackson. New York: Ungar, 1988. 97-119.

FILMOGRAPHY

Colonial and Revolutionary Wars

Allegheny Uprising.** 81m, b/w. Dir. William A. Seiter. With John Wayne, Claire Trevor, George Sanders, Brian Donlevy, Robert Barrat, Moroni Olsen, Chill Wills. RKO, 1939.

America.** 11 reels, b/w. Dir. D.W. Griffith. With Neil Hamilton, Carol Dempster, Erville Alderson, Lionel Barrymore, Louis Wolheim, Charles Emmet Mack. UA, 1924.

April Morning.*** 100m, color. Dir. Delbert Mann. With Tommy Lee Jones, Robert Urich, Chad Lowe, Susan Blakely, Rip Torn. Goldwyn, 1987.

Battles of Chief Pontiac.* 71m, b/w. Dir. Felix Feist. With Lex Barker, Helen Westcott, Lon Chaney, Jr., Berry Kroeger, Roy Robert. Real, 1952.

Cardigan.* 7 reels, b/w. Dir. John W. Noble. With William Collier, Jr., Betty Carpenter, Thomas Cummings. ARC, 1922.

*The Deerslayer.** 76m, color. Dir. Kurt Neumann. With Lex Barker, Rita Moreno, Forrest Tucker. Fox, 1957.

*The Devil's Disciple.**** 82m, b/w. Dir. Guy Hamilton. With Burt Lancaster, Kirk Douglas, Laurence Olivier, Janette Scott, Eva Le Gallienne, Harry Andrews, Basil Sydney. UA, 1959.

*Drums Along the Mohawk.****** 103m, color. Dir. John Ford. With Claudette Colbert, Henry Fonda, Edna May Oliver, Eddie Collins, John Carradine, Dorris Bowden, Jessie Ralph, Arthur Shields. Fox, 1939.

   Poignant pioneer drama. Ford's first color film. Exciting battle scenes of Indians shooting from behind trees and attacking a fort. Based on the novel by Walter D. Edmunds. Notable scene: domestic farewell before battle. Footnote: the movie's flintlock muskets were actually used in the 1930's against Mussolini's forces in Ethiopia.

*Fort Ti.** 73m, color. Dir. William Castle. With George Montgomery, Joan Vohs, Irving Bacon. Columbia, 1953.

*The Howards of Virginia.** 116m, b/w. Dir. Frank Lloyd. With Cary Grant, Martha Scott, Sir Cedric Hardwicke, Alan Marshal, Richard Carlson. Columbia, 1940.

*The Iroquois Trail.** Aka *The Tomahawk Trail*. 85m, b/w. Dir. Phil Karlson. With George Montgomery, Brenda Marshall, Glen Langan, Reginald Denny, Monte Blue. UA, 1950.

*Janice Meredith.*** 11 reels, b/w, color. Dir. E. Mason Hopper. With Marion Davies, Harrison Ford, Holbrook Blinn, Maclyn Arbuckle, Hattie Delaro. Cosmo, 1924.

*John Paul Jones.** 126m, color. Dir. John Farrow. With Robert Stack, Bette Davis, Marisa Pavan, Charles Coburn, Erin O'Brien. WB, 1959.

*Johnny Tremain.*** 80m, color. Dir. Robert Stevenson. With Hal Stalmaster, Luana Patten, Jeff York, Sebastian Cabot, Dick Beymer, Walter Sande. BV, 1957.

*The Last of the Mohicans.** 6 reels, b/w. Dir. Clarence Brown, Maurice Tourneur. With Wallace Beery, Barbara Bedford, Albert Roscoe, Lillian Hall, Henry Woodward. AP, 1920.

*The Last of the Mohicans.*** 91m, b/w. Dir. George B. Seitz. With Randolph Scott, Binnie Barnes, Bruce Cabot, Henry Wilcoxon, Heather Angel. UA, 1936.

*Last of the Redmen.** 78m, color. Dir. George Sherman. With Jon Hall, Michael O'Shea, Evelyn Ankers. Columbia, 1947.

*Mohawk.** 79m, color. Dir. Kurt Neumann. With Scott Brady, Rita Gam, Neville Brand, Lori Nelson. Fox, 1956.

*Northwest Passage.**** 125m, color. Dir. King Vidor. With Spencer Tracy, Robert Young, Walter Brennan, Ruth Hussey, Nat Pendleton, Louis Hector. MGM, 1940.

In their attempt to open up new territory, Rogers' Rangers must fight Indians. Beautifully photographed in early Technicolor. A good actioner with a fine lead performance by Tracy. Based on the novel by Kenneth Rogers. Footnote: only the first part of the novel, which does not deal with the historic northwest passage, was used for the story.

*The Pathfinder.** 78m, color. Dir. Sidney Salkow. With George Montgomery, Helena Carter, Jay Silverheels, Walter Kingsford. Columbia, 1952.

*Revolution.***** 123m, color. Dir. Hugh Hudson. With Al Pacino, Donald Sutherland, Natassja Kinski. 1985.

An American frontiersman and his son become involved in the struggle against British rule. Universally panned by critics, this film is significant for its realistic, unheroic treatment of history. Best sequence: the British attack on the American position conveys a vividly accurate picture of 18th century military tactics.

*The Scarlet Coat.** 101m, color. Dir. John Sturges. With Cornel Wilde, Michael Wilding, George Sanders, Anne Francis, Robert Douglas. MGM, 1955.

*The Seats of the Mighty.** 6 reels, b/w. Dir. T. Hayes Hunter. With Lionel Barrymore, Millicent Evans, Lois Meredith, Thomas Jefferson. World, 1914.

*1776.** 141m, color. Dir. Peter H. Hunt. With William Daniels, David Ford, Howard Da Silva, Donald Madden, Emory Bass. Columbia, 1972.

*Washington at Valley Forge.** 4 reels, b/w. Dir. Francis Ford, Grace Cunard. With Francis Ford, Grace Cunard. Universal, 1914.

*When the Redskins Rode.** 78m, color. Dir. Lew Landers. With Jon Hall, Mary Castle, James Seay. Columbia, 1951.

Barbary Pirates and War of 1812

*Barbary Pirate.** 64m, b/w. Dir. Lew Landers. With Donald Woods, Trudy Marshall, Lenore Aubert. Columbia, 1949.

*Brave Warrior.** 73m, color. Dir. Spencer G. Bennet. With Jon Hall, Christine Larson, Jay Silverheels, Michael Ansara, Harry Cording. Columbia, 1952.

*The Buccaneer.*** 124m, b/w. Dir. Cecil B. DeMille. With Fredic March, Franciska Gaal, Akim Tamiroff, Margot Grahame, Walter Brennan. Paramount, 1938.

The Buccaneer.**** 121m, color. Dir. Anthony Quinn. With Yul Brynner, Charlton Heston, Claire Bloom, Charles Boyer, Inger Stevens. Paramount, 1958.

A lavish costume drama that manages to convey a vivid sense of the Battle of New Orleans and the roles of General Andrew Jackson (Heston) and pirate Jean LaFitte (Brynner). Best sequence: the assault of British forces through the early morning fog against the American position is faithful to the events. Footnote: Because Cecil B. DeMille, who had directed the earlier version of *Buccaneer*, was ill, his son-in-law (Quinn) was given the director's job.

Captain Caution.* 84m, b/w. Dir. Richard Wallace. With Victor Mature, Louise Platt, Leo Carrillo, Bruce Cabot, Robert Barrat. UA, 1940.

Magnificent Doll.* 93m, b/w. Dir. Frank Borzage. With Ginger Rogers, David Niven, Burgess Meredith, Stephen McNally. Universal, 1946.

Mutiny.* 77m, color. Dir. Edward Dmytryk. With Mark Stevens, Angela Lansbury, Patric Knowles, Gene Evans, Rhys Williams. UA, 1952.

Old Ironsides.*** 11 reels, b/w. Dir. James Cruze. With Esther Ralston, Wallace Beery, George Bancroft, Charles Farrell, Johnny Walker. Paramount, 1926.

Tripoli.* 95m, color. Dir. Will Price. With Maureen O'Hara, John Payne, Howard Da Silva, Philip Reed. Paramount, 1950.

4

Wars with Mexico

CHRONOLOGY

Texas War for Independence (1822-1836):

Prelude. American expansion (1822-1836) from Texas to California puts pressure on Mexico's sparsely populated and little developed northern provinces.

1822. American settlers begin moving into Mexico's northern borderland of Texas at Mexico City's invitation, but serious cultural differences develop.

1835. General Santa Anna, dictator of Mexico, leads an expedition into the region to suppress unrest and agitation for independence.

23 February-6 March 1836. Santa Anna lays siege to the Alamo (see *The Alamo*, 1960).

21 April 1836. Texas leader Sam Houston defeats Santa Anna at the Battle of San Jacinto. Texas independence is assured.

Mexican War (1846-1848):

July 1846. American troops clash with Mexican cavalry in the disputed area along the southern boundary of Texas.

May 1846-January 1847. The northern region (including California) falls to the Americans. The Mexican government refuses to concede the territories.

March 1847-September 1847. American forces under Winfield Scott invade Mexico proper at Veracruz and march inland to capture Mexico City.

1848. The war ends. The United States gains a vast new western empire.

COMMENTARY

Of the turbulent period, from 1836 to 1848, of American territorial expansion and Manifest Destiny, one event alone stands out--the siege of the Alamo during the Texas war for independence. To be sure, there is enough material in these years to fill more than a few movie screens, but the defense of the old Spanish mission buildings at San Antonio has focused filmmakers' attention.

The Battle of the Alamo is inherently a military engagement of superior dramatic possibilities: a small band of brave men fight to the death against repeated attacks by an army thirty times their number. All the mythic elements are present: heroes larger than life (Davy Crockett and Jim Bowie among others), sturdy American frontiersmen facing a horde of peons led by a ruthless tyrant (General Antonio Lopez de Santa Anna), and a story with more than enough truth mixed in with legend to give it historical credibility and popular appeal. Whatever the reality (good evidence now suggests that Crockett surrendered and was executed, for instance), the thirteen-day siege is firmly fixed in the popular imagination, and is endlessly appealing.

Of the eight feature films based on the battle, John Wayne's *The Alamo* (1960) is the best. It pays careful attention to historical research: the reconstructed Alamo and the military uniforms and frontier costumes all have an authentic look. Wayne, aided by uncredited director John Ford, even manages to temper patriotic American fervor with respect for the Mexican soldiers. But Don Graham (52) says that "no Alamo movie comes close to capturing what must have been the fury of that fight." He wishes for a version with the fire of Sam Peckinpah's violent western *The Wild Bunch* (1969).

The later two-year war with Mexico, however, has produced nothing of consequence with regard to filmmaking despite its scope (the American acquisition of the northern half of Mexico) and its many dramatic engagements (for instance, the storming of the Mexican fortress at Chapultepec immortalized in song as "the Halls of Montezuma"). Mexicans lost not only the wars but also suffered "cinematic degradation" at Hollywood's hands (Pettit 131). Like the Indian, the Mexican has been stereotyped on the screen. And wars with Mexico have been fodder for B-westerns.

Graham, Don. "History Lesson." *Cowboys and Cadillacs: How Hollywood Looks at Texas*. Austin: Texas Monthly, 1983. 41-53.

Pettit, Arthur G. *Images of the Mexican American in Fiction and Film*. Ed. with afterword Dennis E. Showalter. College Station: Texas A&M UP, 1980.

FILMOGRAPHY

The Alamo.**** 192m, color. Dir. John Wayne. With John Wayne, Richard Widmark, Laurence Harvey, Richard Boone, Carlos Arruza, Frankie Avalon, Patrick Wayne. UA, 1960.

    Wide-screen spectacle focuses on three heroes: Crockett (Wayne), Bowie (Widmark), and Travis (Harvey). Meticulous attention to settings, costumes, uniforms. Respects the patriotism of both Texans and Mexicans (but was banned in Mexico). Wayne's story moves slowly but surely to the rousing final battle, the storming of the mission. Footnote: John Ford gave Wayne uncredited assistant direction.

California.** 5 reels, b/w. Dir. W.S. Van Dyke. With Tim McCoy, Dorothy Sebastian, Fred Warren, Lillian Leighton, Edwin Terry. MGM, 1927.

A California Romance.** 4 reels, b/w. Dir. Jerome Storm. With John Gilbert, Estelle Taylor, George Seigmann, Jack McDonald, Charles Anderson. Fox, 1922.

The First Texan.* 82m, color. Dir. Byron Haskin. With Joel McCrea, Felicia Farr, Jeff Morrow, Wallace Ford, Abraham Sofaer. AA, 1956.

Frontier Uprising.* 68m, b/w. Dir. Edward L. Cahn. With James Davis, Nancy Hadley, Ken Mayer, Nestor Paiva. UA, 1961.

Heroes of the Alamo.* 74m, b/w. Dir. Harry Fraser. With Lane Chandler, Earle Hodgins, Ruth Findlay, Roger Williams. Columbia, 1938.

*Kit Carson.*** 97m, b/w. Dir. George B. Seitz. With Jon Hall, Lynn Bari, Dana Andrews, Harold Huber, Ward Bond. UA, 1940.

*The Last Command.*** 110m, color. Dir. Frank Lloyd. With Sterling Hayden, Anna Maria Alberghetti, Richard Carlson, Arthur Hunnicutt, Ernest Borgnine. Republic, 1955.

*The Man From the Alamo.*** 79m, color. Dir. Budd Boetticher. With Glenn Ford, Julia Adams, Chill Wills, Victor Jory, Hugh O'Brian. Universal, 1953.

*Man of Conquest.*** 105m, b/w. Dir. George Nicholls, Jr. With Richard Dix, Gail Patrick, Edward Ellis, Joan Fontaine, Victor Jory. Republic, 1939.

*The Martyrs of the Alamo.*** 5 reels, b/w. Dir. W. Christy Cabanne. With Sam De Grasse, Walter Long, Tom Wilson, A.D. Sears, Alfred Paget. Triangle, 1915.

*Pirates of Monterey.** 78m, color. Dir. Alfred Werker. With Maria Montez, Rod Cameron, Mikhail Rasummy, Philip Reed, Gilbert Roland. Universal, 1947.

5

American Civil War

CHRONOLOGY

Prelude (1856-1861):

1856. Terrorism erupts on the Kansas-Missouri border between pro- and anti-slavery elements (see *Seven Angry Men*, 1955).

1859. John Brown raids the federal arsenal at Harper's Ferry, Virginia, in an attempt to incite a slave rebellion (see *Santa Fe Trail*, 1940).

November 1860. Abraham Lincoln is elected President. The South begins to secede (see *Abe Lincoln in Illinois*, 1940).

12-14 April 1861. Confederates fire on the federal fort in the harbor at Charleston, South Carolina.

Campaigns (1861):

21 July. Rebel forces rout Union troops at Bull Run. The real fighting begins.

10 August. The Union tactical defeat at Wilson's Creek in Missouri results in a strategic victory: blocking the Confederate rush to Missouri.

Campaigns (1862):

February. Union forces begin an offensive aimed at control of the Mississippi River line. Union General Ulysses S. Grant moves against Forts Henry and Donelson, Tennessee.

8-9 March. The Union ironclad ship *Monitor* duels the rebel ironclad *Merrimack* at Hampton Roads, Virginia.

6-7 April. Union forces win the Battle of Shiloh, Tennessee (see the Shiloh sequence in *How the West Was Won*, 1963).

22 April. Andrews' Raid or "The Great Locomotive Chase" (see *The General*, 1927).

May. Confederate General Thomas J. "Stonewall" Jackson defeats Union armies in the Shenandoah Valley.

1 May. Combined Union army and navy forces take New Orleans.

1 June. Confederate General Robert E. Lee is appointed commander of the Army of Northern Virginia.

25 June-1 July. The Seven Days' Battles: Mechanicsville, Gaines' Mill, and Malvern Hill. The Union invasion of Virginia is stymied.

17 September. The Battle of Antietam stops Lee's raid into Maryland.

22 September. Lincoln issues the Preliminary Emancipation Proclamation.

13 December. Union forces are defeated at Fredericksburg.

Year of Decision (1863):

17 April-2 May. "Grierson's Raid." Union cavalry raid through Mississippi as part of Grant's Vicksburg campaign (see *The Horse Soldiers*, 1959).

1-4 May. Battle of Chancellorsville. Lee's greatest victory is spoiled by the death of "Stonewall" Jackson from friendly fire.

1-3 July. Battle of Gettysburg. The largest battle ever fought on the North American continent results in a Union victory (see *The Battle of Gettysburg*, 1914).

4 July. Confederates surrender at Vicksburg (see *The Crisis*, 1915).

18 July. The 54th Massachusetts Colored Infantry attacks the rebel position at Fort Wagner, SC, but is thrown back (see *Glory*, 1989).

24-25 November. Rebel forces lose at Chattanooga, Tennessee.

By the end of the year, the South had suffered three decisive defeats--Gettysburg, Vicksburg and Chattanooga. Southerners could no longer win victory on the battlefield. Their only remaining hope was to achieve victory by dragging out the war, thereby destroying the Northern will to continue.

Campaigns (1864):

9 March. U.S. Grant takes command of all Union forces.

5-6 May. Grant's forces hammer Lee's army in the Battle of the Wilderness in Virginia.

November 15. The burning of Atlanta (see *Gone With the Wind*, 1939). Union General William T. Sherman begins his "March to the Sea" (see *Raintree County*, 1957).

June. Grant begins the siege of Petersburg (see *The Birth of a Nation*, 1915).

August-October. Union General Phil Sheridan destroys the rebel resources in the Shenandoah Valley.

Campaigns (1865):

19 January. Sherman moves from Savannah, Georgia, through South Carolina. The heart of the Confederacy is torn out (see *The Birth of a Nation*, 1915).

January-April. Grant continues unrelenting pressure on Lee's army.

9 April. Lee surrenders to Grant at Appomattox Court House, Virginia.

COMMENTARY

Ken Burns, producer and director of *The Civil War*, an extraordinarily popular documentary series for the Public Broadcasting System, wrote about the relationship of photographs and history. The Civil War, he reminded us, was the first war to be photographed extensively; the images of the aftermath of battle gripped viewers with a grotesque fascination. Following the Battle of Antietam in 1862, the *New York Times* commented on a series of violent photographs of the mutilated corpses taken by pioneer photographer Mathew Brady: "Mr. Brady has done something to bring us the terrible reality and earnestness of war. If he has not brought bodies and laid them in our dooryards and along our streets, he has done something very like it" (Burns 1). These graphic horrors were shocking, but over the last 125 years, we have gradually become inured to such scenes: "In many ways, our relationship to imagery has changed, the *value* of one picture down from the cliched *1000 words* to substantially less: devalued by familiarity and the inability of images to shock as they once did, and by a new medium, television, which always seems to impose itself between the picture and its ability to impress, to make memories, to make history" (Burns 1).

We can add, of course, feature films to television as an instrument of this devaluation. Horror films come first to mind, but war movies have had the same effect. Yet, even in their devalued state, scenes of war, fiction and nonfiction, "make memories" and "make history." In this sense the Civil War was not only the first photographer's war, it was the first filmmaker's war as well; it inspired D.W. Griffith's movie classic *The Birth of a Nation* (1915).

The appeal of the American Civil War--above all other American wars--to D.W. Griffith and millions of others lies first with the Myth of the Lost Cause: "Against forces most formidable the southerner pitted himself, his small fortune, his Lilliputian industry, his life, and his girded honor. He lost, but lost magnificently. He lost wholly, utterly, but out of the ashes of his homes, his cities, his broken generation, he salvaged his sacred honor. And with this scrap of victory he could build the myth that has sustained him" (Vandiver 147). William Faulkner called it the defeated Southerner's "ability to walk backward slow and stubborn and to endure" (347).

Ironically, the "Lost Cause" was soon adopted by Northerners and eventually the Hollywood film industry who came to see the rebels as gallant underdogs. Hollywood Westerns frequently told the story of a returning rebel soldier who must fight post-war corruption. Other reasons for the appeal of the Civil War lie in its pageantry, its scope, and its human drama. Quite simply, there has been no war like it before or since, no event in American history as vital, intense, meaningful or dramatic.

"No other American conflict--indeed, no other episode in our history--has so gripped the popular imagination as has the Civil War, the struggle between the United States and the Confederate States, the North and the South. It is the most written about, read about, and known about of all our wars," wrote historian T. Harry Williams. The story of that war "possesses unusual human interest and rare drama" and "an unparalleled cast of military characters--heroes and greats, might-have-been greats, and failures. It also offers speculative suspense--fateful battles that either side might have won." It was "a great dramatic experience and a searing national tragedy" (198).

This, of course, is the stuff of great motion pictures: a story and scenes attuned to the popular imagination, a strong cast, human interest, suspense, epic battles and tragedy. It is not surprising, then, that the American Civil War has provided the storyline for two of the greatest motion pictures ever made--*The Birth of a Nation* (1915) and *Gone With the Wind* (1939). Although no Civil War film since these has matched or surpassed their qualities, it is a subject of unending interest to a vast number of Americans, both North and South. The Civil War is still within living memory and the issue of race, so central to that conflict, remains a matter of concern in our public and private lives. What is surprising, however, is that a subject of such fascination and film potential has not received the kind of attention it deserves. Looking over the hundred or so best known Civil War movies, we can point only to a handful--like *Birth of a Nation*, *Gone With the Wind*, *The Red Badge of Courage* (1951), *Raintree County* (1957), *The Horse Soldiers* (1959) and *Glory* (1989)--of first-class productions that deal seriously with the war and its issues. And of these only *Birth of a Nation*, *Red Badge of Courage*, *Horse Soldiers* and *Glory* contain extended battle scenes. Others are mostly hybrid westerns: a "curious blend of cavalry-vs-Indian and Civil War action" (Langman and Borg 20).

Interestingly, one of the most authentic films is a comedy: Buster Keaton's *The General* (1927) has "the look of the unavoidable Mathew Brady photographs and the final scenes are treated with a realism unusual in a film of this kind" (Butler 40-41).

The last of the old wars and the first of the modern ones, the Civil War foreshadowed the shape of things to come. The great narrative historian Bruce Catton wrote this passage which has in it the epic qualities and largely neglected cinematic possibilities of America's greatest war. During Pickett's charge at Gettysburg, on that hot July day in 1863, he found a scene that could "make memories" and "make history":

> The smoke lifted like a rising curtain, and all of the great amphitheater lay open at last, and the Yankee soldiers could look west all the way to the belt of trees on Seminary Ridge. They were old soldiers and had been in many battles, but what they saw then took their breath away, and whether they had ten minutes or seventy-five years yet to live, they remembered it until they died. There it was, for the last time in this war, perhaps for the last time anywhere, the grand pageantry of war in the old style, beautiful and majestic and terrible: fighting men lined up for a mile and a half from flank to flank, slashed red flags overhead, soldiers marching forward elbow to elbow, officers with drawn swords, sunlight gleaming from thousands of musket barrels, lines dressed as if for parade (Catton 33).

No studio's feature film has managed to capture the grand proportions--though *Birth of a Nation* and *Glory* come close--of Civil War combat. But an independent's short film deserves special mention for suggesting the war's essence. In *A Time Out of War* (1954), a rarely seen low-budget film by a college film student, two Yankees and one rebel soldier agree to a temporary truce so they can relax their guard on opposite banks of a river. "They chat, rest, float coffee and tobacco to one another across the river." But their discovery of a soldier's corpse reminds them of their sworn purpose to kill each other. The theme of instinctive brotherhood, unnaturally broken, is poignantly depicted. "In the brief twenty-three minutes of this visually beautiful little masterpiece more is said on its subject than a dozen overblown epics" (Butler 97).

Burns, Ken. "The Painful, Essential, Images of War." *New York Times* 27 Jan. 1991, sec. 2: 1.

Butler, Ivan. *The War Film*. Cranbury, NJ: A.S. Barnes, 1974.
Catton, Bruce. *Glory Road*. New York: Doubleday, 1952.
Faulkner, William. *Absalom, Absalom!* 1936. New York: Modern Library, 1951.
Langman, Larry, and Ed Borg. *Encyclopedia of American War Films*. New York: Garland, 1989.
Vandiver, Frank. "The Confederate Myth." *Myth and Southern History*. Ed. Patrick Gerster and Nicholas Cords. Chicago: Rand, 1974. 147-53.

FILMOGRAPHY

Abraham Lincoln.* aka *The Dramatic Life of Abraham Lincoln*. 12 reels, b/w. Dir. Phil Rosen. With Fay McKenzie, Westcott B. Clark, George A, Billings, Ruth Clifford, Nell Craig. AFN, 1924.

Abraham Lincoln.** 97m, b/w. Dir. D.W. Griffith. With Walter Huston, Una Merkal, Kay Hammond, E. Alyn Warren, Hobart Bosworth. UA, 1930.

Advance to the Rear.* 97m, b/w. Dir. George Marshall. With Glenn Ford, Stella Stevens, Melvyn Douglas, Jim Backus, Joan Blondell. MGM, 1964.

Alvarez Kelly.* 110m, color. Dir. Edward Dmytryk. With William Holden, Richard Widmark, Janice Rule, Victoria Shaw, Patrick O'Neal. Columbia, 1966.

Arizona Bushwackers.* 87m, color. Dir. Lesley Selander. With Howard Keel, Yvonne De Carlo, John Ireland, Marilyn Maxwell, Scott Brady. Paramount, 1968.

The Battle of Gettysburg.* 5 reels, b/w. Dir. Thomas H. Ince. With Willard Mack, Charles French, Enid Bennett, Herschal Mayall, Walter Edwards. Mutual, 1914.

The Beguiled.* 105m, color. Dir. Don Seigel. With Clint Eastwood, Geraldine Page, Elizabeth Hartman, Jo Ann Harris. Universal, 1971.

The Birth of a Nation.**** 12 reels, b/w. Dir. D.W. Griffith. With Lillian Gish, Mae Marsh, Henry B. Walthall, Miriam Cooper, Robert Harron, Wallace Reid, Joseph Henabery. Epoch, 1915.

Originally tinted for dramatic effect and accompanied by a symphonic score, this stunning production set the Hollywood standard in filmmaking. U.S. President Woodrow Wilson said it was "History written in lightning." Remarkable panoramic battlefield scenes (filmed in Southern

California). Based on a Thomas Dixon novel, *The Clansman*. Evocative shot: screen title "War's peace" fades to reveal dead soldiers strewn in trenches. Still controversial for its favorable depiction of the Ku Klux Klan. Footnote: most films then were made from only 100 separate shots, but Griffith edited 1544 shots.

Border River.* 80m, color. Dir. George Sherman. With Joel McCrea, Yvonne De Carlo, Pedro Armendariz, Howard Petrie, Erika Nordin. Universal, 1954.

Charley-One-Eye.* 107m, color. Dir. Don Chaffey. With Richard Roundtree, Roy Thinnes, Nigel Davenport, Jill Pearson. Paramount, 1973.

The Coward.** b/w. Dir. Reginald Barker. With Frank Keenan, Charles Ray, Gertrude Claire. Triangle, 1915.

Dan.* 5 reels, b/w. With Lew Dockstader, Lois Meredith, Gail Kane, Beatrice Clevener. All Star Feature, 1914.

The Dark Command.* 91m, b/w. Dir. Raoul Walsh. With John Wayne, Claire Trevor, Walter Pidgeon, Roy Rogers, Gabby Hayes. Republic, 1940.

Drums in the Deep South.* 87m, color. Dir. William Cameron Menzies. With Craig Stevens, James Craig, Barbara Payton, Guy Madison. RKO, 1951.

Escape From Fort Bravo.* 98m, color. Dir. John Sturges. With William Holden, Eleanor Parker, John Forsythe, William Demarest, William Campbell. MGM, 1953.

The Fastest Guitar Alive.* 87m, b/w. Dir. Michael Moore. With Roy Orbison, Sammy Jackson, Maggie Pierce, Joan Freeman, Lyle Bettger. MGM, 1967.

Friendly Persuasion.*** 137m, color. Dir. Willliam Wyler. With Gary Cooper, Dorothy McGuire, Marjorie Main, Anthony Perkins, Richard Eyer. AA, 1956.

Frontier Scout.* 60m, b/w. Dir. Sam Newfield. With George Houston, Al St. John, Beth Marion, Dave O'Brien. Fine, 1939.

The General.**** 8 reels, b/w. Dir. Buster Keaton. With Buster Keaton, Marian Mack, Glen Cavender, Jim Farley. UA, 1927.

Keaton's romantic-slapstick masterpiece (much of it improvised during shooting). Based on true story. Best scene: the engineer (Keaton) fails to notice he has passed retreating Southerners on his way to recapture his train ("the General"). Footnote: filmed in Oregon with great attention to the look of Mathew Brady photographs.

Glory.**** 122m, color. Dir. Edward Zwick. With Matthew Broderick, Denzel Washington, Cary Elwes, Morgan Freeman. Tri-Star, 1989.

Based on true story of the 54th Massachusetts Colored Infantry's suicidal attack on Fort Wagner, SC. Best scene: the unit faces its first test in turning back an infantry-cavalry charge in a smoky wooded clearing. Slow moving but gorgeous cinematography helps glorify the heroism of bickering individuals turning into a unit. Supporting Oscar for Washington.

Gone With the Wind.**** 220m, color. Dir. Victor Fleming. With Clark Gable, Vivien Leigh, Olivia de Havilland, Leslie Howard, Thomas Mitchell, Barbara O'Neil, Hattie McDaniel, Butterfly McQueen, Victor Jory, Evelyn Keyes, Ann Rutherford, Laura Hope Crews, Harry Davenport, Jane Darwell, Ona Munson, Ward Bond. MGM, 1939.

Incomparable. Oscars for best film, actress, supporting actress, direction, screenwriting, and 5 other categories. Best scene: camera on 125-foot crane pulls back to reveal masses of wounded Confederates. Uncredited directors include George Cukor, William Cameron Menzies, David O. Selznick, and Sam Wood. Based on the novel by Margaret Mitchell. Footnote: burning of Atlanta is actually the burning of Pathe studio's 30-acre backlot.

Grandma's Boy.** 5 reels, b/w. Dir. Fred Newmeyer. With Harold Lloyd, Mildred Davis, Anna Townsend, Charles Stevenson. Exhibitors, 1922.

Great Day in the Morning.* 91m, color. Dir. Jacques Tourneur. With Virginia Mayo, Robert Stack, Ruth Roman, Alex Nichol. RKO, 1956.

The Great Locomotive Chase.** aka *Andrews' Raiders.* 87m, color. Dir. Francis D. Lyon. With Fess Parker, Jeffrey Hunter, John Lupton, Jeff York. Disney, 1956.

Hands Up.** 6 reels, b/w. Dir. Clarence Badger. With Raymond Griffith, Marion Nixon, Virginia Lee Corbin, Mack Swain, Montagu Love. Paramount, 1926.

The Heart of Maryland.* 6 reels, b/w. Dir. Tom Terriss. With Catherine Calvert, Crane Wilbur, Felix Krembs, Ben Lyon. FN, 1921.

Hearts In Bondage.* 72m, b/w. Dir. Lew Ayres. With James Dunn, Mae Clarke, David Manners, Charlotte Henry. Republic, 1936.

The Hellbenders.* 92m, color. Dir. Sergio Corbucci. With Joseph Cotton, Norma Bengell, Julian Mateos. Embassy, 1967.

Horse Soldiers.*** 119m, color. Dir. John Ford. With John Wayne, William Holden, Constance Towers, Althea Gibson, Hoot Gibson, Anna Lee. UA, 1959.

Incident at Phantom Hill.* 88m, color. Dir. Earl Bellamy. With Robert Fuller, Jocelyn Lane, Dan Durtea, Tom Simcox. Universal, 1966.

Jesse James.* 8 reels, b/w. Dir. Lloyd Ingraham. With Fred Thompson, Nora James, Montagu Love, Mary Carr, James Pierce. Paramount, 1927.

Johnny Ring & the Captain's Sword.* 5 reels, b/w. Dir. Norman L. Stevens. With Ben Warren, Frank Walker. Temple, 1921.

Journey to Shiloh.* 101m, color. Dir. William Hale. With James Caan, Michael Sarrazin, Brenda Scott, Don Stroud, Paul Peterson, Harrison Ford. Universal, 1968.

Kansas Raiders.* 80m, color. Dir. Ray Enright. With Audie Murphy, Brian Donlevy, Marguerite Chapman, Scott Brady, Tony Curtis. Universal, 1950.

The Last Outpost.* 88m, color. Dir. Lewis R. Foster. With Ronald Reagan, Rhonda Flemming, Bruce Bennett, Bill Williams, Peter Hanson, Noah Beery, Jr. Paramount, 1951.

The Man from Dakota.* aka *Arouse and Beware.* 74m, b/w. Dir. Leslie Fenton. With Wallace Beery, John Howard, Dolores Del Rio, Donald Meek, Robert Barrat. MGM, 1940.

May Blossom.* 4 reels, b/w. Dir. Allan Dwan. With Gertrude Robinson, Russell Bassett, Marshall Neilan, Donald Crisp. Famous, 1915.

Morgan's Last Raid.* 6 reels, b/w. Dir. Nick Grinde. With Tim McCoy, Dorothy Sebastian, Wheeler Oakman. MGM, 1929.

No Drums, No Bugles.* 85m, color. Dir. Clyde Ware. With Davey Davidson, Rod McCarey, Martin Sheen, Denine Terry. Cinerama, 1971.

Occurence at Owl Creek Bridge.*** 29m, b/w. Dir. Robert Enrico. With Roger Jaquet, Anne Cornally. Cappagariff, 1962.

Only the Brave.* 66m, b/w. Dir. Frank Tuttle. With Gary Cooper, Mary Brian, Philips Holmes, James Neill, Morgan Farley. Paramount, 1930.

Operator 13.* 86m, b/w. Dir. Richard Boleslavsky. With Marion Davies, Gary Cooper, Jean Parker, Katherine Alexander, Ted Healy. MGM, 1934.

Quantrill's Raiders.* 68m, color. Dir. Edward Bernds. With Steve Cochran, Diane Brewster, Leo Gordon, Gale Robbins, Will Wright. AA, 1958.

The Raid.** 82m, color. Dir. Hugo Fregonese. With Van Heflin, Anne Bancroft, Richard Boone, Lee Marvin, Tommy Rettig. Fox, 1954.

Raintree County.*** 157m, color. Dir. Edward Dmytryk. With Montgomery Clift, Elizabeth Taylor, Eva Marie Saint, Rod Taylor, Lee Marvin. MGM, 1957.

Reason to Live, A Reason to Die.* aka *Massacre at Fort Holman.* 92m, color. Dir. Tonino Valerii. With James Coburn, Telly Savalas, Bud Spencer, Ralph Goodwin. Heritage, 1974.

Rebel City.* 62m, b/w. Dir. Thomas Carr. With Wild Bill Elliott, Marjorie Lord, Robert Kent, Keith Richards. AA, 1953.

The Red Badge of Courage.**** 69m, b/w. Dir. John Huston. With Audie Murphy, Bill Mauldin, Douglas Dick, Royal Dano, Andy Devine, John Dierkes, Arthur Hunnicutt. MGM, 1951.

A young infantryman (Murphy) learns about fear and bravery in combat. Based on the classic novel by Stephen Crane. Best scene: untested soldiers discuss how they will react to the coming battle. Footnote: Lillian Ross in her book *Picture* gives us a trenchant insider's view into the making of this film in particular, and the business of filmmaking in general.

Red Mountain.* 84m, color. Dir. William Dieterle. With Alan Ladd, Lizabeth Scott, Arthur Kennedy, John Ireland, Jeff Corey. Paramount, 1951.

Revolt at Fort Laramie.* 73m, color. Dir. Lesley Selander. With John Dehner, Gregg Palmer, Frances Helm, Don Gordon. UA, 1957.

Rocky Mountain.* 83m, b/w. Dir. William Keighley. With Errol Flynn, Patrice Wymore, Scott Forbes, Guinn Williams, Dick Jones, Howard Petrie. WB, 1950.

The Romance of Rosy Ridge* 105m, b/w. Dir. Roy Rowland. With Van Johnson, Thomas Mitchell, Janet Leigh, Marshall Thompson, Selena Royle. MGM, 1947.

Secret Service.* 69m, b/w. Dir. J. Walter Ruben. With Richard Dix, Shirley Grey, William Post, Jr., Gavin Gordon. RKO, 1931.

Seven Angry Men.* 90m, b/w. Dir. Charles Marquis Warren. With Raymond Massey, Debra Paget, Jeffrey Hunter, Larry Pennell, Leo Gordon. AA, 1955.

Shenandoah.** 105m, color. Dir. Andrew V. McLaglen. With James Stewart, Doug McClure, Glenn Corbett, Patrick Wayne, Rosemary Forsyth. Universal, 1965.

The Siege at Red River.* 86m, color. Dir. Rudolph Mate. With Van Johnson, Joanne Dru, Richard Boone, Milburn Stone. Fox, 1954.

So Red the Rose.* 82m, b/w. Dir. King Vidor. With Margaret Sullavan, Walter Connally, Janet Beecher, Harry Ellerbe. Paramount, 1935.

A Southern Yankee.* aka *My Hero!* 90m, b/w. Dir. Edward Sedgwick. With Red Skelton, Brian Donlevy, Arlene Dahl, George Coulouris, Lloyd Gough, John Ireland. MGM, 1948.

Springfield Rifle.* 93m, color. Dir. Andre de Toth. With Gary Cooper, Phyllis Thaxter, David Brian, Paul Kelly, Philip Carey. WB, 1952.

Tap Roots.** 109m, color. Dir. George Marshall. With Van Heflin, Susan Hayward, Boris Karloff, Julie London, Whitfield Conner, Ward Bond. Universal, 1948.

Thirteen Fighting Men.* 69m, b/w. Dir. Harry Gerstad. With Grant Williams, Brad Dexter, Carole Mathews, Robert Dix, Richard Garland. Fox, 1960.

Those Without Sin.* 5 reels, b/w. Dir. Marshall Neilan. With Blanche Sweet, Tom Forman, C.H. Geldert, Guy Oliver, James Neill. Paramount, 1917.

A Time For Killing.* 83m, color. Dir. Phil Karlson. With Glenn Ford, George Hamilton, Inger Stevens, Paul Peterson, Timothy Carey. Columbia, 1967.

A Time Out of War.**** 23m, b/w. Dir. Denis Sanders. With Barry Atwater, Robert Sherry, Alan Cohen. Sanders, 1954.
A remarkable film (the only short judged important enough to list in this guide), based on Robert W. Chambers' short story "Pickets." Two Yanks and one Reb take a one-hour break from war to fish, talk and eat; then go back to exchanging gunfire. Footnote: the film is Sanders' master's project at the University of California.

Two Flags West.* 92m, b/w. Dir. Robert Wise. With Joseph Cotten, Linda Darnell, Jeff Chandler, Cornel Wilde, Dale Robertson. Fox, 1950.

The Undefeated.* 119m, color. Dir. Andrew V. McLaglen. With John Wayne, Rock Hudson, Tony Aguilar, Marian McCargo. Fox, 1969.

The Vanquished.* 84m, color. Dir. Edward Ludwig. With John Payne, Coleen Gray, Jan Sterling, Lyle Bettger. Paramount, 1953.

Virginia City.* 121m, b/w. Dir. Michael Curtiz. With Errol Flynn, Miriam Hopkins, Randolph Scott, Humphrey Bogart, Frank McHugh, Alan Hale. WB, 1940.

The Warrens of Virginia.* 5 reels, b/w. Dir. Cecil B. DeMille. With Blanche Sweet, James Neill, House Peters, Page Peters, Mabel Van Baren. Lasky, 1915.

The Warrens of Virginia.* 7 reels, b/w. Dir. Elmer Clifton. With George Backus, Rosemary Hill, Martha Mansfield, Robert Andrews. Fox, 1924.

Yellowneck.* 83m, color. Dir. Arthur Lubin. With Lin McCarthy, Stephen Courtleigh, Berry Kroeger, Harold Gordon, Bill Mason. Republic, 1955.

6

Indian Wars

CHRONOLOGY

Seventeenth and Eighteenth Centuries:

1622-1644. Uprising of tidewater Virginia tribes under Opechancanough.

1637. Puguot War (Connecticut).

1675. King Philip's War (New England).

1711. Tuscarora War (North Carolina).

1756-1763. French and Indian War (see also Chapter 3, "Early American Wars") or the Seven Years' War (see *The Last of the Mohicans*, 1936; *Northwest Passage*, 1940).

1776-1783. The American Revolution inspired Indian uprising along the western frontier (see *Drums Along the Mohawk*, 1939). Iroquois nations fight on both sides--Mohawks, Senecas, and Onondagas with the British; Oniedas and Tuscaroras with Americans in the Old Northwest; Cherokees attack American colonial settlements in southern frontier area.

Early to Mid-Nineteenth Century:

1812. Tecumseh's uprising in the Old Northwest (upper Mississippi region).

1817-1818. First Seminole War. Seminole and Lower Creeks attack Georgia and Spanish Florida border area.

1832. Black Hawk War. Sac and Fox uprising along the upper Mississippi.

1835-1843. Second Seminole War. Guerrilla warfare is led by Osceola in the swamps of Florida (see *Distant Drums*, 1951; *Seminole*, 1953).

Mid to Late Nineteenth Century:

Approximately 100,000 out of 250,000 Indians resist the white advance in the Great Plains region.

1850's. The U.S. Army acts to: (1) defend migrants and railroads along central Great Plains routes to Oregon and California from attacks by Sioux, Cheyennes, Arapahos, and Comanches, (2) protect settlers on the Texas and New Mexico frontier from raids by Kiowas, Comanches, Utes, and Apaches and (3) build a series of western fronts in the Indian Country and Southwest frontier.

1862-1868. Santee Sioux uprising in Minnesota spreads to central and southern Great Plains.

1864. Battle of Sand Creek, Colorado. Southern Cheyennes under Black Kettle are massacred.

1874. Red River War in the southern Great Plains. Kiowas, Cheyennes, Arapahos and Comanches are forced onto reservations in the Indian Territory.

1876-1877. Sioux and Cheyenne hostiles under Crazy Horse and Sitting Bull leave reservation areas in the Dakotas and gather in Montana along the Little Big Horn River; Custer's unit of the Seventh Cavalry Regiment is annihilated ("Custer's Last Stand") on 26 June 1876 (see

They Died With Their Boots On, 1941; *The Great Sioux Massacre*, 1965; *Custer of the West*, 1968; *Little Big Man*, 1970). The Federal government is now determined to end Indian resistance once and for all.

1870's-1886. Apache resistance in Arizona, New Mexico, and west Texas is led by Cochise and Geronimo (see *Tomahawk Trail*, 1957; *Ulzana's Raid*, 1972). Search and destroy operations finally end resistance.

1890. Ghost Dance movement leads to unrest and confrontation on the Sioux reservation in South Dakota. Massacre of Wounded Knee in December (see *Soldier Blue*, 1970). Indian wars end.

COMMENTARY

White society has, since the first contacts with the native peoples of North America, exhibited a curiously schizophrenic cultural attitude. On the one hand, the Indian was the Child of Nature or Noble Savage--a view both romantic and philosophical. Here were people who lived in harmony with nature in an ideal society of "sexual innocence, equality of condition and status, peaceful simplicity, healthful and handsome bodies, and vigorous minds unsullied by the wiles, complexities, and sophistication of modern civilization" (Berkhofer 72). The good Indian was admired for his skills, bravery, and innate democratic ways--a "master of the wilderness and possessor of physical prowess" (98). The bad Indian was a vicious brute who impeded the advance of civilization: "In the negative image the Indian was the usual bloodthirsty savage, often crazed, seeking vengeance or just malicious fun at the expense of innocent Whites, especially woman" (98). The great historian Francis Parkman, for example, saw the Oglala Sioux "as a troublesome and dangerous species of wild beast" (qtd. in Berkhofer 95).

Literature, art, and film have all reflected this confusion of images. The good Indian and the bad Indian exist in our movies side by side. Whether Wild Savage or Noble Red Man, there were other confusions as well. The Hollywood western or cavalry movie seldom gets its anthropology right: "the Indian was generally depicted as a person of little culture and less language. Speaking *how!* and *ugh!* dialogue and wearing combination, if not phony, tribal dress, Indians were usually portrayed with little concern for tribal differences in language, customs, or beliefs. Whites and Asians frequently acted the leading Indian parts." Thus, "because of the ignorance of writers, directors, and actors, the Indian was usually as stereotyped in a film supposedly sympathetic to the Native American cause as in one openly hostile to his plight" (Berkhofer 103).

Broken Arrow (1950) illustrates the point. Although it is a "landmark film in its sympathetic treatment of the American Indian," the viewer has to accept the Teutonic-looking Jeff Chandler as Cochise and Debra Paget as an Indian maiden. With regard to the Indian-white conflict, the film gets to have it both ways. The fighting is instigated by "unscrupulous whites," but "treacherous Apaches" contribute to the strife "until the cavalry is forced to intervene" (Langman and Borg 80).

Also noteworthy is *Little Big Man* (1970), a quirky film that attempts an overview of mistreating Native Americans through the reminiscences of the only "survivor" of Custer's Last Stand, the 121-year old Jack Crabb.

Yet "even those films of the 1960's and 1970's hailed as realistic and sympathetic of Native American society still contain stereotypes typical of the motion-picture industry in the past, for all they usually did was to reverse the traditional imagery by making the Indian good and the White bad." The counterculture movement influenced filmmakers to create movies (like *Soldier Blue* and *Little Big Man*, both 1970) whose "action and locale purport to be laid in the past" yet whose "dialogue and thrust of plot speak more to the recent conflict in Vietnam than to the battle over the American plains and mountains" (Berkhofer 103).

In *Dances with Wolves* (1990), Kevin Costner, director and star of the compelling but anachronistic film, plays a "New Age" cavalry lieutenant who comes to see the environment, the animals of the Plains and the Sioux as friends (Morris H11). First he cleans up the pollution around an abandoned army outpost. Eventually he is adopted by the local tribe and "turns Indian." By the end of the film, the hero's identification with the Native American is complete. He comes to see whites as "without character or soul" because they have no respect for "Sioux rights." "Every one of the soldiers is made a loutish brute, so...we understand why he helps [the Sioux] to kill" them (Kauffmann). Really, Costner's film shows little understanding of the history or culture of the aggressive Sioux or their Indian enemies. But the film, a "politically correct" box office hit for the 1990s, won seven Oscars. It makes an interesting contrast to John Ford's classic *She Wore a Yellow Ribbon* (1949) which treats the Cheyenne with historical accuracy, respect and understanding; it also accurately records the details of army dress and celebrates the heroism and traditions of the cavalry. It is part of Ford's brilliant trilogy about the U.S. Cavalry during the Indian wars: *Fort Apache* (1948), *She Wore a Yellow Ribbon* (1949), and *Rio Grande* (1950). Ford's attention to detail is, of course, his hallmark. He shows women trying to maintain civilized standards on the frontier; military routine in an outpost; costumes and scenery based on Frederic Remington's western paintings; the songs and culture of the ordinary cavalrymen.

If *Dances with Wolves* turns the Myth of the West upside down, it nevertheless achieves a genuineness of detail (a brilliantly reenacted buffalo hunt, for example) seldom seen in film. The cast includes real Sioux Indians (Nathan Lee Chasing His Horse, Jason Lone Hill, and Michael Spears, for example) and "cackling, toothless old women and tubby little boys up to mischief." And too, "the quest for authenticity is reflected in the costumes of tanned deer hide and buffalo wraps, at times decorated with elaborate beadwork and porcupine-quill weaving..." (Morris H22). These Indians do not speak in "how! and ugh! dialogue"; they converse in Pawnee or Lakota translated in English subtitles. The realities of Indian warfare are pictured in accurate detail as well: "This is not the kind of Hollywood film in which men die neatly with an arrow crisply through the heart. Here, more true to life, they die slowly, crawling in shock with a dozen arrows sticking out of their sides and arms and calves" (Morris H22). Yet even this film is not free of confusion of perception. Conflicting images of the Child of Nature and the Bloodthirsty Savage exist side by side. The Sioux's "Pawnee enemies are painted a primal blue, like some cannibalistic tribe from the jungle" (Morris H22).

It is with some little irony (or calculation) that *Dances with Wolves* appeared in movie houses exactly one hundred years following the Battle (Massacre) of Wounded Knee which marked the end of Indian resistance, and a century after the Census of 1890 announced the end of the American Frontier.

Berkhofer, Jr, Robert F. *The White Man's Indian: Images of the American Indian from Columbus to the Present*. New York: Knopf, 1978.

Kauffman, Stanley. "Review of *Dances with Wolves*." *New Republic* 10 Dec. 1990: 28.

Langman, Larry, and Ed Borg. *Encyclopedia of American War Films*. New York: Garland, 1989.

Morris, Richard C. "Kevin Costner Journeys to a New Frontier."
New York Times 4 Nov. 1990: H11+.

FILMOGRAPHY

*Ambush.** 89m, b/w. Dir. Sam Wood. With Robert Taylor, John
Hodiak. Arlene Dahl. MGM, 1950.

*Apache.*** 91m, color. Dir. Robert Aldrich. With Burt Lancaster,
Jean Peters, John McIntire, Charles (Bronson) Buchinsky.
UA, 1954.

*Apache Drums.*** 74m, color. Dir. Hugo Fregonese. With Stephen
McNally, Coleen Gray, Willard Parker, Arthur Shields,
James Griffith. Universal, 1951.

*Apache Rifles.** 90m, color. Dir. William H. Witney. With Audie
Murphy, Michael Dante, Linda Lawson. Fox, 1964.

*Apache Uprising.** 90m, color. Dir. R.G. Springsteen. With Rory
Calhoun, Corinne Calvet, John Russell, DeForest Kelley.
Paramount, 1966.

*Apache Warrior.*** 73m, b/w. Dir. Elmo Williams. With Keith
Larson, Jim Davis, Rodolfo Acosta, John Miljan, Eddie
Little. Fox, 1957.

*Arrowhead.*** 105m, color. Dir. Charles Marquis Warren. With
Charlton Heston, Jack Palance, Katy Jurado, Brian Keith,
Mary Sinclair. Paramount, 1953.

*Badlands of Dakota.*** 74m, b/w. Dir. Alfred E. Green. With
Robert Stack, Ann Rutherford, Richard Dix, Frances
Farmer, Broderick Crawford, Hugh Herbert. Universal, 1941.

*The Battle at Apache Pass.** 85m, color. Dir. George Sherman.
With John Lund, Jeff Chandler, Beverly Tyler, Bruce
Cowling, Susan Cabot. Universal, 1952.

*The Black Dakotas.** 65m, color. Dir. Ray Nazarro. With Gary
Merrill, Wanda Hendrix, John Bromfield, Noah Beery, Jr.,
Fay Roope. Columbia, 1954.

*Broken Arrow.**** 93m, color. Dir. Delmer Daves. With James
Stewart, Jeff Chandler, Debra Paget, Basil Ruysdael, Will
Geer, Joyce McKenzie, Arthur Honnicutt. Fox, 1950.

*Bugles in the Afternoon.*** 85m, color. Dir. Roy Rowland. With
Ray Milland, Forrest Tucker, George Reeves, Helena Carter,
Gertrude Michael. WB, 1952.

*Cheyenne Autumn.**** 159m, color. Dir. John Ford. With Richard
Widmark, Carroll Baker, Karl Malden, James Stewart,
Edward G. Robinson, Sal Mineo, Ricardo Montalban. WB,
1964.

Chief Crazy Horse.** 86m, color. Dir. George Sherman. With Victor Mature, Suzan Ball, John Lund, Ray Danton, Keith Larson. Universal, 1955.

Comanche.** 87m, color. Dir. George Sherman. With Dana Andrews, Kent Smith, Linda Cristal, Nestor Paiva, Henry Brandon. UA, 1956.

Comanche Territory.* 76m, color. Dir. George Sherman. With Maureen O'Hara, MacDonald Carey, Will Geer, Charles Drake. Universal, 1950.

Conquest of Cochise.* 70m, color. Dir. William Castle. With John Hodiak, Robert Stack, Joy Page, Rico Alniz, Fortunio Bonanova. Columbia, 1953.

Custer of the West.** 143m, color. Dir. Robert Siodmak. With Robert Shaw, Mary Ure, Jeffrey Hunter, Robert Ryan, Ty Hardin, Charles Stalnaker, Robert Hall, Lawrence Tierney. Cinerama, 1968

Dances with Wolves.**** 180m, color. Dir. Kevin Costner. With Kevin Costner, Nathan Lee Cashing His Horse, Jason Lone Hill, Michael Spears. 1990.

    Sympathetic view of the land, the animals, and the strengths and gentleness of the Sioux. Awarded 7 Oscars. Best scene: a thrilling buffalo hunt is restaged with live and mechanical animals. Footnote: Pauline Kael (*New Yorker*, 17 Dec. 1990) called the movie "New Age Daydreams" and said its popularity is due to its presenting complex issues in simpleminded terms.

Daniel Boone, Trail Blazer.* 76m, color. Dir. Albert C. Gannaway. With Bruce Bennett, Lon Chaney, Jr., Faron Young, Kem Dibbs, Damian O'Flynn. Republic, 1957.

The Deserter.* 90m, color. Dir. Burt Kennedy. With Bekim Fehmiu, Richard Crenna, Chuck Conners, Ricardo Montalban. Paramount, 1971.

Distant Drums.** 100m, color. Dir. Raoul Walsh. With Gary Cooper, Mari Aldon, Richard Webb, Ray Teal. WB, 1951.

A Distant Trumpet.** 117m, color. Dir. Raoul Walsh. With Troy Donahue, Suzanne Pleshette, Kent Smith, Claude Akins, James Gregory. WB, 1964.

Drum Beat.** 111m, color. Dir. Delmer Daves. With Alan Ladd, Audrey Dalton, Marisa Pavan, Robert Keith, Rodolfo Acosta. WB, 1954.

Duel at Diablo.* 105m, color. Dir. Ralph Nelson. With James Garner, Sidney Poitier, Bibi Anderson, Dennis Weaver, Bill Travers. UA, 1966.

Escape from Fort Bravo.** 98m, color. Dir. John Sturges. With
William Holden, Eleanor Parker, John Forsythe, William
Demarest, William Campbell. MGM, 1953.

Flaming Frontier.* 70m, b/w. Dir. Sam Newfield. With Bruce
Bennett, Jim Davis, Paisley Maxwell, Cecil Linder, Peter
Humphreys. Fox, 1958.

Fort Apache.**** 127m, b/w. Dir. John Ford. With Henry
Fonda, John Wayne, Shirley Temple, John Agar, Anna Lee,
Ward Bond, Victor McLaglen. RKO, 1948.

   The first of Ford's cavalry trilogy. Epic story, panoramic
scenes (filmed in Monument Valley), attention to detail.
Based on the short stories of James W. Bellah. The best
scenes deal with the routine life of the Irish soldiers.
Footnote: Fonda's character is based upon George Custer.

Fort Bowie.* 80m, b/w. Dir. Howard W. Koch. With Ben
Johnson, Jan Harrison, Kent Taylor, Jane Davi, Larry
Chance. UA, 1958.

Fort Massacre.** 80m, color. Dir. Joseph M. Newman. With
Joel McCrea, Forrest Tucker, Susan Cabot, John Russell,
Anthony Caruso. UA, 1958.

Fort Yuma.* 78m, color. Dir. Lesley Selander. With Peter
Graves, Joan Vohs, John Hudson, Joan Taylor. UA, 1955.

Geronimo.** 89m, b/w. Dir. Paul H. Sloane. With Preston Foster,
Ellen Drew, Andy Devine, Gene Lockhart, Ralph Morgan,
Marjorie Gateson, Chief Thundercloud. Paramount, 1939.

Geronimo.* 101m, color. Dir. Arnold Laven. With Chuck Conners,
Kamala Devi, Ross Martin, Pat Conway, Adam West. UA,
1962.

The Glory Guys.** 111m, color. Dir. Arnold Laven. With Tom
Tryon, Harve Presnell, Senta Berger, Andrew Duggan, Slim
Pickens, James Caan, Michael Anderson, Jr. UA, 1965.

The Great Sioux Massacre.** aka *Custer Massacre; The Massacre
at Rosebud.* 92m, color. Dir. Sidney Salkow. With Joseph
Cotten, Darren McGavin, Philip Carey, Julie Sommars,
Nancy Kovack, John Matthews, Frank Ferguson. Columbia,
1965.

The Great Sioux Uprising.* 79m, color. Dir. Lloyd Bacon. With
Jeff Chandler, Faith Domerque, Lyle Bettger, Stacy Harris,
Peter Whitney. Universal, 1953.

The Gun That Won the West.* 69m, color. Dir. William Castle.
With Dennis Morgan, Paula Raymond, Richard Denning,
Chris O'Brein. Columbia, 1955.

The Guns of Fort Petticoat. * 81m, color. Dir. George Marshall.
With Audie Murphy, Kathryn Grant, Hope Emerson, Jeff
Donnell, Jeanette Nolan. Columbia, 1957.

*I Killed Geronimo.** 72m, b/w. Dir. John Hoffman. With James
     Ellison, Chief Thunder Cloud, Virginia Herrick, Smith
     Ballew. EL, 1950.
*I Will Fight No More Forever.*** 100m, color. Dir. Richard T.
     Heffron. With James Whitmore, Ned Romero, Linda
     Redfern, Sam Elliott. Wolper, 1975.
*Indian Fighter.*** 88m, color. Dir. Andre de Toth. With Kirk
     Douglas, Elsa Martinelli, Walter Abel, Walter Matthau,
     Diana Douglas, Lon Chaney. UA, 1955.
*Indian Uprising.** 75m, color. Dir. Ray Nazarro. With George
     Montgomery, Audrey Long, Carl Benton Reid, Eugene
     Iglesias. Columbia, 1951.
*The Invaders.** 7 reels, b/w. Dir. J.P. McGowan. With Bob Steele,
     Edna Aslin, Thomas Lindham, J.P. McGowan. Syndicate,
     1929.
*Last of the Comanches.** aka *The Sabre and the Arrow.* 85m,
     color. Dir. Andre de Toth. With Broderick Crawford,
     Barbara Hale, Johnny Stewart, Lloyd Bridges, Mickey
     Shaughnessy. Columbia, 1952.
*Last Outpost.*** 88m, color. Dir. Lewis R. Foster. With Ronald
     Reagan, Rhonda Fleming, Bruce Bennett, Bill Williams,
     Peter Hanson. Paramount, 1951.
*Little Big Horn.** 5 reels, b/w. Dir. Harry L. Fraser. With John
     Beck, Roy Stewart, Helen Lynch, Edmund Cobb. Oxford,
     1927.
*Little Big Horn.*** 86m, b/w. Dir. Charles Marquis Warren. With
     Lloyd Bridges, John Ireland, Marie Windsor, Reed Hadley,
     Jim Davis. Lippert, 1951.
*Little Big Man.*** 147m, color. Dir. Arthur Penn. With Dustin
     Hoffman, Faye Dunaway, Martin Balsam, Richard Mulligan,
     Chief Dan George, Jeff Corey, Amy Eccles. National, 1970.
*Major Dundee.*** 124m, color. Dir. Sam Peckinpah. With Charlton
     Heston, Richard Harris, Jim Hutton, James Coburn,
     Michael Anderson, Jr. Columbia, 1965.
*Massacre.** 74m, b/w. Dir. Alan Crosland. With Richard
     Barthelmess, Ann Dvorak, Dudley Digges, Clare Dodd,
     Henry O'Neill. FN, 1934.
*Massacre.** 76m, color. Dir. Louis King. With Dane Clark, James
     Craig, Marta Roth. Fox, 1956.
*Only the Valiant.** 105m, b/w. Dir. Gordon Douglas. With
     Gregory Peck, Barbara Payton, Ward Bond, Gig Young,
     Lon Chaney. WB, 1951.
*The Plainsman.*** 115m, b/w. Dir. Cecil B. DeMille. With Gary
     Cooper, Jean Arthur, James Ellison, Charles Bickford,
     Porter Hall, Helen Burgess. Paramount, 1937.

Pursuit.* 86m, color. Dir. Thomas Quillen. With Ray Danton, DeWitt Lee, Troy Nabors. Key, 1975.

Red Tomahawk.* 82m, color. Dir. R.G. Springsteen. With Howard Keel, Joan Caulfield, Broderick Crawford, Scott Brady, Wendell Corey. Paramount, 1967.

Rio Grande.**** 105m, b/w. Dir. John Ford. With John Wayne, Maureen O'Hara, Ben Johnson, Harry Carey, Jr., Victor McLaglen, Claude Jarman, Jr. Republic, 1950.

   The third of Ford's cavalry trilogy. New recruit (Jarman) learns about hardship from tough commander (Wayne). Realistic treatment of dirty, tired men who fight Indians, play practical jokes, and worship romance. Based on the short stories of James W. Bellah. Footnote: Sentimental Irish songs are sung by the Sons of the Pioneers.

Run of the Arrow.** 86m, color. Dir. Samuel Fuller. With Rod Steiger, Sarita Montiel, Brian Keith, Ralph Meeker, Jay C. Flippen. RKO, 1957.

Santa Fe Trail.** 110m, b/w. Dir. Michael Curtiz. With Errol Flynn, Olivia de Haviland, Raymond Massey, Ronald Reagan, Alan Hale, Van Heflin, Gene Reynolds. WB, 1940.

Saskatchewan.** 87m, color. Dir. Raoul Walsh. With Alan Ladd, Shelley Winters, J. Carroll Naish, Hugh O'Brian, Robert Douglas. Universal, 1954.

The Savage.** 95m, color. Dir. George Marshall. With Charlton Heston, Susan Morrow, Peter Hanson, Joan Taylor, Richard Rober. Paramount, 1953.

Seminole.** 87m, color. Dir. Budd Boetticher. With Rock Hudson, Barbara Hale, Anthony Quinn, Richard Carlson, Hugh O'Brian. Universal, 1953.

Seminole Uprising.* 74m, color. Dir. Earl Bellamy. With George Montgomery, Karin Booth, William Faucett, Steve Ritch. Columbia, 1955.

She Wore a Yellow Ribbon.**** 103m, color. Dir. John Ford. With John Wayne, Joanne Dru, Harry Carey, Jr., John Agar, Ben Johnson, Victon McLaglen, Mildred Natwick. RKO, 1949.

   The second and best of Ford's cavalry trilogy. Forced to retire, Capt. Brittles (Wayne) goes out on one last mission. Based on the short stories of James W. Bellah. Poignant scene: Brittles needs eyeglasses to read the inscription "Lest we forget" on the watch given him by his men. Footnote: Cinematographer Winton Hoch won an Oscar but filed a protest over Ford's order to film during a thunderstorm.

*Sitting Bull.*** 105m, color. Dir. Sidney Salkow. With Dale Robertson, Mary Murphy, J. Carrol Naish, Iron Eyes Cody, John Litel. UA, 1954.

*Soldier Blue.** 112m, color. Dir. Ralph Nelson. With Candice Bergen, Peter Strauss, Donald Pleasence, Bob Carraway. Avco, 1970.

*Taza, Son of Cochise.*** 79m, color. Dir. Douglas Sirk. With Rock Hudson, Barbara Rush, Gregg Palmer, Bart Roberts, Morris Ankrum. Universal, 1954.

*They Died with Their Boots On.**** 140m, b/w. Dir. Roaul Walsh. With Errol Flynn, Olivia de Haviland, Arthur Kennedy, Charles Grapewin, Gene Lockhart, Anthony Quinn, Stanley Ridges, Sydney Greenstreet. WB, 1942.

*A Thunder of Drums.** 97m, color. Dir. Joseph M. Newman. With Richard Boone, George Hamilton, Luana Patton, Arthur O'Connell. MGM, 1961.

*Tomahawk.** 82m, color. Dir. George Sherman. With Van Heflin, Yvonne De Carlo, Preston Foster, Jack Oakie. Universal, 1951.

*Tomahawk Trail.** 60m, b/w. Dir. Robert Parry. With Chuck Conners, John Smith, Susan Cummings, Lisa Montell. UA, 1957.

*Tonka.*** 97m, color. Dir. Lewis R. Foster. With Sal Mineo, Philip Carey, Jerome Courtland, Rafael Campos, H.M. Wynant, Joy Page. Disney, 1958.

*Two Flags West.*** 92m, b/w. Dir. Robert Wise. With Joseph Cotton, Linda Darnell, Jeff Chandler, Cornel Wilde. Fox, 1950.

*Two Rode Together.*** 108m, color. Dir. John Ford. With James Stewart, Richard Widmark, Linda Cristal, Shirley Jones, Andy Devine, Mae Marsh, Henry Brandon, Anna Lee. Columbia, 1961.

*Ulzana's Raid.***** 103m, color. Dir. Robert Aldrich. With Burt Lancaster, Bruce Davison, Jorge Luke, Richard Jaeckel, Joaquin Martinez, Lloyd Bochner, Karl Swenson. Universal, 1972.

A fascinating, complex treatment of the cavalry's response to atrocities by Apache leader Ulzana (Martinez) in the 1880s. It is more successful and less heavy handed than *Soldier Blue* (1970), a film with similar themes. Footnote: the film's indictment of American imperialism was influenced by the growing public outcry against the Vietnam War.

*The Vanishing American.** 90m, b/w. Dir. Joseph Kane. With
Scott Brady, Audrey Totter, Forrest Tucker, Gene Lockhart,
Jim Davis. Republic, 1955.

*Walk the Proud Land.** 88m, color. Dir. Jesse Hibbs. With
Audie Murphy, Anne Bancroft, Pat Crowley, Charles Drake,
Tommy Rall. Universal, 1956.

*War Arrow.*** 78m, color. Dir. George Sherman. With Maureen
O'Hara, Jeff Chandler, John McIntire, Suzan Ball, Noah
Berry, Jr. Universal, 1953.

*War Drums.** 75m, color. Dir. Reginald LeBorg. With Lex Barker,
Joan Taylor, Ben Johnson, Larry Chance. UA, 1957.

*War Party.** 72m, b/w. Dir. Lesley Selander. With Michael T.
Mikler, Davey Davison, Donald Barry, Laurie Mock. Fox,
1965.

*Warpath.*** 95m, color. Dir. Byron Haskin. With Edmond O'Brien,
Dean Jagger, Forrest Tucker, Polly Bergen. Paramount,
1951.

*White Feather.*** 102m, color. Dir. Robert D. Webb. With Robert
Wagner, John Lund, Debra Paget, Jeffrey Hunter, Eduard
Franz. Fox, 1955.

*The Yellow Tomahawk.** 82m, color. Dir. Lesley Selander. With
Rory Calhoun, Peggie Castle, Noah Beery, Jr., Warner
Anderson. UA, 1954.

7

New Imperial Wars

CHRONOLOGY

Prelude (1895-1898):

The Cuban War for Independence. Spain attempts to maintain control of the island of Cuba in face of a nationalist revolt. The United States, out of humanitarian and economic interests, is sympathetic to the rebels (see *Santiago*, 1956).

15 February 1898. The USS *Maine* explodes in Havana Harbor. Pro-war elements in the United States blame the Spanish.

Spanish-American War (May-August 1898):

1 May. Admiral George Dewey defeats the Spanish squadron at Manila in the Philippines.

24 June. Las Guasimas. U.S. troops under General Joseph Wheeler defeat a Spanish force holding a ridge near Santiago de Cuba (see *Message to Garcia*, 1936).

1 July. El Caney. American troops drive the Spanish away from a village near the port of Santiago de Cuba.

1 July. San Juan Hill. American troops (including Teddy Roosevelt and his dismounted cavalry unit) push the Spanish back toward Santiago de Cuba (see *The Rough Riders*, 1927).

29 May-17 July. American naval and army action results in the defeat of the Spanish fleet off Cuba and the surrender of the Spanish troops.

June-August. Manila. Combined American naval and army action under Admiral Dewey and General Wesley Merritt results in the capitulation of the Spanish forces in the Philippines.

Philippine and Moro Insurrections (1899-1913):

Filipinos believe that the American defeat of Spanish overlords will result in independence for the islands. Nationalists, along with some bandit elements, begin a conventional and then a guerrilla war when it becomes clear that Americans will not leave.

4 February 1899. Filipinos attack American troops outside Manila.

23 March 1901. Filipino leader Emilio Aguinaldo is captured.

31 March 1902. American soldiers capture the rebel headquarters at Malolos.

4 July 1902. President Teddy Roosevelt declares the Philippine insurrection over.

1902-1903. The Moro guerrilla war (see *The Real Glory*, 1939).

COMMENTARY

"Remember the *Maine!*" and Teddy Roosevelt's charge up the San Juan Hill are prominent among the slogans and iconography of American popular history. This would seem to be a rich source for motion picture screenplays--war adventure in exotic lands. The 1890s were heady times, "The Good Years," when a vibrant young industrial nation emerged as a world power. Nevertheless, it is not surprising that the war with Spain, lasting only four months and fought against a weak enemy unwilling to put up little more than token resistance, would have produced little to inspire filmmakers. The bloody, vicious war against the Filipino nationalist guerrillas and Moro Muslim rebels was even less inspirational, though; the victory over Spain and these events marked the fall of one empire and the rise of another.

The Spanish-American War was certainly a popular war at the time, but the war against the Filipinos and Moros (America's "little brown brothers") was different. Some Americans saw that the annexation of the Philippine archipelago violated basic American principles. The United States had joined *old* imperial nations, Britain, France and others, in the age of the *new* imperialism. Henry Adams said, "I turn green in bed at midnight if I think of the horror of a year's warfare in the Philippines...where...we must slaughter a million or two of foolish Malays in order to give them the comforts of flannel petticoats and electric railways" (qtd. in Wolff 195).

Actual casualties were lower than that (7,000 Americans dead or wounded and about 50,000 Filipinos dead of causes direct and indirect) but high enough. Granted that America ruled the Philippines with progressive policies and much justice afterwards, it nevertheless was a distasteful affair marked by various atrocities on both sides. The United States had become a new imperial power in the Caribbean, Central American, and Southeast Asian regions, although nothing like the real or imagined glories of the British Empire ever attached itself to the founding of America's little empire. "Enough of blood an enough of tears and desolation," cried Emilio Aguinaldo. When the war ended in 1902, "the public reacted...with muted relief and the nation's press mostly gave the news perfunctory treatment" (Karnow 195). Very few Americans had opposed a war fought with regulars and volunteers.

Although the earliest of all war movies--a 90-second nickleodeon feature called *Tearing Down the Spanish Flag*--is about the Spanish-American War (Garland 2), Hollywood has largely ignored it. With the exception of the ahistorical *A Message to Garcia* (1936), the Spanish-American War is relegated to silent films, and few of them at that. Only two movies have portrayed the Philippine insurrection: *Across the Pacific* (1926) and *Cavalry Command* (1963) which views American imperialism with favor. Although Vietnam inspired anti-war films of an allegorical nature (*Soldier Blue*, 1970, and *M*A*S*H*, 1970, for example), the Philippine experience produced none. The Moro war provided the subject matter for *The Real Glory* (1939), an action film (similar in message to the classic film of British imperialism *Gunga Din*, 1939) depicting the siege of a remote outpost by the Muslim fanatics of Mindanao. In it, a young idealistic surgeon (Gary Cooper), rallies natives to defend themselves against Moro rebels and thereby prove themselves capable of independence. America's new imperialism is seen as a school for civilization.

Garland, Brock. *War Movies*. New York: Facts on File, 1987.

Karnow, Stanley. *In Our Image: America's Empire in the Philippines*. New York: Ballantine, 1989.

Wolff, Leon. *Little Brown Brother: America's Forgotten Bid for Empire Which Cost 250,000 Lives*. New York: Longmans, 1960; rpt. 1970.

FILMOGRAPHY

*Across the Pacific.** 7 reels, b/w. Dir. Roy Del Ruth. With Monte Blue, Jane Winton, Myrna Loy, Charles Stevens, Tom Wilson. WB, 1926.

*A Message to Garcia.*** Dir. George Marshall. With Wallace Beery, Barbara Stanwyck, John Boles, Alan Hale, Mona Barrie. Fox, 1936.

*The Real Glory.**** Dir. Henry Hathaway. With Gary Cooper, David Niven, Andrea Leeds, Reginald Owen, Kay Johnson, Broderick Crawford. 1939.

*Rough Riders.** 10 reels, b/w. Dir. Victor Fleming. With Charles Farrell, Noah Beery, George Bancroft, Charles Emmett Mack, Mary Astor. Paramount, 1927.

*Santiago.*** 92m, color. Dir. Gordon Douglas. With Alan Ladd, Rossana Podespa, Lloyd Nolan, Chill Wills, L.Q. Jones. WB, 1956.

*The Tangle.**. 4 reels, b/w. Dir. Harry Lambart. With Darwin Karr, Naomi Childers. Vitagraph, 1914.

*Tearing Down the Spanish Flag.***** 90 seconds. Dir. J. Stuart Blackton. With J. Stuart Blackton. Vitagraph, 1898.

   The first war film made. A soldier (Blackton) replaces the Spanish with the American flag in Cuba. The movie, said to have been shot on location, was actually photographed atop a New York City office building. Nonetheless, it was extremely popular and showed that audiences would pay to see battle footage, even if faked. Former President Teddy Roosevelt was so impressed that in 1915 he persuaded Blackton to produce the first propaganda feature film designed to make isolationist Americans want to get into the Great War on the side of the French and British.

*Yellow Jack.** Dir George B. Seitz. With Robert Montgomery, Virginia Bruce, Lewis Stone. MGM, 1938.

8

The Great War

CHRONOLOGY

Prelude (June-August 1914):

28 June. The Sarajevo Crisis. Slav terrorists assassinate Archduke Franz Ferdinand, heir to the Austro-Hungarian empire.

July-August. Mobilization of the armies and declarations of war by the major European powers.

Best Laid Plans (August-September 1914):

August. Germany invades northern France through Belgium (the Schlieffen Plan). France launches a counterattack into the German-occupied provinces of Alsace and Lorraine (Plan XVII). Russia attacks Germany in East Prussia.

26-30 August. Germans defeat Russians at the Battle of Tannenberg.

6-8 September. French stop the German invasion at the Battle of the Marne River north of Paris.

Stalemate (1915-1917):

The development of trench warfare results from a lethal balance of fire power. A war of attrition sets in. Approximately seventy major land engagements take place during the conflict on the Western, Eastern, Italian, Balkan, and Turkish fronts.

July-November 1916. Battle of the Somme on the Western Front (British vs. Germans).

February-December 1916. Battle of Verdun (French vs. Germans) on the Western Front: the war in microcosm.

American Intervention (1917-1918):

2 April 1917. Unrestricted German submarine warfare precipitates America's entry into the conflict. President Woodrow Wilson delivers his war message to Congress.

6 April 1917. U.S. Congress votes for war.

July-December 1917. Battle of Passchendaele (British vs. Germans).

May 1917. Mutinies in the French army. Executions and better treatment restore discipline (see *Paths of Glory*, 1957).

October 1917. American Expeditionary Force (A.E.F.) sees limited fighting for the first time on the Western Front in the Lorraine area.

October-November 1917. Battle of Caporetto (Italians vs. Germans and Austrians) on the Italian Front (see *A Farewell to Arms*, 1932; 1957).

March-May 1918. Germany launches a series of major offensives on the Western Front.

May-June 1918. Battles of Chateau Thierry (see *Rails*, 1924) and Belleau Wood. Americans experience heavy fighting as the Allies counterattack.

July-August 1918. Second Battle of the Marne. Americans participate with British and French troops to stop the German offensive.

September 1918. Battle of the Saint-Mihiel salient (see *Wings*, 1927). American-French offensive.

September-November 1918. The Meuse-Argonne Offensive (see *The Big Parade*, 1925; *Sergeant York*, 1940). Combined American, British and French offensive.

11 November 1918. The war ends with an armistice forced upon
    Germany.

COMMENTARY

The images of the Great War of 1914-1918 are firmly fixed in
hundreds of documentary and feature films: trench warfare, attacks
and counterattacks across "No Man's Land," machine guns and
biplanes, massive artillery bombardments and poison gas. This was
not the kind of war that anyone had anticipated.

From the end of the Napoleonic Wars until the summer of
1914, a period of almost one hundred years, a general peace had
existed in Europe. There had been, of course, little wars fought
for limited ends on the continent and overseas, but no general
war involving all the Great Powers. There were, however, rumors
of some great war to come. What surprised everyone was the
nature of the conflict.

"The strategy and diplomacy of the war had everywhere been
based on the assumption that the war would be a short war,"
wrote James Joll. "The French soldiers scribbled 'A Berlin' on the
railroad coaches taking them to the front; the British assured one
another that 'It will all be over by Christmas'; the Germans
expected a 'bright and jolly' war. Within a few months, however,
these hopes were buried in the mud of the Western Front (3).
Those who planned the war failed to take into account the
maxim which holds that a war once begun often takes on a life
of its own irrespective of the good intentions of the general staff,
that a war can become, like Frankenstein's creation, an
uncontrollable monster.

The Germans sought to defeat France in a speedy campaign
lasting no more that six weeks or so, followed by a quick victory
over the Russians. Nothing went as planned. By 1915 it became
a war of stalemate and attrition that no one could find a way to
win or stop. Leon Wolff describes the situation that existed on
the eve of the American intervention: "soldiers were no longer
betting that the war would be over by next year. They had
begun to whisper, 'It might last a lifetime,' and the ancient joke
followed: 'They say the first seven years will be the worst.'
Nobody sang 'Tipperary' any more--that dashing, inspiring tune of
earlier days" (5). The disillusionment reflected the high hopes of
summer and the disappointments of winter.

In 1914 Rupert Brooke's sonnet "Peace" illustrates eager
anticipation of war: "Now, God be thanked Who has matched us

with His hour." By 1917 Wilfred Owen's *"Dulce et Decorum Est"* concentrates on the mind-numbing horrors suffered by war's victims: "you could hear, at every jolt, the blood / Come gargling from the froth-corrupted lungs / Obscene as cancer, bitter as the cud" (qtd. in Fussell 60, 294). A similar comparison can be found in the American films of the Great War. In *The Common Cause* (1918), the heroes find their lives purified by "the great fire of patriotism" which "burned the dross from their lives." But by the time of *All Quiet on the Western Front* (1930), a young German soldier (Lew Ayres) has lost all sense of a purpose: "When it comes to dying for your country, it is better not to die at all."

Many critics have disagreed about the evolution of cinematic attitude toward the war. Jack Spears found a clear movement from pacifism and neutrality at the war's start, to militancy and vengeance, and then finally to disillusion just before the outbreak of the next world war. But Michael Isenberg found no such movement in Hollywood, which simply produced a variety of films with a variety of themes. "Although *All Quiet on the Western Front* was a legitimate masterpiece, its success was not the signal for a exclusive onrush of war-protest pictures. It must be remembered that *All Quiet* was conterminous with the blood-and-thunder *Hell's Angels*." Therefore, the 1930s can "in no sense be classified as a decade in which the American cinema was given over to anti-war film" (Isenberg 140).

There is also disagreement about the American treatment. John Gillett found that while British postwar films were concerned about the good sides of the war (for example tradition, heroism, and a stiff upper lip), American postwar films offered "a dehumanised obsession with the sound and fury of conflict...a belief in stern discipline and toughness for their own sake..a neurosis of power, in fact" (121, ellipses his). But Isenberg found American movies dominated by the themes of commitment, adventure, sacrifice, honor, duty, or glory. If by 1918 and after Europeans saw the Great War as "nothing less than a political, economic, social, intellectual, and moral holocaust," Americans "continued to view it as the supreme adventure of the democratic conscience." Although novels and poetry "showed a mounting repulsion with the war and its results, and even with the Americans' role in the war, motion pictures continued to outline the war experience in honorable and heroic terms" (Isenberg 218).

Likewise, one historian claimed, films of the Great War "all share one feature: the capacity to mythologize the war, to recreate it in a form which was much more palatable to live with than was the event itself. Hence many war films, in particular those of the interwar years, served (and still serve) an essential purpose: to bury the past and help people recreate it in a form they can accept" (Winter 238).

Uncompromising antiwar films were made. *Paths of Glory* (1957), *Oh! What a Lovely War* (1969), and *Johnny Got His Gun* (1970) send clear pacifist or anti-military messages, but the last two were inspired less by the Great War than the Vietnam conflict. Ambivalence about the war is also reflected in two Australian films widely seen in America: *Gallipoli* (1981) is anti-war but *The Lighthorsemen* (1987) depicts the war on the Turkish Front in romantic and heroic terms.

Fussell, Paul. *The Great War and Modern Memory*. New York: Oxford UP, 1975.

Gillett, John. "Westfront 1957." *Sight and Sound* 27.3 (Winter 1957-1958): 122-27.

Isenberg, Michael. *War on Film: The American Cinema and World War I, 1914-1941*. East Brunswick, NJ: AUP, 1981.

Joll, James. "Introduction," L.L. Farrar, Jr., *The Short War Illusion: German Policy, Strategy & Domestic Affairs, August-December 1914*. Santa Barbara: ABC-CLIO, 1973.

Spears, Jack. "World War I on the Screen." *Films in Review* 17.5-6 (1966): 247-92, 347-65.

Winter, J. M. *The Experience of World War I*. New York: Oxford UP, 1989.

Wolff, Leon. *In Flanders Fields: the 1917 Campaign*. New York: Viking, 1958.

FILMOGRAPHY

Ace of Aces.** 76m, b/w. Dir. J. Walter Ruben. With Richard Dix, Elizabeth Allan, Ralph Bellamy, Theodore Newton. RKO, 1933.

Aces High.*** 104m, color. Dir. Jack Gold. With Malcolm McDowell, Christopher Plummer, Simon Ward. EMI, 1976.

Adele.** 6 reels, b/w. Dir. Wallace Worsley. With Kitty Gordon, Mahlon Hamilton, Wedgewood Nowell. UPTA, 1919.

Afraid to Fight.** 5 reels, b/w. Dir. William Worthington. With Frank Mayo, Lillian Rich, Peggy Cartwright, Lydia Knott. Universal, 1922.

The African Queen.**** 105m, color. Dir. John Huston. With Humphrey Bogart, Katharine Hepburn, Robert Morley, Peter Bull, Theodore Bikel, Walter Gotell, Gerald Onn. UA, 1951.

A legendary film about human resiliency and romance in an African backwater at the start of the war. Based on the novel by C.S. Forester. Bogart's only Oscar. Ugly intrusion of war is seen in burning of a native village. Footnote: Hepburn adopted the mannerisms of Eleanor Roosevelt for the role of Rose Sayer.

*After Tonight.** 70m, b/w. Dir. George Archainbaud. With Constance Bennett, Gilbert Roland, Edward Ellis, Sam Godfrey. RKO, 1933.

*Alias Mike Moran.*** 5 reels, b/w. Dir. James Cruze. With Wallace Reid, Ann Little, Emory Johnson, Charles Ogle. Paramount, 1919.

*An Alien Enemy.*** 5 reels, b/w. Dir. Wallace Worsley. With Louise Glaum, Mary Jane Irving, Thurston Hall, Albert Alladt. Paralta, 1918.

*All Quiet on the Western Front.***** 140m, b/w. Dir. Lewis Milestone. With Lew Ayres, Louis Wolheim, Slim Summerville, John Wray, Russell Gleason, William Bakewell, Beryl Mercer. Universal, 1930.

Classic anti-war film about ordinary infantrymen. An American film about German soldiers, based on Erich Maria Remarque's novel. Oscars for best picture and direction. Key battle scene: The camera takes a machine gun's point of view, mowing down soldiers caught in its path. Footnote: Banned in Poland as pro-German; banned in Germany as anti-German, following Nazi-instigated riots.

*All Quiet on the Western Front.**** 150m, color. Dir. Delbert Mann. With Richard Thomas, Ernest Borgnine, Patricia Neal, Ian Holm, Donald Pleasence. ITC, 1979.

*Anybody's War.** 90m, b/w. Dir. Richard Wallace. With Charles Mack, George Moran. Paramount, 1930.

*Armageddon.*** 6 reels, b/w. Dir. H. Bruce Woolfe. BI, 1923.

*Arms and the Girl.** 5 reels, b/w. Dir. Joseph Kaufman. With Billie Burke, Thomas Meighan, Louis Bales. Paramount, 1917.

*Army Surgeon.** 63m, b/w. Dir. A. Edward Sutherland. With James Ellison, Jane Wyatt, Kent Taylor. RKO, 1942.

*As in a Looking Glass.*** 5 reels, b/w. Dir. Frank H. Crane. With Kitty Gordon, F. Lumsden Hare, Frank Goldsmith, Gladden James. World, 1916.

*Barbed Wire.**** 7 reels, b/w. Dir. Rowland V. Lee. With Pola Negri, Clive Brook, Einar Hanson, Claude Gillingwater. Paramount, 1927.

The Battle Cry of Peace.*** 9 reels, b/w. Dir. J. Stuart Blackton. With Charles Richman, L. Rogers Lytton, Charles Kent, James Morrison, Julia Swayne Gordon, Mary Maurice. Vitagraph, 1915.

Battle of Paris.* 80m, b/w. Dir. Lloyd Kaufman. With Lloyd Kaufman, Lynn Lowry, Andy Kay. Standard, 1929.

The Battles of the Coronel and Falkland Islands.** aka *The Deeds Men Do.* 8 reels, b/w. Dir. Walter Summers. With Craighall Sherry. BI, 1928.

Behind the Front.** 6 reels, b/w. Dir. A. Edward Sutherland. With Wallace Beery, Mary Brian, Raymond Hatton, Richard Arlen, Tom Kennedy, Chester Conklin. Famous, 1926.

The Better 'Ole.** 9 reels, b/w. Dir. Charles Reisner. With Sydney Chaplin, Doris Hill, Harold Goodwin, Theodore Lorch, Ed Kennedy. WB, 1926.

Beware!* 5 reels, b/w. Dir. William Nigh. With Maurine Powers, Frank Norcross, Julia Hurley. WB, 1919.

Beyond Victory.* 70m, b/w. Dir. John Robertson. With Bill Boyd, ZaSu Pitts, Lew Cody, Marion Shilling. RKO, 1931.

The Big Parade.**** 13 reels, b/w. and color. Dir. King Vidor. With John Gilbert, Renee Adoree, Hobart Bosworth, Claire McDowell, Claire Adams, Karl Dane, Tom O'Brien. MGM, 1925.

The best silent film about combat. Three young men, enticed by patriotism and romance to follow the "big parade" to war, enlist, become pals and discover war's actual horrors. Romantic comedy provides effective relief and deepens our sympathy for the characters. Best scene: Vidor had the footsoldiers advance slowly in file through the woods and fall dead in time to an off-camera drumbeat.

The Black Watch.** 91m, b/w. Dir. John Ford. With Victor McLaglen, Myrna Loy, David Rollins, Lumsden Hare, Roy D'Arcy. Fox, 1929.

Blaze O' Glory.** 78m, b/w. Dir. Renaud Hoffman. With Eddie Dowling, Betty Compson, Ferdinand Schumann-Heink, Frankie Darro. Sonofilms, 1930.

Blockade.* 78m, b/w. Dir. Geoffrey Barkas. With J.P. Kennedy, Roy Travers, Johnny Butt. New Era, 1928.

Blockheads.** 58m, b/w. Dir. John G. Blystone. With Stan Laurel, Oliver Hardy, Patricia Ellis, Billy Gilbert. MGM, 1938.

The Blue Max.** 155m, color. Dir. John Guillermin. With George Peppard, James Mason, Ursula Andress, Jeremy Kemp, Anton Diffring, Karl Michael Vogler, Carl Schell. Fox, 1966.

*Body and Soul.*** 82m, b/w. Dir. Alfred Santell. With Charles Farrell, Elissa Landi, Humphrey Bogart, Myrna Loy, Donald Dillaway. Fox, 1931.

*Bonnie Annie Laurie.** 5 reels, b/w. Dir Harry Millarde. With Peggy Hyland, William Bailey, Henry Hallam, Sidney Mason. Fox, 1918.

*Born for Glory.*** aka *Brown on Resolution.* 70m, b/w. Dir. Walter Forde. With Betty Balfour, John Mills, Jimmy Hanley, Barry Mackay. Gaumont, 1935.

*British Intelligence.*** 62m, b/w. Dir. Terry Morse. With Boris Karloff, Margaret Lindsey, Maris Wrixon. WB, 1940.

*Broken Lullaby.**** 77m, b/w. Dir. Ernst Lubitsch. With Phillips Holmes, Nancy Carroll, Lionel Barrymore, Lucien Littlefield, Tully Marshall, Zasu Pitts. Paramount, 1932.

*Captain Eddie.*** 107m, b/w. Dir. Lloyd Bacon. With Fred McMurray, Lynn Bari, Charles Bickford, Thomas Mitchell. Fox, 1945.

*Captain Swagger.** 5 reels, b/w. Dir. Edward H. Griffith. With Rod La Rocque, Sue Carol, Richard Tucker. Pathe, 1928.

*Captured!** 72m, b/w. Dir. Roy Del Ruth. With Leslie Howard, Douglas Fairbanks, Jr., Paul Lukas, Maragret Lindsay, Arthur Hohl. WB, 1933.

*The Case of Sergeant Grischa.** 73m, b/w. Dir. Herbert Brenon. With Chester Morris, Betty Compson, Jean Hersholt, Alec B. Francis. RKO, 1930.

*Chances.*** 72m, b/w. Dir. Allan Dwan. With Douglas Fairbanks, Jr., Anthony Bushell, Mary Forbes, Rose Hobart, Holmes Hebert. FN, 1931.

*The Charmer.** 6 reels, b/w. Dir. Sidney Olcott. With Pola Negri, Wallace McDonald, Robert Frazer, Trixie Friganza. Paramount, 1925.

*Civilian Clothes.** 6 reels, b/w. Dir. Hugh Ford. With Thomas Meighan, Martha Mansfield, Maude Turner Gordon, Alfred Hickman. Paramount, 1920.

*Civilization.** 7 reels, b/w. Dir. Thomas H. Ince. With J. Barney Sherry, Howard Hickman, Enid Markey, Herschel Mayall. Ince, 1916.

*Cock of the Air.** 72m, b/w. Dir. Tom Buckingham. With Chester Morris, Billie Dove, Matt Moore. UA, 1932.

*The Cockeyed World.*** 115m, b/w. Dir. Raoul Walsh. With Victor McLaglen, Edmund Lowe, Lily Damita, El Brendel, Lelia Karnelly, Stuart Erwin. Fox, 1929.

*Come On In.** 5 reels, b/w. Dir. John Emerson. With Shirley Mason, Ernest Truex, Charles De Planta, Joseph Burke. Paramount, 1918.

*Comrades.** 6 reels, b/w. Dir. Cliff Wheeler. With Donald Keith, Helene Costello, Gareth Hughes, Lucy Beaumont. FD, 1928.

*Convoy.** 8 reels, b/w. Dir. Joseph C. Boyle. With Lowell Sherman, Dorothy Mackaill, William Collier, Jr., Lawrence Gray, Ian Keith. FN, 1927.

*Corporal Kate.** 8 reels, b/w. Dir. Paul Sloane. With Vera Reynolds, Julia Faye, Majel Coleman, Kenneth Thompson, Fred Allen. DeMille, 1926.

*The Court Marshall of Billy Mitchell.**** 100m, color. Dir. Otto Preminger. With Gary Cooper, Charles Bickford, Ralph Bellamy, Rod Steiger, Elizabeth Montgomery, James Daly, Darren McGavin, Jack Lord, Fred Clark. WB, 1955.

*Crimson Romance.*** 70m, b/w. Dir. David Howard. With Ben Lyon, Sari Maritza, Erich von Stroheim, Hardie Albright, James Brush. Mascot, 1934.

*The Cross Bearer.** 8 reels, b/w. Dir. George Archainbaud. With Montagu Love, Jeanne Engles, Anthony Marlo, George Morgan. World, 1918.

*The Crowded Hour.** 7 reels, b/w. Dir. E. Mason Hopper. With Bebe Daniels, Kenneth Harlan, T. Roy Barnes, Frank Morgan. Paramount, 1925.

*Dangerous Business.** 5 reels, b/w. Dir. Roy William Neill. With Constance Talmadge, Kenneth Harlan, George Fawcett, Mathilde Brundage. FN, 1920.

*The Dark Angel.**** 8 reels, b/w. Dir. George Fitzmaurice. With Vilma Banky, Ronald Colman, Helen Jerome Eddy, Wyndham Standing. UA, 1925.

*The Dark Angel.*** 105m, b/w. Dir. Sidney Franklin. With Fredric March, Merle Oberon, Herbert Marshall, Janet Beecher, John Halliday, Frieda Inescort. UA, 1935.

*The Dark Road.*** 5 reels, b/w. Dir. Charles Miller. With Dorothy Dalton, Robert McKim, Jack Livingston, Jack Gilbert, Walt Whitman. Triangle, 1917.

*Darling Lili.** 136m, color. Dir. Blake Edwards. With Julie Andrews, Rock Hudson, Jeremy Kemp, Lance Percival. Paramount, 1970.

*Dawn.** b/w. Dir. Herbert Wilcox. With Sybil Thorndike, Mary Brough, Marie Ault, Ada Bodart, Haddon Mason. BD, 1928.

*The Dawn Patrol.*** 112m, b/w. Dir. Howard Hawks. With Richard Barthelmes, Douglas Fairbanks, Jr., Neil Hamilton, William Janney. WB, 1933.

*The Dawn Patrol.**** 103m, b/w. Dir. Edmund Goulding. With Errol Flynn, Basil Rathbone, David Niven, Donald Crisp, Melville Cooper, Barry Fitzgerald, Carl Esmond. WB, 1938.

*Devil Dogs.** 6 reels, b/w. Dir. Fred Windermere. With Alexander
    Alt, Pauline Curley, Stuart Holmes. Anchor, 1928.
*Dishonored.*** 91m, b/w. Dir. Josef von Sternberg. With Marlene
    Detrich, Victor McLaglen, Lew Cody, Gustav von Seyffertitz,
    Warner Oland. Paramount, 1931.
*Dog of the Regiment.*** 5 reels, b/w. Dir. Ross D. Lederman.
    With Rin-Tin-Tin, Dorothy Gulliver, Tom Gallery, John
    Peters. WB, 1927.
*Doing Their Bit.*** 5 reels, b/w. Dir. Kenean Buel. With Jane
    Lee, Katherine Lee, Franklyn Hanna, Gertrude Le Brandt,
    Beth Ivins. Fox, 1918.
*Don't Write Letters.** 5 reels, b/w. Dir. William Bertram. With
    Gareth Hughs, Bartine Burkett, Herbert Hayes, Harry
    Lorraine. Metro, 1922.
*The Doomed Battalion.** 95m, b/w. Dir. Luis Trenker. With Tala
    Birell, Luis Trenker, Victor Varconi. Universal, 1932.
*Dough Boys.**** 80m, b/w. Dir. Edward Sedgwick. With Buster
    Keaton, Sally Eilers, Cliff Edwards, Edward Brophy, Victor
    Potel. MGM, 1930.
*The Eagle and the Hawk.**** 72m, b/w. Dir. Stuart Walker. With
    Frederic March, Cary Grant, Jack Oakie, Carole Lombard,
    Sir Guy Standing, Douglass Scott. Paramount, 1933.
*The Enchanted Cottage.*** 7 reels, b/w. Dir. John S. Robertson.
    With Richard Barthelmess, May McAvoy, Ida Waterman,
    Alfred Hickman. FN, 1924.
*Ever in My Heart.** 70m, b/w. Dir. Archie Mayo. With Barbara
    Stanwyck, Otto Kruger, Ralph Bellamy. WB, 1933.
*False Faces.*** 6 reels, b/w. Dir. Irvin Willat. With Henry B.
    Walthall, Mary Anderson, Lon Chaney, Milton Ross,
    Thornton Edwards. Paramount, 1919.
*A Farewell to Arms.**** 90m, b/w. Dir. Frank Borzage. With
    Helen Hayes, Gary Cooper, Adolphe Menjou, Mary Phillips,
    Jack LaRue, Blanche Frederici, Henry Armetta. Paramount,
    1932.
*A Farewell to Arms.** 152m, color. Dir. Charles Vidor. With Rock
    Hudson, Jennifer Jones, Vittorio de Sica, Alberto Sordi,
    Mercedes McCambridge, Elaine Stritch, Oscar Homolka,
    Victor Francen. Fox, 1957.
*Fields of Honor.** 6 reels, b/w. Dir. Ralph Ince. With Mae
    Marsh, Marguerite Marsh, George Cooper, John Wessell.
    Goldwyn, 1918.
*The Fighting 69th.**** 90m, b/w. Dir. William Keighley. With
    James Cagney, Pat O'Brien, George Brent, Alan Hale,
    Dennis Morgan, William Lundigan, Jeffrey Lynn, Frank
    McHugh, Dick Foran. WB, 1940.

*The Flames of Chance.** 5 reels, b/w. Dir. Raymond Wells. With Margery Wilson, Jack Mulhall, Anna Dodge, Wilbur Higbee, Percy Challenger. Triangle, 1918.

*For Better, For Worse.** 7 reels, b/w. Dir. Cecil B. DeMille. With Elliott Dexter, Gloria Swanson, Tom Forman, Sylvia Ashton. Art, 1919.

*For France.** 5 reels, b/w. Dir. Wesley Ruggles. With Edward Earle, Betty Howe, Arthur Donaldson, Mary Maurice. Vitagraph, 1917.

*For Liberty.** 5 reels, b/w. Dir. Bertram Bracken. With Gladys Brockwell, Charles Clary, Bertram Grassby. Fox, 1918.

*For the Freedom of the East.** 7 reels, b/w. Dir. Ira M. Lowry. With Lady Tsen Mei, Robert Elliott, Lai Mon Kim, Herbert Horton Pattee. Goldwyn, 1918.

*For the Freedom of the World.** 8 reels, b/w. Dir. Ira M. Lowry, F.J. Carroll. With E.K. Lincoln, Barbara Castleton, Romaine Fielding, Neil Moran. Goldwyn, 1917.

*For Valour.** 5 reels, b/w. Dir. Albert Parker. With Winifred Allen, Richard Barthelmess, Henry Weaver, Mabel Ballin. Triangle, 1917.

*Forever After.*** 7 reels, b/w. Dir. F. Harmon Weight. With Lloyd Hughes, Mary Astor, Hallam Cooley, David Torrence, Eulalie Jensen. FN, 1926.

*The Fountain.** 85m, b/w. Dir. John Cromwell. With Ann Harding, Brian Aherne, Paul Lukas, Jean Hersholt, Ralph Forbes. Radio, 1934.

*The Four Horsemen of the Apocalypse.*** 11 reels, b/w. Dir. Rex Ingram. With Rudolph Valentino, Alice Terry, Pomeroy Cannon, Wallace Beery, Stuart Holmes. MGM, 1921.

*Four Sons.**** 10 reels, b/w. Dir. John Ford. With James Hall, Margaret Mann, Earle Foxe, Charles Morton, Francis X. Bushman, Jr. Fox, 1928.

*Friendly Enemies.** 7 reels, b/w. Dir. George Melford. With Lew Fields, Joe Weber, Virginia Brown Faire, Jack Mulhall. Producers Distr, 1925.

*Fugitive Road.** 69m, b/w. Dir. Frank Strayer. With Erich von Stroheim, Wera Engels, Leslie Fenton, George Humbert, Harry Holman. Chester, 1934.

*Gallipoli.**** 110m, color. Dir. Peter Weir. With Mark Lee, Mel Gibson, Bill Kerr, Ron Graham, Harold Hopkins. Paramount, 1981.

*The Gay Diplomat.** 66m, b/w. Dir. Richard Boleslavsky. With Ivan Lebedeff, Genevieve Tobin, Betty Compson, Ilka Chase, Purnell Pratt. RKO, 1931.

*The Gay Retreat.*** 6 reels, b/w. Dir. Ben Stoloff. With Ted
McNamara, Sammy Cohen, Gene Cameron, Betty Francisco,
Judy King. Fox, 1927.

*Gigolo.** 8 reels, b/w. Dir. William K. Howard. With Rod La
Rocque, Jobyna Ralston, Louise Dresser, Cyril Chadwick.
Producers Distr, 1926.

*The Girl Who Stayed at Home.**** 6 reels, b/w. Dir. D.W.
Griffith. With Carol Dempster, Adolphe Lestina, Frances
Parkes, Richard Barthelmess. Paramount, 1919.

*Golden Dawn.** 81m, color. Dir. Ray Enright. With Walter Woolf,
Vivienne Segal, Noah Beery, Alice Gentle, Lupino Lane.
WB, 1930.

*The Good-bye Kiss.** 8 reels, b/w. Dir. Mack Sennett. With
Johnny Burke, Sally Eilers, Matty Kemp, Wheeler Oakman,
Irving Bacon. FN, 1928.

*The Great Impersonation.** 7 reels, b/w. Dir. George Melford.
With James Kirkwood, Ann Forrest, Winter Hall, Truly
Shattuck. Universal, 1921.

*The Great Love.*** 7 reels, b/w. Dir. D.W. Griffith. With Robert
Harron, Henry B. Walthall, Gloria Hope, Lillian Gish,
Maxfield Stanley. Paramount, 1918.

*The Greater Glory.** 11 reels, b/w. Dir. Curt Rehfeld. With
Conway Tearle, Anna Q. Nilsson, May Allison, Ian Keith.
FN, 1926.

*The Greatest Thing in Life.**** 7 reels, b/w. Dir. D.W. Griffith.
With Lillian Gish, Robert Harron, Adolphe Lestina, David
Butler, Elmo Lincoln. Art, 1918.

*The Green Temptation.** 6 reels, b/w. Dir. William D. Taylor.
With Betty Compson, Mahlon Hamilton, Theodore Kosloff,
Neely Edwards. Paramount, 1922.

*Half Shot at Sunrise.*** 75m, b/w. Dir. Paul Sloane. With Bert
Wheeler, Robert Woolsey, John Rutherford, George
MacFarlane. RKO, 1930.

*Ham and Eggs at the Front.*** aka *Ham and Eggs.* 6 reels, b/w.
Dir. Roy Del Ruth. With Tom Wilson, Heinie Conklin,
Myrna Loy, William J. Irving. WB, 1927.

*Heart Trouble.*** 6 reels, b/w. Dir. Harry Langdon. With Harry
Langdon, Doris Dawson, Lionel Belmore. FN, 1928.

*Heartbreak.** 63m, b/w. Dir. Alfred Werker. With Charles Farrell,
Madge Evans, Hardie Albright, Paul Cavanagh. Fox, 1931.

*Hearts of the World.*** 12 reels, b/w. Dir. D.W. Griffith. With
Lilian Gish, Dorothy Gish, Robert Harron, Kate Bruce, Ben
Alexander, George Fawcett, George Siegmann, Noel Coward.
Art, 1918.

Hell Below.** 105m, b/w. Dir. Jack Conway. With Robert Montgomery, Walter Huston, Madge Evans, Jimmy Durante. MGM, 1933.

Hell in the Heavens.* 79m, b/w. Dir. John G. Blystone. With Warner Baxter, Conchita Montenegro, Russell Hardie, Andy Devine. Fox, 1934.

Hell on Earth.* aka *No Man's Land*. 64m, b/w. Dir. Victor Trivas. With Georges Peclet, Hugh Douglas, Wladimir Sokoloff, Ernest Busch. Rescofilm, 1934.

The Hell's Angels.**** 135m, b/w, color. Dir. Howard Hughes, Marshall Neilan, Luther Reed. With Ben Lyon, James Hall, Jean Harlow, John Darrow. UA, 1930.

Startling aerial war scenes. Brothers fight over girl (Harlow) and for the Royal Flying Corps. Footnote: Harlow became a star when she said, "Would you be shocked if I put on something more comfortable?"

The Hero.** 7 reels, b/w. Dir. Louis J. Gasnier. With Gaston Glass, Barbara La Marr, John Sainpolis, Martha Mattox. Preferred, 1923.

His Master's Voice.** 6 reels, b/w. Dir. Renaud Hoffman. With Thunder the Dog, George Hackathorne, Marjoria Daw, Mary Carr. Gotham, 1925.

Hotel Imperial.* 67m, b/w. Dir. Robert Florey. With Isa Miranda, Ray Milland, Reginald Owen, Gene Lockhart, J. Carroll Naish. Paramount, 1939.

How I Won the War.*** 109m, color. Dir. Richard Lester. With Michael Crawford, John Lennon, Roy Kinnear, Lee Montague, Jack MacGowan. UA, 1967.

The Hun Within.*** 5 reels, b/w. Dir. Chester Withey. With Dorothy Gish, George Fawcett, Charles Gerard, Douglas MacLean, Herbert Sutch. Paramount, 1918.

I Was a Spy.* 72m, b/w, color. Dir. Victor Saville. With Madeleine Carroll, Conrad Veidt, Herbert Marshall. Fox, 1934.

In Again-Out Again.** 5 reels, b/w. Dir. John Emerson. With Douglas Fairbanks, Arline Pretty, Walter Walker, Arnold Lucy. Art, 1917.

Inside the Lines.** 6 reels, b/w. Dir. David M. Hartford. With Lewis S. Stone, Marguerite Clayton, Carl Herlinger, Nick Cogley. World, 1918.

Inside the Lines.* 72m, b/w. Dir. Roy J. Pomeroy. With Betty Compson, Ralph Forbes, Montagu Love. RKO, 1930.

Into No Man's Land.** 7 reels, b/w. Dir. Cliff Wheeler. With Tom Santschi, Josephine Norman, Jack Daugherty, Betty Blythe. Excellent, 1928.

*The Iron Major.*** 85m, b/w. Dir. Ray Enright. With Pat O'Brien, Ruth Warrick, Robert Ryan, Leon Ames, Russell Wade. RKO, 1943.

*Joan of Plattsburg.*** 6 reels, b/w. Dir. George Loane Tucker, William Humphrey. With Mabel Normand, Robert Elliott, William Fredericks, Edward Elkas. Goldwyn, 1918.

*Joan the Woman.**** 10 reels, b/w. Dir. Cecil B. DeMille. With Geraldine Farrar, Hobart Bosworth, Wallace Reid, Raymond Hatton, Theodore Roberts, Charles Clay. Lasky, 1916.

*Johnny Got His Gun.***** 111m, b/w. Dir. Dalton Trumbo. With Timothy Bottoms, Kathy Fields, Marsha Hunt, Diane Varsi, Jason Robards, Donald Sutherland. Cinemation, 1971.

A well made, disturbing anti-war film. A legless, armless and faceless WWI veteran (Bottoms) lives as a vegetable in a hospital (sequences filmed in black-and-white) but dreams and remembers vividly (filmed in color). Based on a novel by Dalton Trumbo, who also wrote the script. Footnote: Trumbo, who arranged the financing, gives screen credit to Robert Rich, one of Trumbo's pseudonyms from his days of being blacklisted in Hollywood.

*Journey's End.*** 130m, b/w. Dir. James Whale. With Colin Clive, David Manners, Ian MacLaren, Billy Bevan, Anthony Bushell. Tiffany, 1930.

*The Kaiser, or the Beast of Berlin.*** 7 reels, b/w. Dir. Rupert Julian. With Rupert Julian, Allan Sears, Nigel de Brulier, Lon Chaney. Jewel, 1918.

*The Kaiser's Finish.*** 8 reels, b/w. Dir. John Joseph Harvey, Clifford P. Saum. With Earl Schenck, Claire Whitney, Percy Standing, Louis Dean. WB, 1918.

*The Kaiser's Shadow.** 5 reels, b/w. Dir. Thomas H. Ince. With Dorothy Dalton, Thurston Hall, Edward Cecil, Clemont Boyd. Paramount, 1918.

*Keep 'em Rolling.** 65m, b/w. Dir. George Archainbaud. With Walter Huston, Frances Dee, Minna Gombell, Frank Conroy. RKO, 1934.

*King of Hearts.**** 100m, color. Dir. Philippe de Broca. With Alan Bates, Genevieve Bujold, Pierre Brasseur, Jean-Claude Brialy, Adolfo Celi. UA, 1967.

*Kiss Barrier.** 6 reels, b/w. Dir. R. William Neill. With Edmund Lowe, Claire Adams, Diana Miller, Marion Harlan. Fox, 1925.

*Lafayette Escadrille.*** 93m, b/w. Dir. William A. Wellman. With Tab Hunter, David Janssen, Etchika Choureau, Bill Wellman, Jr., Jody McCrea. WB, 1958.

Lancer Spy.** 84m, b/w. Dir. Gregory Ratoff. With Dolores Del Rio, George Sanders, Peter Lorre, Virginia Field, Sig Rumann. Fox, 1937.

The Last Outpost.* 72m, b/w. Dir. Charles Barton, Louis J. Gasnier. With Cary Grant, Claude Rains, Gertrude Michael, Kathleen Burke. Paramount, 1935.

The Last Parade.* 82m, b/w. Dir. Erle C. Kenton. With Jack Holt, Tom Moore, Constance Cummings, Gaylord Pendleton. Columbia, 1931.

Lawrence of Arabia.**** 220m, color. Dir. David Lean. With Peter O'Toole, Alec Guinness, Anthony Quinn, Jack Hawkins, Claude Rains, Anthony Quayle, Arthur Kennedy, Omar Sharif, Jose Ferrer, Donald Wolfit, Michael Ray. Columbia, 1962.

A wide-screen spectacle of Arab tribes fighting Ottoman Turks. Seven Oscars include picture, direction, cinematography, and score. Reissued in a restored version in 1991. Best sequence: a British-led Arab force crosses the desert to attack the port at Aqaba. Footnote: O'Toole (as the brilliant but strange British guerrila leader T.E. Lawrence) plays his first and best starring role.

The Leech.* 5 reels, b/w. Dir. Herbert Hancock. With Ray Howard, Alex Hall, Claire Whitney, Katherine Leon. Pioneer, 1921.

Light of Victory.** 5 reels, b/w. Dir. William Wolbert. With Bob Edmonds, Fred Wilson, Monroe Salisbury, Fred Kelsey, Betty Compson. Universal, 1919.

The Lighthorsemen.** 111m, color. Dir. Simon Wincer. With John Blake, Peter Phelps, Nick Wateres. RKO, 1987.

Lilac Time.** 11 reels, b/w. Dir. George Fitzmaurice. With Gary Cooper, Colleen Moore, Burr McIntosh, Kathryn McGuire. FN, 1928.

Little Miss Hoover.** aka *The Golden Bird.* 5 reels, b/w. Dir. John Stuart Robertson. With Marguerite Clark, Eugene O'Brien. Alfred Hickman, Forrest Robinson, Frances Kaye. Paramount, 1918.

A Little Patriot.* 5 reels, b/w. Dir. William Bertram. With Baby Marie Osborne, Herbert Standing, Marian Warner, Jack Connolly. Pathe, 1917.

Little Wildcat.* 5 reels, b/w. Dir. David Divad. With Alice Calhoun, Ramsey Wallace, Herbert Fortier, Oliver Hardy. Vitagraph, 1922.

The Lone Eagle.** 6 reels, b/w. Dir. Emory Johnson. With Raymond Keane, Barbara Kent, Nigel Barrie, Jack Pennick, Donald Stuart. Universal, 1927.

The Lost Patrol.*** 74m, b/w. Dir. John Ford. With Victor McLaglen, Boris Karloff, Wallace Ford. RKO, 1934.

Love in a Hurry.* aka *Allies*. 5 reels, b/w. Dir. Dell Henderson. With Carlyle Blackwell, Evelyn Greeley, Isabel O'Madigan, George MacQuarrie. World, 1919.

The Love Light.** 8 reels, b/w. Dir. Frances Marion. With Mary Pickford, Evelyn Dumo, Fred Thompson, Edward Philips, Albert Prisco. UA, 1921.

Luck and Pluck.** 5 reels, b/w. Dir. Edward Dillon. With George Walsh, Virginia Lee, Joe Smiley. Fox, 1919.

The Mad Parade.* aka *Forgotten Women*. 63m, b/w. Dir. William Beaudine. With Evelyn Brent, Irene Rich, Louise Fazenda, Lilyan Tashman. Paramount, 1931.

Madame Spy.** 5 reels, b/w. Dir. Douglas Gerrard. With Jack Mulhall, Wadsworth Harris, Jean Hersholt, Donna Drew. Butterfly, 1918.

Madame Spy.* 70m, b/w. Dir. Karl Freund. With Fay Wray, Nils Asther, Edward Arnold, John Miljan. Universal, 1934.

Mamba.* 78m, color. Dir. Al Rogell. With Jean Hersholt, Eleanor Boardman, Ralph Forbes, Josef Swickard, Claude Fleming. Tiffany, 1930.

A Man From Wyoming.* 71m, b/w. Dir. Rowland V. Lee. With Gary Cooper, June Collyer, Regis Toomey, Morgan Farley. Paramount, 1930.

The Man From Yesterday. * 71m, b/w. Dir. Berthold Viertel. With Claudette Colbert, Clive Brook, Charles Boyer, Andy Devine, Alan Mowbray. Paramount, 1932.

The Man Who Reclaimed His Head.** 82m, b/w. Dir. Edward Ludwig. With Claude Rains, Joan Bennett, Lionel Atwill, Juanity Quigley, Bessie Barriscale. Universal, 1935.

Mare Nostrum.*** 10 reels, b/w. Dir. Rex Ingram. With Uni Apollon, Alex Nova, Kada-Abd-el-Kader, Antonio Moreno, Alice Terry. MGM, 1926.

Marianne.** 84m, b/w. Dir. Robert Z. Leonard. With Marion Davies, Cliff Edwards, Lawrence Gray, Benny Rubin, Scott Kolk. MGM, 1929.

The Melody of Love.** 83m, b/w. Dir. A.B. Heath. With Walter Pigeon, Mildred Harris, Jane Winton, Tommy Dugan. Universal, 1928.

Men of the Sky.* 71m, b/w. Dir. Alfred E. Green. With Irene Delroy, Jack Whiting, Bramwell Fletcher. WB, 1931.

Merry-Go-Round.** 10 reels b/w. Dir. Rupert Julian, Erich von Stroheim. With Norman Kerry, Mary Philbin, Cesare Gravina, Edithe Yorke, George Hackethorne. Universal, 1923.

*The Mighty.** 74m, b/w. Dir. John Cromwell. With George Bancroft, Esther Ralston, Warner Oland, Raymond Hatton. Paramount, 1929.

*Mrs. Slacker.** 5 reels, b/w. Dir. Hobart Henley. With Gladys Hulette, Creighton Hale, Paul Clerget. Pathe, 1918.

*My Buddy.** 67m, b/w. Dir. Steve Sekely. With Donald Barry, Ruth Terry, Lynne Roberts, Alexander Granach, Emma Dunn. Republic, 1944.

*My Four Years in Germany.** 9 reels, b/w. Dir. William Nigh. With Halbert Brown, Willard Dashiell, Louis Dean, Earl Schneck. WB, 1918.

*The New Commandment.*** 7 reels, b/w. Dir. Howard Higgin. With Blanche Sweet, Ben Lyon, Holbrook Blinn, Clare Eames, Effie Shannon. FN, 1925.

*New Lives for Old.** 7 reels, b/w. Dir. Clarence Badger. With Betty Compson, Wallace MacDonald, Theodore Kosloff, Sheldon Lewis. Paramount, 1925.

*The Night Watch.*** 7 reels, b/w. Dir. Alexander Korda. With Billie Dove, Paul Lukas, Donald Reed, Nicholas Soussanin. FN, 1928.

*Now We're in the Air.*** 6 reels, b/w. Dir. Frank Strayer. With Wallace Beery, Raymond Hatton, Russell Simpson, Louise Brooks, Emile Chataurd. Paramount, 1927.

*Nurse Edith Cavell.*** 95m, b/w. Dir. Herbert Wilcox. With Anna Neagle, George Sanders, Edna May Oliver, ZaSu Pitts. RKO, 1939.

*Oh! What a Lovely War.**** 144m, color. Dir. Richard Attenborough. With Laurence Olivier, John Gielgud, Ralph Richardson, Michael Redgrave, John Mills, Vanessa Redgrave, Dirk Bogarde, Susannah York. Paramount, 1969.

*The Ordeal.*** 5 reels, b/w. With William H. Tooker, George De Carlton, Harry Spingler, Anna Laughlin. Life Photo, 1914.

*Pack Up Your Troubles.*** 68m, b/w. Dir. George Marshall, Raymond McCarey. With Stan Laurel, Oliver Hardy, Mary Carr, James Finlayson, Charles Middleton, Grady Sutton, Billy Gilbert. Roach, 1932.

*Pack Up Your Troubles.*** 75m, b/w. Dir. H. Bruce Humberstone. With Jane Withers, the Ritz Brothers, Lynn Bari, Joseph Schildkraut. Fox, 1939.

*Paris Green.*** 5 reels, b/w. Dir. Jerome Storm. With Charles Ray, Ann May, Bert Woodruff, Gertrude Claire, Donald MacDonald. Paramount, 1920.

*Passport to Hell.** 75m, b/w. Dir. Frank Lloyd. With Elissa Landi, Paul Lukes, Warner Oland, Alex Kirkland. Fox, 1932.

*Passport to Hell.** 75m, b/w. Dir. Ray McCarey. With Elsa
     Lanchester, Gordon Oliver, Lenore Aubert, Lionel Royce.
     RKO, 1944.
*Paths of Glory.**** 86m, b/w. Dir. Stanley Kubrick. With Kirk
     Douglas, Ralph Meeker, Adolphe Menjou, George Macready,
     Wayne Morris, Richard Anderson, Timothy Carey. UA,
     1957.
        Kubrick's first signature film, an anti-war masterpiece.
     Incompetent comfortable officers botch an attack then cover
     up by accusing three enlisted men of mutiny. Based on
     the 1935 novel by Humphrey Cobb. Great combat scene:
     Suicide charge up "The Ant Hill." Visual impact of contrast
     between conditions in the rear and in the trenches.
     Footnote: the film was banned in France and even on
     American military installations for a time.
*Paws of the Bear.** 5 reels, b/w. Dir. Reginald Barker. With
     William Desmond, Clara Williams, Robert McKim. Triangle,
     1917.
*Poppies of Flanders.** 9 reels, b/w. Dir. Arthur Maude. With
     Jameson Thomas, Eve Gray, Malcolm Todd, Gibb
     McLaughlin. Wardour, 1927.
*Private Izzy Murphy.** 8 reels, b/w. Dir. Lloyd Bacon. With
     George Jessel, Patsy Ruth Miller, Vera Gordon, Nat Carr.
     WB, 1926.
*Private Jones.** 86m, b/w. Dir. Russell Mack. With Lee Tracy,
     Donald Cook, Gloria Stuart, Shirley Grey. Universal, 1933.
*Private Peat.*** 5 reels, b/w. Dir. Edward Jose. With Harold R.
     Peat, Miriam Fouche, William T. Sorelle, Edwin Grant.
     Paramount, 1918.
*Puppets.** 8 reels, b/w. Dir. George Archainbaud. With Milton
     Sills, Gertrude Olmstead, Francis McDonald. FN, 1926.
*Recompense.** 7 reels, b/w. Dir. Harry Beaumont. With Marie
     Provost, Monte Blue, John Roche, George Siegmann. WB,
     1925.
*Rendezvous.*** 91m, b/w. Dir. William K. Howard. With William
     Powell, Rosalind Russell, Binnie Barnes, Lionel Atwill,
     Cesar Romero. MGM, 1935.
*The Road to Glory.**** aka *Wooden Crosses, Zero Hour.* 95m,
     b/w. Dir. Howard Hawks. With Frederic March, June
     Lang, Lionel Barrymore, Warner Baxter. Fox, 1936.
*A Romance of the Air.*** 7 reels, b/w. Dir. Harry Revier. With
     Bert Hall, Edith Day, Florence Billings, Stuart Holmes,
     Brian Donlevy. Crest, 1919.
*Roses of Picardy.** 9 reels, b/w. Dir. Maurice Elvey. With Lillian
     Hall-Davis, John Stuart, Humbertson Wright, Jameson

Thomas. Gaumont, 1927.

The Royal African Rifles.* 75m, color. Dir. Lesley Selander. With Louis Hayward, Veronica Hurst, Michael Pate, Angela Greene. AA, 1953.

Scotland Yard.* 65m, b/w. Dir. William K. Howard. With Edmund Lowe, Joan Bennett, Donald Crisp, Georges Renavent. Fox, 1930.

The Seas Beneath.** 99m, b/w. Dir. John Ford. With George O'Brien, Marion Lessing, Mona Maris, Walter C. Kelly, Walter McGrail. Fox, 1931.

The Secret Game.** 5 reels, b/w. Dir. William C. De Mille. With Sessue Hayakawa, Jack Holt, Florence Vidor, Mayme Kelso. Paramount, 1917.

Sergeant York.**** 134m, b/w. Dir. Howard Hawks. With Gary Cooper, Walter Brennan, Joan Leslie, Stanley Ridges, George Tobias, Margaret Wycherly, David Bruce, Dickie Moore, Ward Bond. WB, 1941.

Earnest film biography of pacifist turned combat hero: "There weren't nothing anybody could do but to stop them guns." Cooper's first Oscar. Best comic battle scene: during the Argonne offensive, York (Cooper) gobbles like a turkey to lure Germans into poking their heads up. Footnote: when released, the film was criticized as interventionist propaganda for America to fight in the new European war.

Seven Days Leave.* 80m, b/w. Dir. Richard Wallace. With Gary Cooper, Beryl Mercer, Daisy Belmore, Nora Cecil, Tempe Piggott. Paramount, 1930.

Seventh Heaven.*** 12 reels, b/w. Dir. Frank Borzage. With Janet Gaynor, Charles Farrell, Ben Bard, David Butler, Marie Mosquini. Fox, 1927.

She Goes to War.** 87m, b/w. Dir. Henry King. With Eleanor Boardman, John Holland, Edmund Burns, Alma Rubens, Al St. John. UA, 1929.

Shock.* 70m, b/w. Dir. Roy J. Pomeroy. With Ralph Forbes, Gwenllian Gill, Monroe Owsley, Reginald Sharland. Monogram, 1934.

Shootin' for Love.** 5 reels, b/w. Dir. Edward Sedgwick. With Hoot Gibson, Laura La Plante, Alfred Allen, William Welsh, William Steele. Universal, 1923.

The Shopworn Angel.** 82m, b/w. Dir. Richard Wallace. With Nancy Carroll, Gary Cooper, Paul Lukas, Emmett King. Paramount, 1929.

The Shopworn Angel.*** 852m, b/w. Dir. H.C. Potter. With Margaret Sullavan, James Stewart, Sam Levene, Walter Pidgeon. Paramount, 1938.

The Sideshow of Life.** 8 reels, b/w. Dir. Herbert Brenon. With Ernest Torrence. Anna Q. Nilsson, Louise Lagrange, Maurice Cannon. Paramount, 1924.

Sins of Man.* 77m, b/w. Dir. Gregory Ratoff, Otto Brower. With Jean Hersholt, Don Ameche, Allen Jenkins, J. Edward Bromberg. Fox, 1936.

Sky Devils.* 90m, b/w. Dir. A. Edward Sutherland. With Spencer Tracy, William Boyd, George Cooper. UA, 1932.

Sky Hawk.** 67m, b/w. Dir. John G. Blystone. With Helen Chandler, John Garrick, Gilbert Emery, Lennox Pawle, Lumsden Hare. Fox, 1929.

A Soldier's Plaything.* 71m, b/w. Dir. Michael Curtiz. With Lotti Loder, Harry Langdon, Ben Lyon, Jean Hersholt, Noah Beery, Sr. WB, 1931.

The Somme.** 8 reels, b/w. Dir. M.A. Wetherell. New Era, 1927.

Sons o' Guns.** 82m, b/w. Dir. Lloyd Bacon. With Joe E. Brown, Joan Blondell, Beverly Roberts. WB, 1936.

Sonny.*** 7 reels, b/w. Dir. Henry King. With Richard Berthelmess, Margaret Seddon, Pauline Garon, Lucy Fox, Herbert Grinwood. AFN, 1922.

Spuds.* 5 reels, b/w. Dir. Larry Semon. With Larry Semon, Dorothy Dwan, Edward Hearn. Pathe, 1927.

Stamboul Quest.*** 88m, b/w. Dir. Sam M. Wood. With Myrna Loy, George Brent, Lionel Atwill, C. Henry Gordon, Douglas Dumbrille, Rudolf Amendt. MGM, 1934.

Storm at Daybreak.* 68m, b/w. Dir. Richard Boleslavsky. With Kay Francis, Nils Asther, Walter Huston, Phillips Holmes. MGM, 1933.

The Strong Man.** 7 reels, b/w. Dir. Frank Capra. With Harry Langdon, Priscilla Bonner, Gertrude Astor. FN, 1926.

Submarine Patrol.** 95m, b/w. Dir. John Ford. With Richard Greene, Nancy Kelly, Preston Foster, George Bancroft. Fox, 1938.

Suicide Fleet.* 84m, b/w. Dir. Albert S. Rogell. With Bill Boyd, Robert Armstrong, James Gleason, Ginger Rogers. RKO, 1931.

Surrender.* 69m, b/w. Dir. William K. Howard. With Warner Baxter, Leila Hyams, Ralph Bellamy, William Pawley. Fox, 1931.

Suzy.* 99m, b/w. Dir. George Fitzmaurice. With Jean Harlow, Franchot Tone, Cary Grant, Benita Hume, Lewis Stone. MGM, 1936.

*This Hero Stuff.** 5 reels, b/w. Dir. Henry King. With William Russell, Winifred Westover, J. Barney Sherry, Charles K. French. AIP, 1919.

*This Mad World.** 70m, b/w. Dir. William C. De Mille. With Kay Johnson, Basil Rathbone, Louise Dresser, Veda Buckland, Louis Natheaux. MGM, 1930.

*Three Comrades.**** 100m, b/w. Dir. Frank Borzage. With Robert Taylor, Franchot Tone, Margaret Sullavan, Robert Young, Lionel Atwill, Guy Kibbee, Monty Woolley. MGM, 1938.

*Three Faces East.*** 71m, b/w. Dir. Roy Del Ruth. With Constance Bennett, Erich von Stroheim, Anthony Bushell, William Courtenay, Crauford Kent. WB, 1930.

*The Three Sisters.** 77m, b/w. Dir. Paul Sloane. With Louise Dresser, Tom Patricola, Kenneth MacKenna, Joyce Compton, June Collyer. Fox, 1930.

*Thunder Afloat.*** 94m, b/w. Dir. George B. Seitz. With Wallace Beery, Chester Morris, Virginia Grey, Douglas Dumbrille, Cark Esmond. MGM, 1939.

*Till We Meet Again.*** aka *Forgotten Faces.* 72m, b/w. Dir. Robert Florey. With Herbert Marshall, Gertrude Michael, Lionel Atwill, Rod LaRocque, Guy Bates Post. Paramount, 1936.

*Today We Live.*** 113m, b/w. Dir. Howard Hawks. With Joan Crawford, Gary Cooper, Robert Young, Franchot Tone, Roscoe Karns. MGM, 1933.

*Tomorrow is Forever.** 105m, b/w. Dir. Irving Pichel. With Claudette Colbert, Orson Welles, George Brent, Lucile Watson, Natalie Wood. RKO, 1946.

*Von Richthofen and Brown.*** 97m, color. Dir. Roger Corman. With John Phillip Law, Don Stroud, Barry Primus, Peter Masterson. UA, 1970.

*The "W" Plan.** 87m, b/w. Dir. Victor Saville. With Brian Aherne, Madeleine Carroll, Gordon Harker, Gibb McLaughlin, Milton Rosmer. RKO, 1930.

*Wanted for Murder.*** 5 reels, b/w. Dir. Frank H. Crane. With Elaine Hammerstein, Mrs. Walker, Lillian Hall, Charles Raven. Chatham, 1919.

*The War Horse.*** 5 reels, b/w. Dir. Lambert Hillyer. With Buck Jones, Lola Todd, Lloyd Whitlock, Stanley Taylor. Fox, 1927.

*War Nurse.** 79m, b/w. Dir. Edgar Selwyn. With Robert Montgomery, Robert Ames, June Walker, Anita Page, ZaSu Pitts. MGM, 1930.

*Waterloo Bridge.*** 72m, b/w. Dir. James Whale. With Mae
    Clarke, Kent Douglas, Doris Lloyd, Frederick Kerr, Bette
    Davis. Universal, 1931.
*Waterloo Bridge.**** 103m, b/w. Dir. Mervyn LeRoy. With Vivien
    Leigh, Robert Taylor, Lucile Watson, C. Aubrey Smith,
    Maria Ouspenskaya, Virginia Field. MGM, 1940.
*What Price Glory?***** 12 reels, b/w. Dir. Raoul Walsh. With
    Victor McLaglen, Edmund Lowe, Delores Del Rio, William
    V. Mong, Phyllis Haver. Fox, 1926.
        A silent classic. Captain Flagg (McLaglen) and Sgt.
    Quirt (Lowe) fight good-naturedly over a French girl (Del
    Rio). In between they battle Germans in grisly battle
    scenes. Based on a play by Laurence Stallings and
    Maxwell Anderson. Footnote: The actors clearly speak
    profanities that never make it into subtitles.
*What Price Glory?** 111m, color. Dir. John Ford. With James
    Cagney, Dan Dailey, Corinne Calvet, James Gleason,
    William Demarest, Robert Wagner. Fox, 1952.
*The White Cliffs of Dover.*** 126m, b/w. Dir. Clarence Brown.
    With Irene Dunne, Alan Marshall, Frank Morgan, Roddy
    McDowall, Peter Lawford, Dame May Whitty. MGM, 1944.
*The White Sister.**** 12 reels, b/w. Dir. Henry King. With Lillian
    Gish, Ronald Colman, Gail Kane, J. Barney Sherry,
    Charles Lane. Metro, 1923.
*The White Sister.*** 110m, b/w. Dir. Victor Fleming. With Helen
    Hayes, Clark Gable, Lewis Stone, Louise Closser Hale, May
    Robson. MGM, 1933.
*Wife Savers.*** 6 reels, b/w. Dir. Ralph Cedar. With Wallace
    Beery, Raymond Hatton, ZaSu Pitts, Sally Blane.
    Paramount, 1928.
*The Winding Stair.*** 6 reels, b/w. Dir. John Griffith. With Alma
    Rubens, Edmund Lowe, Warner Oland, Mahlon Hamilton.
    Fox, 1925.
*Wings.***** 13 reels, b/w. Dir. William A. Wellman. With Clara
    Row, Richard Arlen, Buddy Rogers, Jobyna Ralston, Gary
    Cooper. Paramount, 1927.
        Last big silent made and the first film to win the best
    picture Oscar. The most authentic WWI dogfights ever
    filmed: used actual Army pilots and war equipment (tanks,
    trucks, bombs). Contains Cooper's first role, a brief but
    memorable appearance as a doomed flyboy. Footnote: the
    picture was released the same year as Charles Lindbergh's
    famous solo flight across the Atlantic.

The Woman from Monte Carlo. * 65m, b/w. Dir. Michael Curtiz. With Lil Dagover, Walter Huston, Warren William, John Wray, George E. Stone. WB, 1932.

The Woman I Love. ** 85m, b/w. Dir. Anatole Litvak. With Paul Muni, Mirium Hopkins, Louis Hayward, Colin Clive, Minor Watson. RKO, 1937.

A Woman of Experience. * 65m, b/w. Dir. Harry Joe Brown. With Helen Twelvetrees, William Bekewell, Lew Cody, ZaSu Pitts, H.B. Warner. RKO, 1931.

The World Moves On. * 104m, b/w. Dir. John Ford. With Madeleine Carroll, Franchot Tone, Lumsden Hare, Raul Roulien. Fox, 1934.

Young Eagles. ** 70m, b/w. Dir. William A. Wellman. With Charles Rogers, Jean Arthur, Paul Lukas, Stuart Erwin, Virginia Bruce. Paramount, 1930.

World War II (Wartime Films)

CHRONOLOGY

This chronology refers both to wartime and postwar films (see Chapter 10).

Prelude (1931-1939):

1931-1932. Japan seizes Manchuria (see *Blood on the Sun*, 1945, also the Italian-made film, *The Last Emperor*, 1987).

1935. Italy conquers Ethiopia. Germany begins to re-arm.

1936. Germany re-militarizes the Rhineland. The Spanish Civil War begins (see *Blockade*, 1938; *For Whom the Bell Tolls*, 1943).

1937. Japan invades China proper.

1938. Germany annexes Austria. The Munich Conference takes place. Germany annexes the Sudetenland (see *Four Sons*, 1940).

1939. Fascists win the Spanish Civil War (see *Behold a Pale Horse*, 1964). Germany and Russia sign a peace pact.

Blitzkrieg (1939-1940):

September 1939. Germany and Russia annex parts of Poland.

June 1940. Germany defeats France. The British Army is forced into the sea at Dunkirk (see *A Yank in the RAF*, 1941).

Fall 1940. Hitler is victorious on the continent, but England holds out during the Battle of Britain.

The "World War" Begins (1941):

June 1941. Germany invades Russia (see *The North Star*, 1943); Allied supply convoys are sent to Murmansk and Archangel (see *Action in the North Atlantic*, 1943). In August, U.S. "commercial" pilots fight in China (see *Flying Tigers*, 1942).

December 1941. Japan launches offensives in the Pacific and Southeast Asia: Pearl Harbor (see *From Here to Eternity*, 1953; *Tora! Tora! Tora!* 1970), the Philippines, Singapore, Wake Island (see *Wake Island*, 1942). Germany declares war on the United States.

The Turning Point (1942-1943):

April 1942. Doolittle air raid on Tokyo (see *Thirty Seconds Over Tokyo*, 1944).

June 1942. Japan is defeated at Midway (see *Midway*, 1976).

August 1942-February 1943. American troops take Guadalcanal (see *Guadalcanal Diary*, 1943); Marines raid Makin atol (see *Gung Ho!* 1943).

August 1942-December 1943. Germany is defeated at Stalingrad.

January 1943. The combined British-American air offensive begins against Germany (see *Twelve O'Clock High*, 1949; *Memphis Belle*, 1990).

May-September 1943. The Allied invasion of Sicily and the Italian mainland begins (see *A Walk in the Sun*, 1945).

October-November 1943. Under General Bernard Montgomery, the British Eighth Army defeats German Field Marshal Erwin Rommel's Afrika Korps at El Alamein (see *Sahara*, 1943).

November-December 1943. Allied victory against German U-boats in
the Battle of the Atlantic.

By the end of 1943, following their defeats at Stalingrad,
Midway, and in the North Atlantic, there is no longer a chance
that Germany and Japan can win the war. The Allies gradually
grind them down.

Allied Offensives (1944-1945):

7 June 1944. The Western Allies invade Normandy (see *The
Longest Day*, 1962).

December 1944. The Battle of the Bulge is the last major
German counterattack (see *Battleground*, 1949). Russians
advance into Eastern Europe.

February-June 1945. America wins Pacific victories at Iwo Jima
(see *The Sands of Iwo Jima*, 1949) and Okinawa.

May 1945. Germany surrenders (see *The Victors*, 1963).

August 1945. Atom bombs (see also Chapter 14, "Nuclear
Warfare") are dropped on Hiroshima and Nagasaki (see
Above and Beyond, 1952). Japan surrenders.

1945-1946. Surviving Nazi leaders are tried for war crimes at
Nuremberg (see *Judgment at Nuremberg*, 1961). Similar
war crimes trials are also held in Japan.

COMMENTARY

Trying to understand the scope, purpose, and mood of World
War II is difficult, partly because it was such an enormous
undertaking and so truly global. Unlike World War I, World War
II began with no celebration or optimism. Not even the Germans
looked forward to this conflict.

It can best be understood as not one war but at least four
separate wars: the Eastern European and Russian War; the
Western European, Mediterranean and North African War; the
China War; and the Pacific War.

For purposes of film analysis, Roger Manvell, a British film critic and historian, organized the conflict into four major stages: the prelude to war; the British Commonwealth versus Germany, 1939-41; the middle phase--the war until Hitler's defeat at Stalingrad, January, 1943; and victory in Europe and Asia, 1943-45. His study includes over 700 feature films and documentaries from Britain, France, the United States, the Soviet Union, Italy, Japan, Germany, China, Czechoslovakia, Poland, Hungary, and Yugoslavia. Perhaps it is not surprising, that an event so vast and so complex has attracted such a tremendous amount of historical writing and filmmaking.

Paul Fussell, however, has said that only in the letters and diaries of the soldiers can one truly understand the events of the 1940's. He condemned "the sentimentality of much patriotic wartime journalism and deceptiveness of official emissions, and...the false conceptions of character and motivation nourished by Hollywood and by writing aimed at Hollywood" in films like *Desperate Journey* (1942). And he found combat experience ineffable: "Experience in the library, film theater, debating society, or classroom will" not convey "what a hopeless and senseless mockery this war is" (313-314).

Such concerns did not stop filmmakers from attempting to explain its meaning and experience. In the United States alone, about 400 World War II films were produced between 1939 and 1945 (Langman and Borg 668-70). Like films of the Great War, they touch on every conceivable topic: including the causes of the war, the nature of the enemy, spies, the homefront, and, of course, the experience of combat from Europe to the Pacific and Asia.

"We were war-lovers in my movie-going generation [the 1940s] and lovers of war movies," wrote Judith Crist. At the war's start, "the Hollywood factory mill was aimed at...the twelve-year-old mentality that Hollywood served until the mid-fifties." Not until later did "a reality begin to creep in, with real footage of air battles, of naval encounters and of infantry attacks spliced in. True accounts and diaries of men who knew war emerged and on rare occasions the feel and the grit of experience penetrated a film, for the most part in movies that appeared as the war ended" (5-6). As time went by glamorous recruiting films like *A Yank on the Burma Road* (1942) would give way to more realistic, gritty films like *The Story of G.I. Joe* (1945).

Crist, Judith. "Introduction." Joe Morella, Edward Z. Epstein and John Graggs. *The Films of World War II: A Pictorial*

Treasury of Hollywood's War Years. Secaucus: Citadel, 1973. 5-6.

Fussell, Paul. *Wartime: Understanding and Behavior in the Second World War.* New York: Oxford UP, 1989.

Langman, Larry, and Ed Borg. *Encyclopedia of American War Films.* New York: Garland, 1989.

Manvell, Roger. *Films and the Second World War.* New York: A.S. Barnes, 1974.

FILMOGRAPHY (Wartime Films)

The following films were released during the war years (from the Spanish Civil War to 1945):

Above Suspicion.*** 90m, b/w. Dir. Richard Thorpe. With Joan Crawford, Fred MacMurray, Conrad Veidt, Basil Rathbone, Reginald Owen, Richard Ainley. MGM, 1943.

Abroad With Two Yanks.* 80m, b/w. Dir. Allan Dwan. With William Bendix, Helen Walker, Dennis O'Keeefe, John Loder, George Cleveland. UA, 1944.

Across the Pacific.*** 97m, b/w. Dir. John Huston, Vincent Sherman. With Humphrey Bogart, Mary Astor, Sydney Greenstreet, Charles Halton, Victor Sen Yung, Roland Got, Richard Loo. WB, 1942.

Action in Arabia.** 75m, b/w. Dir. Leonide Moguy. With George Sanders, Virginia Bruce, Gene Lockhart, Robert Armstrong, Michael Ansara. RKO, 1944.

Action in the North Atlantic.*** 126m, b/w. Dir. Lloyd Bacon. With Humphrey Bogart, Raymond Massey, Alan Hale, Julie Bishop, Ruth Gordon, Sam Levene, Dane Clark. WB, 1943.

Address Unknown.*** 80m, b/w. Dir. William Cameron Menzies. With Paul Lukas, Peter Van Eyck, Mady Christians, Carl Esmond, Emory Parnell. Columbia, 1944.

Adventures of a Rookie.* 64m, b/w. Dir. Leslie Goodwins. With Wally Brown, Alan Carney, Richard Martin, Erford Gage, Margaret Landry. RKO, 1943.

Aerial Gunner.** 78m, b/w. Dir. William H. Pine. With Chester Morris, Richard Arlen, Lita Ward, Jimmy Lydon, Dick Purcell. Paramount, 1943.

Air Force.*** 124m, b/w. Dir. Howard Hawks. With John Garfield, John Ridgely, Gig Young, Arthur Kennedy, Charles Drake, Harry Carey, Faye Emerson. WB, 1943.

*Air Raid Wardens.*** 67m, b/w. Dir. Edward Sedgwick. With Stan
    Laurel, Oliver Hardy, Edgar Kennedy, Jacqueline White,
    Horace (Stephen) McNally, Donald Meek. MGM, 1943.
*All Through the Night.**** 107m, b/w. Dir. Vincent Sherman.
    With Humphrey Bogart, Conrad Veidt, Kaaren Verne, Jane
    Darwell, Frank McHugh, Peter Lorre, Judith Anderson,
    Jackie Gleason, Phil Silvers. WB, 1942.
*Allotment Wives Inc.** aka *Woman in the Case.* 80m, b/w. Dir.
    William Nigh. With Kay Francis, Paul Kelly, Otto Kruger,
    Gertrude Michael. Monogram, 1945.
*The Amazing Mrs. Holliday.*** 97m, b/w. Dir. Bruce Manning.
    With Deanna Durbin, Edmond O'Brien, Barry Fitzgerald,
    Arthur Treacher, Frieda Inescort. Universal, 1943.
*Appointment In Berlin.*** 77m, b/w. Dir. Alfred E. Green. With
    George Sanders, Marguerite Chapman, Onslow Stevens, Gale
    Sondergaard, Alan Napier. Columbia, 1943.
*Arise, My Love.**** 100m, b/w. Dir. Mitchell Leisen. With
    Claudette Colbert, Ray Milland, Walter Abel, Dennis
    O'Keefe, Dick Purcell. Paramount, 1940.
*Army Wives.** 68m, b/w. Dir. Phil Rosen. With Elyse Knox,
    Marjorie Rambeau, Rick Vallin. Monogram, 1944.
*Assignment In Brittany.*** 94m, b/w. Dir. Jack Conway. With
    Jean-Pierre Aumont, Susan Peters, Richard Whorf, Margaret
    Wycherly, Signe Hasso, Reginald Owen. MGM, 1943.
*Atlantic Convoy.*** 66m, b/w. Dir. Lew Landers. With Bruce
    Bennett, Virginia Field, John Beal, Clifford Severn, Larry
    Parks. Columbia, 1942.
*Attack Force Z.*** 84m, color. Dir. Tim Burstall. With Mel
    Gibson, John Phillip Law, Sam Neill, John Waters. 1981.
*Back to Bataan.***** 97m, b/w. Dir. Edward Dmytryk. With
    John Wayne, Anthony Quinn, Beulah Bondi, Fely
    Franquelli, Richard Loo, Philip Ahn, Lawrence Tierney.
    RKO, 1945.
    An exciting flag-waving actioner. Includes a poignant
    reconstruction of the infamous Bataan "Death March." Best
    battle scene: Japanese attack in human waves, using their
    bodies as bridges over barbed wire. Footnote: some of the
    American extras had been POWs held by the Japanese in
    Manila's Cambanatuan Prison.
*Background to Danger.*** 80m, b/w. Dir. Raoul Walsh. With
    George Raft, Brenda Marshall, Sydney Greenstreet, Peter
    Lorre, Osa Massen, Kurt Katch. WB, 1943.
*Bataan.*** 113m, b/w. Dir. Tay Garnett. With Robert Taylor,
    George Murphy, Thomas Mitchell, Lloyd Nolan, Lee
    Bowman, Robert Walker, Desi Arnaz. MGM, 1943.

*Beasts of Berlin.*** aka *Hitlerbeast of Berlin.* 87m, b/w. Dir. Sherman Scott. With Roland Drews, Steffi Duna, Greta Granstedt, Alan Ladd, Lucien Prival. Producers Distr, 1939.

*Behind the Rising Sun.*** 88m, b/w. Dir. Edward Dmytryk. With Margo, Tom Neal, J. Carrol Naish, Robert Ryan, Gloria Holden, Don Douglas, George Givot. RKO, 1943.

*A Bell for Adano.**** 104m, b/w. Dir. Henry King. With John Hodiak, Gene Tierney, William Bendix, Glenn Langan, Richard Conte, Stanley Prager, Henry Morgan. Fox, 1945.

*Berlin Correspondent.*** 70m, b/w. Dir. Eugene Forde. With Virginia Gilmore, Dana Andrews, Mona Maris, Martin Kosleck, Sig Rumann. Fox, 1942.

*Betrayal from the East.*** 82m, b/w. Dir. William Berke. With Lee Tracy, Nancy Kelly, Richard Loo, Abner Biberman, Regis Toomey, Philip Ahn. RKO, 1945.

*The Big Noise.** 65m, b/w. Dir. Alex Bryce. With Alastair Sim, Norah Howard, Fred Duprez, Grizelda Hervey. Fox, 1936.

*Black Dragons.** 61m, b/w. Dir. William Nigh. With Bela Lugosi, Joan Barclay, Clayton Moore, George Pembroke, Robert Frazer. Monogram, 1942.

*The Black Parachute.*** 68m, b/w. Dir. Lew Landers. With John Carradine, Osa Massen, Larry Parks, Jeanne Bates, Jonathon Hale. Columbia, 1944.

*Blockade.**** 85m, b/w. Dir. William Dieterle. With Henry Fonda, Madeleine Carroll, Leo Carillo, John Halliday. UA, 1938.

*Blondie for Victory.*** 72m, b/w. Dir. Frank R. Strayer. With Penny Singleton, Arthur Lake, Larry Simms, Majelle White, Stuart Erwin, Jonathan Hale. Columbia, 1942.

*Blood on the Sun.**** 98m, b/w. Dir. Frank Lloyd. With James Cagney, Sylvia Sidney, Wallace Ford, Rosemary DeCamp, Robert Armstrong. UA, 1945.

*Bombardier.*** 97m, b/w. Dir. Richard Wallace. With Pat O'Brien, Randolph Scott, Anne Shirley, Eddie Albert, Walter Reed, Robert Ryan, Barton MacLane. RKO, 1943.

*Bomber's Moon.*** 70m, b/w. Dir. Charles Fuhr. With George Montgomery, Annabella, Kent Taylor, Walter Kingsford, Martin Kosleck. Fox, 1943.

*Bombs Over Burma.*** 67m, b/w. Dir. Joseph H. Lewis. With Anna May Wong, Noel Madison, Dan Seymour, Richard Loo, Nedrick Young, Dennis Moore. Universal, 1942.

*Bowery Blitzrieg.** 62m, b/w. Dir. Wallace Fox. With Leo Gorcey, Bobby Jordan, Huntz Hall, Warren Hall, Charlotte Henry. Monogram, 1941.

Buck Privates.** 82m, b/w. Dir. Arthur Lubin. With Bud Abbott, Lou Costello, Lee Bowman, Alan Curtis, The Andrews Sisters. Universal, 1941.

The Bugle Sounds.** 101m, b/w. Dir. S. Sylvan Simon. With Wallace Beery, Marjorie Main, Lewis Stone, George Bancroft, Henry O'Neill, Donna Reed. MGM, 1941.

Burma Convoy.** 59m, b/w. Dir. Noel Smith. With Charles Bickford, Evelyn Ankers, Frank Albertson, Cecil Kellaway, Keye Luke, Turhan Bey. Universal, 1941.

Busses Roar.** 59m, b/w. Dir. D. Ross Lederman. With Richard Travis, Julie Bishop, Charles Drake, Eleanor Parker, Elisabeth Fraser. WB, 1942.

Cairo.** 101m, b/w. Dir. W.S. Van Dyke II. With Jeanette MacDonald, Robert Young, Ethel Waters, Reginald Owen, Lionel Atwill, Dooley Wilson. MGM, 1941.

Call out the Marines.* 66m, b/w. Dir. Frank Ryan, William Hamilton. With Victor McLaglen, Edmund Lowe, Binnie Barnes, Paul Kelly. RKO, 1942.

The Canterville Ghost.*** 95m, b/w. Dir. Jules Dassin. With Charles Laughton, Margaret O'Brien, William Gargan, Rags Ragland, Una O'Connor, Robert Young, Peter Lawford, Mike Mazurki. MGM, 1944.

Captains of the Clouds.*** 113m, color. Dir. Michael Curtiz. With James Cagney, Dennis Morgan, Alan Hale, Brenda Marshall, George Tobias. WB, 1942.

Careful, Soft Shoulders.* 70m, b/w. Dir. Oliver H.P. Garrett. With Virginia Bruce, James Ellison, Aubrey Mather, Sheila Ryan, Ralph Byrd. Fox, 1942.

Casablanca.**** 102m, b/w. Dir. Michael Curtiz. With Humphrey Bogart, Ingrid Bergman, Paul Henreid, Claude Rains, Conrad Veidt, Sydney Greenstreet, Peter Lorre, Dooley Wilson, S.Z. Sakall, Madeleine LeBeau. WB, 1942.
  One of the best movies Hollywood ever made. Oscars for picture, direction, and screenplay. Memorable psychological portraits of war's impact on non-combatants. Stirring musical battle: the singing of "La Marseillaise" drowns out "Deutschland uber Alles" in Rick's Cafe. Footnote: Actors didn't know which of the several alternative final scenes shot would be used.

Caught in the Draft.*** 82m, b/w. Dir. David Butler. With Bob Hope, Dorothy Lamour, Lynne Overman, Eddie Bracken. Paramount, 1941.

Charlie Chan in Panama.** 66m, b/w. Dir. Norman Foster. With Sidney Toler, Jean Rogers, Kane Richmond, Victor Sen Yung, Lionel Atwill, Mary Nash, Crispin Martin. Fox, 1940.

Charlie Chan in the Secret Service.* 63m, b/w. Dir. Phil Rosen. With Sidney Toler, Mantan Moreland, Gwen Kenyon, Benson Fong, Eddy Chandler. Monogram, 1944.

Chetniks.* 73m, b/w. Dir. Louis Ling. With Philip Dorn, Anna Sten, John Shepard, Virginia Gilmore. Fox, 1943.

China.** 78m, b/w. Dir. John Farrow. With Loretta Young, Alan Ladd, William Bendix, Philip Ahn, Iris Wong, Victor Sen Yung. Paramount, 1943.

China Girl.** 95m, b/w. Dir. Henry Hathaway. With Gene Tierney, George Montgomery, Lynn Bari, Victor McLaglen, Sig Ruman, Bobby Blake, Ann Pennington. Fox, 1942.

China Sky.** 78m, b/w. Dir. Ray Enright. With Randolph Scott, Ruth Warrick, Ellen Drew, Anthony Quinn, Carol Thurston, Richard Loo. RKO, 1945.

China's Little Devils.** 74m, b/w. Dir. Monta Bell. With Harry Carey, Paul Kelly, Ducky Louie, Hayward Soo Hoo, Gloria Ann Chew. Monogram, 1945.

Cipher Bureau.* 64m, b/w. Dir. Charles Lamont. With Leon Ames, Charlotte Wynters, Joan Woodbury, Don Dillaway, Tenen Holtz. GN, 1938.

The Clock.*** 90m, b/w. Dir. Vincente Minnelli. With Judy Garland, Robert Walker, James Gleason, Keenan Wynn, Marshall Thompson. MGM, 1945.

The Commandos Strike at Dawn.** 100m, b/w. Dir. John Farrow. With Paul Muni, Anne Lee, Lillian Gish, Sir Cedric Hardwicke, Robert Coote, Ray Collins, Rosemary DeCamp, Alexander Knox. Columbia, 1942.

Confessions of a Nazi Spy.*** 110m, b/w. Dir. Anatole Litvak. With Edward G. Robinson, Francis Lederer, George Sanders, Paul Lukas, Henry O'Neill, James Stephenson, Sig Ruman. WB, 1939.

Confirm or Deny.** 73m, b/w. Dir. Archie Mayo. With Don Ameche, Joan Bennett, Roddy McDowall, John Loder, Raymond Walburn, Arthur Shields. Fox, 1941.

The Conspirators.** 100m, b/w. Dir. Jean Negulesco. With Hedy Lamarr, Paul Henreid, Sydney Greenstreet, Peter Lorre, Victor Francen, Vladimir Sokoloff, George Macready, Monte Blue, Joseph Calleia. WB, 1944.

Corregidor.** 74m, b/w. Dir. William Nigh. With Otto Kruger, Elissa Landi, Donald Woods, Frank Jenks, Rick Vallin, Wanda McKay, Ian Keith. Producers Rel, 1943.

Corvette K-225.*** 99m, b/w. Dir. Richard Rossen. With Randolph Scott, James Brown, Ella Raines, Barry Fitzgerald, Andy Devine, Walter Sande, Richard Lane. Universal, 1943.

Counter-Attack.** 90m, b/w. Dir. Zoltan Korda. With Paul Muni, Marguerite Chapman, Larry Parks, Philip Van Zandt, George Macready, Roman Bohnen. Columbia, 1945.

Counter-Espionage.** 71m, b/w. Dir. Edward Dmytryk. With Warren William, Eric Blore, Hillary Brooke, Thurston Hall, Fred Kelsey. Columbia, 1942.

Crash Dive.*** 105m, color. Dir. Archie Mayo. With Tyrone Power, Anne Baxter, Dana Andrews, James Gleason, Dame May Whitty, Henry Morgan. Fox, 1943.

Crime by Night.** 72m, b/w. Dir. William Clemens. With Jane Wyman, Jerome Cowan, Faye Emerson, Eleanor Parker, Creighton Hale. WB, 1944.

The Cross of Lorraine.*** 89m, b/w. Dir. Tay Garnett. With Jean-Pierre Aumont, Gene Kelly, Sir Cedric Hardwicke, Richard Whorf, Joseph Calleia, Peter Lorre, Hume Cronyn. MGM, 1943.

Cry Havoc.** 96m, b/w. Dir. Richard Thorpe. With Margaret Sullavan, Ann Sothern, Joan Blondell, Fay Bainter, Marsha Hunt, Ella Raines, Frances Gifford. MGM, 1943.

Danger In the Pacific.* 60m, b/w. Dir. Lewis D. Collins. With Leo Carrillo, Andy Devine, Don Terry. Universal, 1942.

Dangerous Partners.* 74m, b/w. Dir. Edward L. Cahn. With James Craig, Signe Hasso, Edmund Gwen. MGM, 1945.

Dangerously They Live.** 77m, b/w. Dir. Robert Florey. With John Garfield, Nancy Coleman, Raymond Massey, Moroni Olsen, Lee Patrick. WB, 1942.

The Daring Young Man.** 73m, b/w. Dir. Frank R. Strayer. With Joe E. Brown, Marguerite Chapman, William Wright, Roger Clark. Columbia, 1942.

The Dawn Express.* aka *Nazi Spy Ring*. 63m, b/w. Dir. Albert Herman. With Michael Whalen, Anne Nagel, William Bakewell, Constance Worth. Producers Rel, 1942.

Days of Glory.** 86m, b/w. Dir. Jacques Tourneur. With Tamara Toumanova, Gregory Peck, Alan Reed, Maria Palmer, Lowell Gilmore. RKO, 1944.

The Deadly Game.* 65m, b/w. Dir. Phil Rosen. With Charles Farrell, June Lang, John Miljan, Bernadene Hayes, David Clarke. Monogram, 1941.

Desperate Journey.*** 107m, b/w. Dir. Raoul Walsh. With Errol Flynn, Raymond Massey, Ronald Reagan, Nancy Coleman, Alan Hale, Arthur Kennedy, Albert Basserman. WB, 1942.

Destination Tokyo.**** 135m, b/w. Dir. Delmer Daves. With Cary Grant, John Garfield, Alan Hale, John Ridgely, Dane Clark, Warner Anderson, William Prince. WB, 1944.

A submarine crew must put a meteorologist ashore to

guide the first American air raids over Tokyo. The story focuses on vignettes about individual crewmembers. Footnote: this film is important for establishing the formula for later submarine movies. It conveys a chilling sense of silence and claustrophobia underwater.

*Destroyer.*** 99m, b/w. Dir. William A. Seiter. With Edward G. Robinson, Glenn Ford, Marguerite Chapman, Edgar Buchanan, Leo Gorcey, Regis Toomey. Columbia, 1943.

*Devil Pays Off.*** 70m, b/w. Dir. John H. Auer. With J. Edward Bromberg, Osa Massen, William Wright. Republic, 1941.

*The Devil With Hitler.** 44m, b/w. Dir. Gordon Douglas. With Alan Mowbray, Bobby Watson, George E. Stone. UA, 1942.

*Dive Bomber.**** 130m, b/w. Dir. Michael Curtiz. With Errol Flynn, Fred MacMurray, Ralph Bellamy, Alexis Smith, Robert Armstrong, Regis Toomey, Craig Stevens. WB, 1941.

*Doughboys In Ireland.** 61m, b/w. Dir. Lew Landers. With Kenny Baker, Jeff Donnell, Lynn Merrick, Guy Bonham, Red Latham. Columbia, 1943.

*The Doughgirls.*** 102m, b/w. Dir. James V. Kern. With Anne Sheridan, Alexis Smith, Jack Carson, Jane Wyman, Irene Manning. WB, 1944.

*Down In San Diego.** 69m, b/w. Dir. Robert B. Sinclair. With Ray McDonald, Bonita Granville, Dan Dailey, Jr., Leo Gorcey. MGM, 1941.

*Dragon Seed.**** 145m, b/w. Dir. Jack Conway, Harold S. Bucquet. With Katherine Hepburn, Walter Huston, Aline MacMahon, Turhan Bey, Hurd Hatfield, Agnes Moorehead, Frances Rafferty, J. Caroll Naish, Akim Tamiroff. MGM, 1944.

*Eagle Squadron.*** 109m, b/w. Dir. Arthur Lubin. With Robert Stack, Eddie Albert, Diana Barrymore, Nigel Bruce, Jon Hall, Evelyn Ankers, Gladys Cooper. Universal, 1942.

*Edge of Darkness.**** 120m, b/w. Dir. Lewis Milestone. With Errol Flynn, Ann Sheridan, Walter Huston, Nancy Coleman, Helmut Dantine, Judith Anderson, Ruth Gordon, John Beal, Roman Bohnen. WB, 1943.

*Enemy Agents Meet Ellery Queen.** 64m, b/w. Dir. James Hogan. With William Gargan, Gale Sondergaard, Margaret Lindsay, Charley Grapewin, Gilbert Roland. Columbia, 1942.

*Enemy of Women.** aka *The Private Life of Paul Goebbels.* 86m, b/w. Dir. Alfred Zeisler. With Claudia Drake, Paul Andor, Donald Woods, H.B. Warner. Monogram, 1944.

*Escape.**** aka *When the Door Opened.* 104m, b/w. Dir. Mervyn LeRoy. With Norma Shearer, Robert Taylor, Conrad Veidt, Alla Nazimova, Felix Bressart. MGM, 1940.

*Escape From Hong Kong.*** 60m, b/w. Dir. William Nigh. With Leo Carrillo, Andy Devine, Marjorie Lord, Don Terry, Gilbert Emery. Universal, 1942.

*Escape in the Desert.*** 79m, b/w. Dir. Edward A. Blatt. With Jean Sullivan, Philip Dorn, Alan Hale. WB, 1945.

*Escape in the Fog.*** 65m, b/w. Dir. Budd Boetticher. With Nina Foch, William Wright, Otto Kruger. Columbia, 1945.

*Escape to Glory.** aka *Submarine Zone.* 70m, b/w. Dir. John Brahm. With Pat O'Brien, Constance Bennett, John Halliday, Melville Cooper. Columbia, 1940.

*Espionage Agent.*** 74m, b/w. Dir. Lloyd Bacon. With Joel McCrea, Brenda Marshall, George Bancroft, Jeffrey Lynn, James Stephenson, Martin Kosleck. Columbia, 1939.

*The Eve of St. Mark.**** 96m, b/w. Dir. John M. Stahl. With Anne Baxter, William Eythe, Michael O'Shea, Vincent Price, Dickie Moore. Fox, 1944.

*Exile Express.** 70m, b/w. Dir. Eugene Frenke. With Anna Sten, Alan Marshal, Jerome Cowan, Jed Prouty. GN, 1939.

*Eyes in the Night.**** 80m, b/w. Dir. Fred Zinnemann. With Ann Harding, Edward Arnold, Donna Reed, Stephen McNally, Reginald Denny, Rosemary DeCamp, Mantan Moreland. MGM, 1942.

*The Falcon's Brother.** 63m, b/w. Dir. Stanley Logan. With George Sanders, Tom Conway, Jane Randolph, Keye Luke, Charles Arnt. RKO, 1942.

*The Fallen Sparrow.**** 94m, b/w. Dir. Richard Wallace. With John Garfield, Maureen O'Hara, Walter Slezak, Patricia Morison, Martha O'Driscoll, Bruce Edwards. RKO, 1943.

*Federal Fugitives.** 63m, b/w. Dir. William Beaudine. With Neil Hamilton, Doris Day, Victor Varconi, Charles Wilson, George Carleton. Producers Rel, 1941.

*The Fighting Seabees.**** 100m, b/w. Dir. Edward Ludwig. With John Wayne, Susan Hayward, Dennis O'Keefe, William Frawley, Duncan Renaldo. Republic, 1944.

*First Comes Courage.*** 88m, b/w. Dir. Dorothy Arzner. With Merle Oberon, Brian Aherne, Carl Esmond, Fritz Leiber, Erik Rolf. Columbia, 1943.

*First Yank Into Tokyo.*** 82m, b/w. Dir. Gordon Douglas. With Tom Neal, Barbara Hale, Marc Cramer, Richard Loo, Keye Luke, Leonard Strong, Benson Fong. RKO, 1945.

*Five Graves to Cairo.**** 96m, b/w. Dir. Billy Wilder. With Franchot Tone, Anne Baxter, Akim Tamiroff, Erich von Stroheim, Peter Van Eyck. Paramount, 1943.

*Flight Command.*** 113m, b/w. Dir. Frank Borzage. With Robert Taylor, Ruth Hussey, Walter Pidgeon, Paul Kelly, Nat Pendleton, Shepperd Strudwick, Red Skelton, Dick Purcell. MGM, 1940.

*Flight for Freedom.*** 101m, b/w. Dir. Lothar Mendes. With Rosalind Russell, Fred MacMurray, Herbert Marshall, Eduardo Ciannelli, Walter Kingsford. RKO, 1943.

*Fly By Night.*** 74m, b/w. Dir. Robert Siodmak. With Nancy Kelly, Richard Carlson, Albert Basserman, Martin Kosleck, Nestor Piava. Paramount, 1942.

*Flying Blind.** 69m, b/w. Dir. Frank McDonald. With Richard Arlen, Jean Parker, Nils Asther. Paramount, 1941.

*Flying Tigers.*** 102m, b/w. Dir. David Miller. With John Wayne, John Carroll, Anna Lee, Paul Kelly, Mae Clarke, Gordon Jones. Republic, 1942.

*Flying Wild.** 63m, b/w. Dir. William West. With Leo Gorcey, Bobby Jordan, Donald Haines, David Gorcey, Bobby Stone. Monogram, 1941.

*Follow the Boys.*** 122m, b/w. Dir. A. Edward Sutherland. With Marlene Dietrich, George Raft, Orson Welles, Vera Zorina, Dinah Shore, W.C. Fields, Jeanetter MacDonald, Maria Montez, The Andrews Sisters, Sophie Tucker, Nigel Bruce, Gale Sondergaard. Universal, 1944.

*For Whom the Bell Tolls.**** 130m, color. Dir. Sam Wood. With Gary Cooper, Ingrid Bergman, Katina Paxinou, Akim Tamiroff, Arturo de Cordova. Paramount, 1943.

*Foreign Agent.*** 62m, b/w. Dir. William Beaudine. With John Shelton, Gale Storm, Ivan Lebedeff, Hans Schumm, William Halligan. Monogram, 1942.

*Foreign Correspondent.***** 120m, b/w. Dir. Alfred Hitchcock. With Joel McCrea, Laraine Day, Herbert Marshall, George Sanders, Albert Basserman, Robert Benchley, Eduardo Ciannelli, Edmund Gwenn. UA, 1940.
Suspenseful entertainment mixed with anti-Nazi propaganda. Authentic-looking London and Amsterdam were actually recreated in Hollywood. Great scene: After committing murder on crowded steps of the town hall, the killer escapes through a field of open umbrellas. Footnote: Nazi propaganda minister Joseph Goebbels admired the emotional power of this film to move the masses.

*Forever and a Day.**** 104m, b/w. Dir. Rene Clair, Edmund Goulding, Sir Cedric Hardwicke. With Anna Neagle, Ray Milland, Claude Rains, C. Aubrey Smith, Dame May Whitty, Gene Lockhart. RKO, 1943.

*Four Jills in a Jeep.*** 89m, b/w. Dir. William A. Seiter. With Kay Francis, Martha Raye, Carole Landis, Mitzi Mayfair, Phil Silvers, Alice Faye, Betty Grable. Fox, 1944.

*Four Sons.**** 89m, b/w. Dir. Archie Mayo. With Don Ameche, Eugene Leontovich, Mary Beth Hughes, Alan Curtis, George Ernest. Fox, 1940.

*Friendly Enemies.** 95m, b/w. Dir. Allan Dwan. With Charles Winninger, Charlie Ruggles, James Craig, Nancy Kelly, Otto Kruger. UA, 1942.

*G.I. Honeymoon.** 63m, b/w. Dir. Phil Karlstein. With Gale Storm, Peter Cookson, Arline Judge, Frank Jenks, Jerome Cowan. Monogram, 1945.

*The Gang's All Here.*** 103m, color. Dir. Busby Berkeley. With Alice Faye, Carmen Miranda, James Ellison, Charlotte Greenwood, Eugene Pallette, Sheila Ryan, Phil Baker, Benny Goodman. Fox, 1943.

*Gangway for Tomorrow.*** 69m, b/w. Dir. John H. Auer. With Margo, John Carradine, Robert Ryan, Amelita Ward, William Terry, Harry Davenport, James Bell, Charles Arnt, Wally Brown, Alan Carney. RKO, 1943.

*Get Going.*** 57m, b/w. Dir. Jean Yarbrough. With Robert Paige, Grace McDonald, Vera Vague, Walter Catlett, Lois Collier. Universal, 1943.

*God Is My Co-Pilot.**** 90m, b/w. Dir. Robert Florey. With Dennis Morgan, Dane Clark, Raymond Massey, Alan Hale, Andrea King, John Ridgely, Stanley Ridges. WB, 1945.

*The Gorilla Man.*** 64m, b/w. Dir. D. Ross Lederman. With John Loder, Ruth Ford, Marian Hall, Richard Fraser, Creighton Hale. WB, 1942.

*Government Girl.*** 94m, b/w. Dir. Dudley Nichols. With Olivia de Haviland, Sonny Tufts, Anne Shirley, Jess Barker, James Dunn, Paul Stewart, Agnes Moorehead. RKO, 1943.

*The Great Dictator.***** 127m, b/w. Dir. Charles Chaplin. With Charles Chaplin, Paulette Goddard, Jack Oakie, Reginald Gardiner, Maurice Moscovich, Billy Gilbert, Henry Daniell. UA, 1940.

Chaplin's first full talkie, a slaptick-satire. He switches between roles as a Jewish barber and a Hitler-type (Adenoid Hynkel) dictator of Ptomania. Great scene: Hynkel dances obsessively with his own inflated earth globe. Oakie's takeoff on Mussolini (Benzino Napolini) is brilliant. Footnote: the plot was suggested by the remarkable resemblance of Chaplin's "little tramp" to Hitler.

*Great Guns.*** 73m, b/w. Dir. Monty Banks. With Stan Laurel,
Oliver Hardy, Sheila Ryan, Dick Nelson, Edmund
MacDonald. Fox, 1941.

*Great Impersonation.*** 70m, b/w. Dir. John Rawlins. With Ralph
Bellamy, Evelyn Ankers, Aubrey Mather, Edward Norris,
Kaaren Verne. Universal, 1942.

*Guadalcanal Diary.**** 93m, b/w. Dir. Lewis Seiler. With Preston
Foster, Lloyd Nolan, William Bendix, Richard Conte,
Anthony Quinn, Richard Jaeckel. Fox, 1943.

*Gung Ho!***** 88m, b/w. Dir. Ray Enright. With Randolph Scott,
Grace McDonald, Alan Curtis, Noah Berry, Jr., J. Carroll
Naish, David Bruce. Universal, 1943.

Recounts the selection, training, and deployment of
commandos. Based on the true story of the attack on
Makin Island by the Second Marine Raider Battalion
("Carlson's Raiders") on 17 August 1942. Best scene:
volunteers must tell their commander their reasons for
wanting to join the unit. "I fought in Spain," one says.
And another, "I just don't like Japs." Footnote: film
historian Jeanine Basinger sees it as the first of the "dirty
group" films like *The Dirty Dozen* (1967) and *The Devil's
Brigade* (1968).

*A Guy Named Joe.*** 120m, b/w. Dir. Victor Fleming. With
Spencer Tracy, Irene Dunne, Van Johnson, Ward Bond,
James Gleason, Lionel Barrymore, Barry Nelson, Esther
Williams. MGM, 1943.

*Hail the Conquering Hero.**** 101m, b/w. Dir. Preston Sturges.
With Eddie Bracken, Ella Raines, Raymond Walburn,
William Demarest, Elizabeth Patterson, Jimmy Conlin,
Franklin Pangborn, Jack Norton. Paramount, 1944.

A genial satire about hero worship. Bracken plays an
Army reject who fabricates a career as a Marine war hero
to satisfy the needs of his small town. Scene-stealing
performances by Demarest and Pangborn.

*Half Way to Shanghai.** 61m, b/w. Dir. John Rawlins. With
Kent Taylor, Irene Hervey, Henry Stephenson, J. Edward
Bromberg, George Zucco. Universal, 1942.

*Hangmen Also Die.*** aka *Lest We Forget.* 131m, b/w. Dir. Fritz
Lang. With Brian Donlevy, Walter Brennan, Anna Lee,
Gene Lockhart, Dennis O'Keefe. UA, 1943.

*Happy Land.*** 75m, b/w. Dir. Irving Pichel. With Don Ameche,
Frances Dee, Harry Carey, Ann Rutherford, Cara Williams,
Richard Crane, Henry Morgan, Dickie Moore. Fox, 1943.

Here Come the Waves.*** 99m, b/w. Dir. Mark Sandrich. With Bing Crosby, Betty Hutton, Sonny Tufts, Ann Doran, Catherine Craig. Paramount, 1944.

Hers to Hold.** 93m, b/w. Dir. Frank Ryan. With Deanna Durbin, Joseph Cotten, Charles Winninger, Nella Walker, Gus Schilling, Ludwig Stossel. Universal, 1943.

Hey, Rookie.** 71m, b/w. Dir. Charles Barton. With Larry Parks, Ann Miller, Condos Brothers, Joe Sawyer, Jack Gilford, Selmer Jackson. Columbia, 1944.

Hidden Enemy.* 63m, b/w. Dir. Howard Bretherton. With Warren Hull, Kay Linaker, William Von Brinken, George Cleveland, William Costello. Monogram, 1940.

Hillbilly Blitzkrieg.* aka *Enemy Round-Up.* 63m, b/w. Dir. Roy Mack. With Bud Duncan, Cliff Nazarro, Edgar Kennedy, Doris Linden, Lucien Littlefield. Monogram, 1942.

Hitler--Dead or Alive.** 72m, b/w. Dir. Nick Grinde. With Ward Bond, Dorothy Tree, Warren Hymer, Paul Fix, Russell Hicks, Felix Basch, Bobby Watson. Charles House, 1942.

The Hitler Gang.** 101m, b/w. Dir. John Farrow. With Robert Watson, Roman Bohnen, Martin Kosleck, Victor Varconi, Luis Van Rooten, Alexander Pope. Paramount, 1944.

Hitler's Children.*** 80m, b/w. Dir. Edward Dmytryk, Irving Reis. With Tim Holt, Bonita Granville, Kent Smith, Otto Kruger, H.B. Warner, Lloyd Corrigan. RKO, 1942.

Hitler's Madman.** aka *Hitler's Hangman.* 84m, b/w. Dir. Douglas Sirk. With Patricia Morison, John Carradine, Alan Curtis, Ralph Morgan, Howard Freeman, Ludwig Stossel, Edgar Kennedy. MGM, 1943.

Hold Back the Dawn.*** 115m, b/w. Dir. Mitchell Leisen. With Charles Boyer, Olivia de Havilland, Paulette Goddard, Victor Francen, Walter Abel. Paramount, 1941.

Hollywood Canteen.** 124m, b/w. Dir. Delmer Daves. With Joan Crawford, Bette Davis, John Garfield, Sydney Greenstreet, Peter Lorre, Ida Lupino, Eleanor Parker, Alexis Smith, Barbara Stanwyck, Joan Leslie, The Andrews Sisters, Jack Benny, Eddie Cantor, Faye Emerson. WB, 1944.

Hostages.* 88m, b/w. Dir. Frank Tuttle. With Arturo de Cordova, Luise Rainer, William Bendix. Paramount, 1943.

Hotel Berlin.** 98m, b/w. Dir. Peter Godfrey. With Helmut Dantine, Andrea King, Raymond Massey, Faye Emerson, Peter Lorre, Alan Hale, Sr. WB, 1945.

The Hour Before the Dawn.** 74m, b/w. Dir. Frank Tuttle. With Franchot Tone, Veronica Lake, John Sutton, Binnie Barnes, Henry Stephenson, Mary Gordon. Paramount, 1944.

The House on 92nd St.*** 88m, b/w. Dir. Henry Hathaway. With William Eythe, Lloyd Nolan, Signe Hasso, Gene Lockhart, Leo G. Carroll, Lydia St. Clair. Fox, 1945.

The Human Comedy.** 118m, b/w. Dir. Clarence Brown. With Mickey Rooney, Frank Morgan, James Craig, Marsha Hunt, Fay Bainter, Ray Collins. MGM, 1943.

I Escaped From the Gestapo.** aka *No Escape*. 75m, b/w. Dir. Harold Young. With Dean Jagger, John Carradine, Mary Brian, William Henry, Sidney Blackmer. Monogram, 1943.

I Love a Soldier.** 106m, b/w. Dir. Mark Sandrich. With Paulette Goddard, Sonny Tufts, Beulah Bondi, Mary Treen, Barry Fritzgerald. Paramount, 1944.

I Wanted Wings.** 131m, b/w. Dir. Mitchell Leisen. With Ray Milland, William Holden, Wayne Morris, Brian Donlevy, Constance Moore, Veronica Lake. Paramount, 1941.

I'll Be Seeing You.*** 83m, b/w. Dir. William Dieterle. With Ginger Rogers, Joseph Cotton, Shirley Temple, Spring Byington, Tom Tully, Chill Wills. UA, 1944.

Identity Unknown.** 71m, b/w. Dir. Walter Colmes. With Richard Arlen, Cheryl Walker, Roger Pryor, Bobby Driscoll, Lola Lane, Ian Keith. Republic, 1945.

The Immortal Sergeant.** 90m, b/w. Dir. John M. Stahl. With Henry Fonda, Maureen O'Hara, Thomas Mitchell, Allyn Joslyn, Reginald Gardiner, Melville Cooper. Fox, 1943.

The Imposter.** aka *Strange Confession*. 95m, b/w. Dir. Julien Duvivier. With Jean Gabin, Richard Whorf, Allyn Joslyn, Ellen Drew, Peter Van Eyck. Universal, 1944.

In Our Time.* 109m, b/w. Dir. Vincent Sherman. With Ida Lupino, Paul Henreid, Nancy Coleman, Mary Boland, Victor Francen. WB, 1944.

In the Meantime, Darling.** 74m, b/w. Dir. Otto Preminger. With Jeanne Crain, Frank Latimore, Eugene Pallette, Mary Nash, Cara Williams, Reed Hadley, Blake Edwards. Fox, 1944.

In the Navy.** 85m, b/w. Dir. Arthur Lubin. With Bud Abbott, Lou Costello, Dick Powell, The Andrews Sisters, Claire Dodd, Dick Foran. Universal, 1941.

International Lady.** 100m, b/w. Dir. Tim Whelan. With Ilona Massey, George Brent, Basil Rathbone. UA, 1941.

International Squadron.** 85m, b/w. Dir. Lothar Mendes. With Ronald Reagan, James Stephenson, Julie Bishop, Cliff Edwards, Reginald Denny. WB, 1941.

The Invaders.**** aka *49th Parallel*. 105m, b/w. Dir. Michael Powell. With Leslie Howard, Raymond Massey, Sir Laurence Olivier, Anton Walbrook, Eric Portman, Glynis Johns, Niall MacGinnis. Columbia, 1941.

Gripping tale of survivors from a German U-37 submarine, sunk off the Gulf of St. Lawrence, killing their way across Canadian wilderness to get to neutral America. Oscar for best story. Best scene: escape across iced-over Lake Ontario at night. Footnote: the leisurely examination of Hutterite, Eskimo, and Indian culture was influenced by the documentaries of Robert Flaherty.

Invisible Agent.** 79m, b/w. Dir. Edwin L. Marin. With Ilona Massey, Jon Hall, Peter Lorre, Sir. Cedric Hardwicke, J. Edward Bromberg, John Litel. Universal, 1942.

Janie.** 106m, b/w. Dir. Michael Curtiz. With Joyce Reynolds, Edward Arnold, Ann Harding, Robert Benchley, Robert Hutton, Alan Hale, Hattie McDaniel. WB, 1944.

Joan of Ozark.** 80m, b/w. Dir. Joseph Santley. With Judy Canova, Joe E. Brown, Eddie Foy, Jr., Jerome Cowan, Alexander Granach, Anne Jeffreys. Republic, 1942.

Joan of Paris.** 93m, b/w. Dir. Robert Stevenson. With Paul Henreid, Michele Morgan, Thomas Mitchell, Laird Cregar, Alan Ladd. RKO, 1942.

Joe Smith, American.** 63m, b/w. Dir. Richard Thorpe. With Robert Young, Marsha Hunt, Harvey Stephens, Darryl Hickman. MGM, 1942.

Journey for Margaret.*** 81m, b/w. Dir. W.S. Van Dyke II. With Robert Young, Laraine Day, Fay Bainter, Nigel Bruce, Margaret O'Brien, William Severn. MGM, 1942.

Journey Into Fear.*** 71m, b/w. Dir. Norman Foster. With Orson Welles, Joseph Cotten, Delores Del Rio, Ruth Warrick, Agnes Moorehead. RKO, 1942.

Junior Army.* 70m, b/w. Dir. Lew Landers. With Freddie Bartholomew, Billy Halop, Bobby Jordon, Huntz Hall, Boyd Davis. Columbia, 1943.

Keep Your Powder Dry.** 93m, b/w. Dir. Edward Buzzell. With Lana Turner, Laraine Day, Susan Peters, Agnes Moorehead, Bill Johnson, Natalie Schafer. MGM, 1945.

Keeper of the Flame.*** 100m, b/w. Dir. George Cukor. With Spencer Tracy, Katharine Hepburn, Richard Whorf, Margaret Wycherly, Forrest Tucker. MGM, 1942.

Ladies Courageous.** 88m, b/w. Dir. John Rawlins. With Loretta Young, Geraldine Fitzgerald, Diana Barrymore, Evelyn Ankers, Frank Jenks, Ruth Roman, Anne Gwynne, Philip Terry, Lois Collier, Kane Richmond. Universal, 1944.

Ladies of Washington.** 61m, b/w. Dir. Louis King. With Trudy Marshall, Ronald Graham, Anthony Quinn, Sheila Ryan, Robert Bailey, Beverly Whitney. Fox, 1944.

Lady From Chungking.** 71m, b/w. Dir. William Nigh. With Anna May Wong, Harold Huber, Mae Clarke, Rick Vallin, Paul Bryar. Producers Rel, 1942.

The Lady Has Plans.** 77m, b/w. Dir. Sidney Lanfield. With Paulette Goddard, Ray Milland, Roland Young, Albert Dekker, Margaret Hayes, Cecil Kellaway. Paramount, 1942.

Let's Get Tough!* 62m, b/w. Dir. Wallace Fox. With Leo Gorcey, Bobby Jordan, Huntz Hall, Gabriel Dell, Tom Brown, Florence Rice. Monogram, 1942.

A Letter For Evie.** 88m, b/w. Dir. Jules Dassin. With Marsha Hunt, John Carroll, Hume Cronyn, Spring Byington, Pamela Britton. MGM, 1945.

Lifeboat.**** 96m, b/w. Dir. Alfred Hitchcock. With Tallulah Bankhead, William Bendix, John Hodiak, Mary Anderson, Walter Slezak, Canada Lee, Hume Cronyn, Heather Angel, Henry Hull. Fox, 1944.

A survival movie, brilliantly directed on a single set. Stragglers in a lifeboat take aboard the German captain of the U-boat that sank their ship. A revealing study in group behavior and wartime psychology. Best scene: they argue over who will be the captain of the lifeboat. Footnote: Hitchcock appears in this movie as a photograph in a newspaper read by one of the survivors.

Little Tokyo, U.S.A.* 64m, b/w. Dir. Otto Brower. With Preston Foster, Brenda Joyce, Harold Huber, Don Douglas, June Duprez. Fox, 1942.

London Blackout Murders.* 58m, b/w. Dir. George Sherman. With John Abbott, Mary McLeod, Lloyd Corrigan, Lester Matthews, Anita Bolster. Republic, 1942.

The Lone Wolf Spy Hunt.** 67m, b/w. Dir. Peter Godfrey. With Warren William, Ida Lupino, Rita Hayworth, Virginia Weidler, Ralph Morgan, Don Beddoe. Columbia, 1939.

Love Letters.** 101m, b/w. Dir. William Dieterle. With Jennifer Jones, Joseph Cotton, Ann Richards, Anita Louise, Cecil Kellaway. Paramount, 1945.

Lucky Jordan.** 84m, b/w. Dir. Frank Tuttle. With Alan Ladd, Helen Walker, Marie McDonald, Mabel Paige, Sheldon Leonard, Lloyd Corrigan. Paramount, 1942.

Lure of the Islands.* 61m, b/w. Dir. Jean Yarbrough. With Margie Hart, Robert Lowery, Guinn Williams, Ivan Lebedeff, Warren Hymer. Monogram, 1942.

Madame Spy.* 63m, b/w. Dir. Roy William Neill. With Constance Bennett, Don Porter, John Litel, Edward Brophy, John Eldredge. Universal, 1942.

*Main Street After Dark.** 57m, b/w. Dir. Edward L. Cahn. With Edward Arnold, Selena Royle, Tom Trout, Audrey Totter, Dan Duryea. MGM, 1944.

*Make Your Own Bed.** 82m, b/w. Dir. Peter Godfrey. With Jack Carson, Jane Wyman, Alan Hale, Irene Manning, George Tobias, Ricardo Cortez. WB, 1944.

*Man at Large.** 70m, b/w. Dir. Eugene Forde. With Marjorie Weaver, George Reeves, Richard Derr, Steve Geray, Milton Parsons. Fox, 1941.

*The Man From Down Under.*** 103m, b/w. Dir. Robert Z. Leonard. With Charles Laughton, Binnie Barnes, Richard Carlson, Donna Reed, Christopher Severn. MGM, 1943.

*Man Hunt.**** 105m, b/w. Dir. Fritz Lang. With Walter Pidgeon, Joan Bennett, George Sanders, John Carradine, Roddy McDowall. Fox, 1941.

*The Man I Married.**** aka *I Married A Nazi*. 77m, b/w. Dir. Irving Pichel. With Joan Bennett, Francis Lederer, Lloyd Nolan, Anna Sten, Otto Kruger. Fox, 1940.

*Manila Calling.*** 81m, b/w. Dir. Herbert I. Leeds. With Lloyd Nolan, Carole Landis, Cornel Wilde, James Gleason, Martin Kosleck, Ralph Byrd, Elisha Cook, Jr. Fox, 1942.

*Margin for Error.*** 74m, b/w. Dir. Otto Preminger. With Joan Bennett, Milton Berle, Otto Preminger, Carl Esmond, Howard Freeman, Ed McNamara. Fox, 1943.

*Marine Raiders.*** 91m, b/w. Dir. Harold D. Schuster. With Pat O'Brien, Robert Ryan, Ruth Hussey, Frank McHugh, Barton MacLane. RKO, 1944.

*The Marines Come Through.** 60m, b/w. Dir. Louis Gasnier. With Wallace Ford, Toby Wing, Grant Withers. Astor, 1943.

*The Master Race.**** 96m, b/w. Dir. Herbert J. Biberman. With George Coulouris, Stanley Ridges, Osa Massen, Nancy Gates, Lloyd Bridges. RKO, 1944.

*A Medal for Benny.**** 77m, b/w. Dir. Irving Pichel. With Dorothy Lamour, Arturo de Cordova, J. Carrol Naish, Mikhail Rasumny, Fernando Alvarado, Charles Dingle, Frank McHugh. Paramount, 1945.

*Meet the People.*** 99m, b/w. Dir. Charles Reisner. With Lucille Ball, Dick Powell, Virginia O'Brien, Bert Lahr, Rags Ragland, June Allyson, Mata & Hari. MGM, 1944.

*Minesweeper.** 67m, b/w. Dir. William Berke. With Richard Arlen, Jean Parker, Russell Hayden, Guinn Williams, Emma Dunn, Charles D. Brown. Paramount, 1943.

*Ministry of Fear.**** 84m, b/w. Dir. Fritz Lang. With Ray Milland, Marjorie Reynolds, Carl Esmond, Dan Duryea, Hillary Brooke, Alan Napier. Paramount, 1944.

The Miracle of Morgan's Creek.*** 99m, b/w. Dir. Preston Sturges. With Eddie Bracken, Betty Hutton, Diana Lynn, Brian Donlevy, Akim Tamiroff, Porter Hall, Emory Parnell, Alan Bridge. Paramount, 1944.

Miss V From Moscow.* aka *Intrigue in Paris.* 68m, b/w. Dir. Albert Herman. With Lola Lane, Noel Madison, Howard Banks, Paul Weigel, John Vosper. Producers Rel, 1942.

Mission to Moscow.*** 123m, b/w. Dir. Michael Curtiz. With Walter Huston, Ann Harding, Oscar Homolka, George Tobias, Gene Lockhart, Frieda Inescort, Eleanor Parker, Richard Travis. WB, 1943.

Mr. Lucky.*** 100m, b/w. Dir. H.C. Potter. With Cary Grant, Laraine Day, Charles Bickford, Gladys Cooper, Alan Carney, Henry Stephenson, Paul Stewart, Kay Johnson, Florence Bates. RKO, 1943.

Mr. Winkle Goes to War.** 80m, b/w. Dir. Alfred E. Green. With Edward G. Robinson, Ruth Warrick, Ted Donaldson, Robert Armstrong, Ann Shoemaker. Columbia, 1944.

Mrs. Miniver.*** 134m, b/w. Dir. William Wyler. With Greer Garson, Walter Pidgeon, Dame May Whitty, Teresa Wright, Reginald Owen, Henry Travers, Richard Ney, Tom Conway, Henry Wilcoxon. MGM, 1942.

The Moon Is Down.*** 90m, b/w. Dir. Irving Pichel. Sir Cedric Hardwicke, Henry Travers, Lee J. Cobb, Dorris Bowden, Margaret Wycherly, Peter Van Eyck, William Post, Jr. Fox, 1943.

The More the Merrier.*** 104m, b/w. Dir. George Stevens. With Jean Arthur, Joel McCrea, Charles Coburn, Richard Gaines, Bruce Bennett, Ann Savage, Ann Doran, Frank Sully, Grady Sutton. Columbia, 1943.

The Mortal Storm.*** 100m, b/w. Dir. Frank Borzage. With Margaret Sullavan, James Stewart, Robert Young, Frank Morgan, Robert Stack, Bonita Granville, Irene Rich, Maria Ouspenskaya. MGM, 1940.

My Favorite Blonde.*** 78m, b/w. Dir. Sidney Lanfield. With Bob Hope, Madeleine Carroll, Gale Sondergaard, George Zucco, Victor Varconi. Paramount, 1942.

My Favorite Spy.** 86m, b/w. Dir. Tay Garnett. With Kay Kyser, Ellen Drew, Jane Wyman, Robert Armstrong, William Demarest, Una O'Connor, Helen Westley, George Cleveland, Ish Kabibble. RKO, 1942.

My Son, the Hero.* 66m, b/w. Dir. Edgar G. Ulmer. With Patsy Kelly, Roscoe Karns, Joan Blair, Carol Hughes, Maxie Rosenbloom. Producers Rel, 1943.

*Mystery Sea Raider.*** 75m, b/w. Dir. Edward Dmytryk. With Carole Landis, Henry Wilcoxon, Onslow Stevens, Kathleen Howard, Wallace Rairden. Paramount, 1940.

*The Navy Comes Through.*** 81m, b/w. Dir. A. Edward Sutherland. With Pat O'Brien, George Murphy, Jane Wyatt, Jackie Cooper, Carl Esmond, Desi Arnaz. RKO, 1942.

*The Navy Way.** 74m, b/w. Dir. William Berke. With Robert Lowery, Jean Parker, Bill Henry. Paramount, 1944.

*Nazi Agent.** 82m, b/w. Dir. Jules Dassin. With Conrad Veidt, Ann Ayars, Frank Reicher, Dorothy Tree. MGM, 1942.

*Nick Carter, Master Detective.*** 60m, b/w. Dir. Jacques Tourneur. With Walter Pidgeon, Rita Johnson, Henry Hull, Stanley C. Ridges, Donald Meek. MGM, 1939.

*None Shall Escape.**** 85m, b/w. Dir. Andre de Toth. With Marsh Hunt, Alexander Knox, Henry Travers, Richard Crane, Dorothy Morris, Trevor Bardette. Columbia, 1944.

*North Star.***** aka *Armored Attack.* 105m, b/w. Dir. Lewis Milestone. With Dana Andrews, Anne Baxter, Erich von Stroheim, Walter Brennan, Walter Huston, Ann Harding, Jane Withers, Farley Granger. MGM, 1943.

Notable primarily for political reasons as rare pro-Russian propaganda (see also *Mission to Moscow*, 1943). Based on Lillian Hellman's script. Best scene: Blood is taken forcibly from Russian children to aid Nazi wounded. Footnote: in the McCarthy era, the House Un-American Activities Committee questioned filmmakers about their intentions. A 1957 re-release butchered 22 minutes and cut out every mention of the word "comrade."

*Northern Pursuit.*** 94m, b/w. Dir. Raoul Walsh. With Errol Flynn, Julie Bishop, Helmut Dantine, John Ridgely, Gene Lockhart, Tom Tully. WB, 1943.

*Objective, Burma!*** 142m, b/w. Dir. Raoul Walsh. With Errol Flynn, William Prince, James Brown, George Tobias, Henry Hull, Warner Anderson. WB, 1945.

*Once Upon a Honeymoon.*** 117m, b/w. Dir. Leo McCarey. With Ginger Rogers, Cary Grant, Walter Slezak, Albert Dekker, Albert Basserman. RKO, 1942.

*One Night in Lisbon.*** 97m, b/w. Dir. Edward H. Griffith. With Fred MacMurray, Madeleine Carroll, Patricia Morison, Billie Burke, John Loder. Paramount, 1941.

*Over 21.**** 104m, b/w. Dir. Charles Vidor. With Irene Dunne, Alexander Knox, Charles Coburn, Jeff Donnell, Lee Patrick, Phil Brown, Cora Witherspoon. Columbia, 1945.

Pacific Blackout.* 76m, b/w. Dir. Ralph Murray. With Robert Preston, Martha O'Driscoll, Philip Merivale, Eva Gabor. Paramount, 1942.

Pacific Rendezvous.* 75m, b/w. Dir. George Sidney. With Lee Bowman, Jean Rogers, Mona Maris, Carl Esmond, Paul Cavanagh. MGM, 1942.

Panama Hattie.** 79m, b/w. Dir. Norman Z. McLeod. With Ann Sothern, Red Skelton, Rags Ragland, Ben Blue, Marsha Hunt, Virginia O'Brien, Alan Mowbray, Lena Horne, Dan Dailey, Jr., Carl Esmond. MGM, 1942.

Parachute Battalion.** 75m, b/w. Dir. Leslie Goodwins. With Edmond O'Brien, Nancy Kelly, Robert Preston, Harry Carey, Buddy Ebsen, Paul Kelly. RKO, 1941.

Parachute Nurse.* 65m, b/w. Dir. Charles Barton. With Marguerite Chapman, William Wright, Kay Harris, Lauretta M. Schimmoler, Louise Albritton. Columbia, 1942.

Paris After Dark.** 85m, b/w. Dir. Leonide Moguy. With George Sanders, Philip Dorn, Brenda Marshall, Madeleine LeBeau, Marcel Dalio. Fox, 1943.

Paris Calling.*** 93m, b/w. Dir. Edwin L. Marin. With Elisabeth Bergner, Randolph Scott, Basil Rathbone, Gale Sondergaard, Eduardo Ciannelli, Lee J. Cobb. Universal, 1941.

Paris Underground.** 97m, b/w. Dir. Gregory Ratoff. With Constance Bennett, Gracie Fields, George Rigaud, Kurt Kreuger, Leslie Vincent, Charles Andre. UA, 1945.

Passage to Marseille.** 110m, b/w. Dir. Michael Curtiz. With Humphrey Bogart, Michele Morgan, Claude Rains, Philip Dorn, Sydney Greenstreet, Peter Lorre, George Tobias, Helmut Dantine, John Loder, Eduardo Ciannelli. WB, 1944.

Passport to Destiny.** aka *Passport to Adventure.* 65m, b/w. Dir. Ray McCarey. With Elsa Lanchester, Gordon Oliver, Lloyd Corrigan, Gavin Muir, Lenore Aubert. RKO, 1944.

Passport to Suez.* 72m, b/w. Dir. Andre de Toth. With Warren William, Ann Savage, Eric Blore, Robert Stanford, Sheldon Leonard, Lloyd Bridges, Gavin Muir. Columbia, 1943.

Phantom Raiders.** 70m, b/w. Dir. Jacques Tourneur. With Walter Pidgeon, Donald Meek, Joseph Schildkraut, Florence Rice, Nat Pendleton. MGM, 1940.

The Pied Piper.*** 86m, b/w. Dir. Irving Pichel. With Monty Wooley, Roddey McDowall, Anne Baxter, Otto Preminger, J. Carol Naish, Lester Matthews. Fox, 1942.

Pilot No. 5.** 70m, b/w. Dir. George Sidney. With Franchot Tone, Marsha Hunt, Gene Kelly, Van Johnson, Alan Baxter, Dick Simmons. MGM, 1943.

*Pin Up Girl.** 83m, color. Dir. H. Bruce Humberstone. With Betty
Grable, John Harvey, Martha Raye, Joe E. Brown, Eugene
Pallette. Fox, 1944.

*Powder Town.** 79m, b/w. Dir. Rowland V Lee. With Victor
McLaglen, Edmond O'Brien, June Havoc. RKO, 1942.

*Practically Yours.*** 90m, b/w. Dir. Mitchell Leisen. With Claudette
Colbert, Fred MacMurray, Gil Lamb, Robert Benchley,
Rosemary DeCamp, Cecil Kellaway. Paramount, 1944.

*Pride of the Army.** aka *War Dogs.* 65m, b/w. Dir. S. Roy Luby.
With Billy Lee, Addison Richards, Kay Linaker, Bradley
Page. Monogram, 1942.

*Pride of the Marines.**** 119m, b/w. Dir. Delmer Daves. With
John Garfield, Eleanor Parker, Dane Clark, John Ridgely,
Rosemary DeCamp, Ann Doran, Ann Todd, Warren
Douglas. WB, 1945.

*Priorities on Parade.** 79m, b/w. Dir. Albert S. Rogell. With Ann
Miller, Johnnie Johnston, Jerry Colonna, Betty Rhodes,
Vera Vague. Paramount, 1942.

*Prison Ship.** 60m, b/w. Dir. Arthur Dreifuss. With Nina Foch,
Robert Lowery, Richard Loo. Columbia, 1945.

*Prisoner of Japan.** 54m, b/w. Dir. Arthur Ripley. With Alan
Baxter, Gertrude Michael, Ernest Dorian, Corinna Mura,
Tommy Seidel. Producers Rel, 1942.

*The Purple Heart.**** 99m, b/w. Dir. Lewis Milestone. With Dana
Andrews, Farley Granger, Sam Levene, Richard Conte, Tala
Birell, Nestor Paiva, Benson Fong. Fox, 1944.

*The Purple V.** 58m, b/w. Dir. George Sherman. With John
Archer, Mary McLeod, Fritz Kortner. Republic, 1943.

*Pursuit to Algiers.*** 65m, b/w. Dir. Roy William Neill, With
Basil Rathbone, Nigel Bruce, Marjorie Riordan, Rosalind
Ivan, Martin Kosleck. Universal, 1945.

*Quiet Please, Murder.*** 70m, b/w. Dir. John Larkin. With George
Sanders, Gail Patrick, Richard Denning, Sidney Blackmer,
Lynne Roberts, Kurt Katch, Minerva Urecal. Fox, 1942.

*Rainbow Island.*** 97m, color. Dir. Ralph Murphy. With Dorothy
Lamour, Eddie Bracken, Gil Lamb, Barry Sullivan, Forrest
Orr. Paramount, 1944.

*The Ramparts We Watch.** 90m, b/w. Dir. Louis de Rochemont.
With John Adair, John Summers, Julia Kent, Ellen
Prescott, Andrew Brummer. RKO, 1940.

*Rationing.*** 93m, b/w. Dir. Willis Goldbeck. With Wallace Beery,
Marjorie Main, Donald Meek, Gloria Dickson, Henry
O'Neill, Connie Gilchrist. Columbia, 1944.

*Remember Pearl Harbor.** 75m, b/w. Dir. Joseph Santley. With Donald M. Barry, Alan Curtis, Fay McKenzie, Sig Rumann. Republic, 1942.

*Reunion in France.*** 104m, b/w. Dir. Jules Dassin. With Joan Crawford, John Wayne, Philip Dorn, Reginald Owen, Albert Bassermann, John Carradine, Henry Daniell. MGM, 1942.

*Reveille With Beverly.*** 78m, b/w. Dir. Charles Barton. With Ann Miller, William Wright, Dick Purcell, Franklin Pangborn, Larry Parks. Columbia, 1943.

*Rookies in Burma.** 62m, b/w. Dir. Leslie Goodwins. With Wally Brown, Alan Carney, Erford Gage. RKO, 1943.

*Rosie the Riveter.*** 75m, b/w. Dir. Joseph Santley. With Jane Frazee, Frank Albertson, Vera Vague, Frank Jenks, Carl "Alfalfa" Switzer. Republic, 1944.

*Rough, Tough and Ready.** 66m, b/w. Dir. Del Ford. With Chester Morris, Victor McLaglen, Jean Rogers, Veda Ann Borg. Colunbia, 1945.

*Sabotage Squad.** 64m, b/w. Dir. Lew Landers. With Bruce Bennett, Kay Harris, Eddie Norris, Sidney Blackmer, Don Beddoe. Columbia, 1942.

*Saboteur.*** 108m, b/w. Dir. Alfred Hitchcock. With Robert Cummings, Priscilla Lane, Norman Lloyd, Otto Kruger, Murray Alper, Alma Kruger. Universal, 1942.

*Sahara.***** 97m, b/w. Dir. Zoltan Korda. With Humphrey Bogart, Bruce Bennett, Lloyd Bridges, Rex Ingram, J. Carrol Naish, Dan Duryea. Columbia, 1943.

  Thirteen Allied soldiers from different nations form a "lost unit" and hold off 500 Germans of Rommel's Afrika Korps at a desert oasis. The delay allows British reinforcements to arrive before the start of the Battle at El Alamein. Based on *The Thirteen*, a Russian movie. Footnote: *Sahara* established the formula for future desert warfare movies.

*Sailor's Lady.*** 66m, b/w. Dir. Allan Dwan. With Nancy Kelly, Jon Hall, Joan Davis, Dana Andrews, Mary Nash, Larry "Buster" Crabbe, Katherine Aldridge. Fox, 1940.

*Salute for Three.** 74m, b/w. Dir. Ralph Murphy. With Betty Rhodes, MacDonald Carey, Marty May, Cliff Edwards, Minna Gombell. Paramount, 1943.

*Salute to the Marines.*** 101m, color. Dir. S. Sylvan Simon. With Wallace Beery, Fay Bainter, Reginald Owen, Keye Luke, Ray Collins, Marilyn Maxwell. MGM, 1943.

*Samurai.** 78m, b/w. Dir. Raymond Cannon. With Paul Fung, Luke Chan, David Chow, Barbara Woodell. Cavalcade, 1945.

*Secret Agent of Japan.*** 72m, b/w. Dir. Irving Pichel. With Preston Foster, Lynn Bari, Noel Madison, Janis Carter, Sen Yung, Addison Richards, Frank Puglia. Fox, 1942.

*Secret Command.**** 82m, b/w. Dir. A. Edward Sutherland. With Pat O'Brien, Carole Landis, Chester Morris, Ruth Warrick, Wallace Ford. Columbia, 1944.

*Secret Enemies.** 57m, b/w. Dir. Ben Stoloff. With Craig Stevens, Faye Emerson, John Ridgely, Charles Lang, Robert Warwick. WB, 1942.

*Secrets of Scotland Yard.** 68m, b/w. Dir. George Blair. With Edgar Barrier, Stephanie Bachelor, C. Aubrey Smith, Lionel Atwill, Henry Stephenson. Republic, 1944.

*Secrets of the Underground.** 70m, b/w. Dir. William Morgan. With John Hubbard, Virginia Grey, Lloyd Corrigan, Robin Raymond, Miles Mander. Republic, 1943.

*See Here, Private Hargrove.**** 101m, b/w. Dir. Wesley Ruggles. With Robert Walker, Donna Reed, Keenan Wynn, Robert Benchley, Bob Crosby, Grant Mitchell. MGM, 1944.

*Sergeant Mike.** 60m, b/w. Dir. Henry Levin. With Larry Parks, Jeanne Bates, Loren Tindall, Jim Bannon, Robert Williams. Columbia, 1945.

*Seven Miles From Alcatraz.*** 62m, b/w. Dir. Edward Dmytryk. With James Craig, Bonita Granville, Frank Jenks, Cliff Edwards, George Cleveland. RKO, 1942.

*The Seventh Cross.**** 110m, b/w. Dir. Fred Zinnemann. With Spencer Tracy, Signe Hasso, Hume Cronyn, Agnes Moorehead, Jessica Tandy, George Macready, Kaaren Verne, George Zucco, Felix Bressart. MGM, 1944.

*Shadow of Terror.** 60m, b/w. Dir. Lew Landers. With Richard Fraser, Grace Gillern, Cy Kendall. Producers Rel, 1945.

*Sherlock Holmes and the Secret Weapon.*** 68m, b/w. Dir. Roy William Neill. With Basil Rathbone, Nigel Bruce, Lionel Atwill, Kaaren Verne, William Post, Jr., Dennis Hoey, Mary Gordon, Holmes Herbert. Universal, 1942.

*Sherlock Holmes and the Voice of Terror.** 65m, b/w. Dir. John Rawlins. With Basil Rathbone, Nigel Bruce, Evelyn Ankers, Reginald Denny, Thomas Gomez, Henry Daniell, Montagu Love. Universal, 1942.

*Sherlock Holmes in Washington.** 71m, b/w. Dir. Roy William Neill. With Basil Rathbone, Nigel Bruce, Marjorie Lord, Henry Daniell, George Zucco, John Archer, Gavin Muir. Universal, 1943.

*She's in the Army.*** 63m, b/w. Dir. Jean Yarbrough. With Lucille Gleason, Veda Ann Borg, Marie Wilson, Lyle Talbot, Robert Lowerey. Monogram, 1942.

Ship Ahoy.** 96m, b/w. Dir. Edward Buzzell. With Eleanor Powell, Red Skelton, Virginia O'Brien, Bert Lahr, John Emery, Tommy Dorsey Orch, Frank Sinatra, Jo Stafford. MGM, 1942.

Since You Went Away.*** 172m, b/w. Dir. John Cromwell. With Claudette Colbert, Jennifer Jones, Joseph Cotten, Shirley Temple, Monty Woolley, Hattie McDaniel, Nazimova, Robert Walker, Lionel Barrymore. UA, 1944.

Sky Murder.** 71m, b/w. Dir. George B. Seitz. With Walter Pidgeon, Donald Meek, Kaaren Verne, Edward Ashley, Joyce Compton, Tom Conway. MGM, 1940.

The Sky's the Limit.*** 89m, b/w. Dir. Edward H. Griffith. With Fred Astaire, Joan Leslie, Robert Benchley, Robert Ryan, Elizabeth Patterson, Marjorie Gateson. RKO, 1943.

Snafu.* 82m, b/w. Dir. Jack Moss. With Robert Benchley, Vera Vague, Conrad Janis, Nanette Parks. Columbia, 1945.

So Ends Our Night.*** 120m, b/w. Dir. John Cromwell. With Fredric March, Margaret Sullavan, Frances Dee, Glenn Ford, Anna Sten, Erich von Stroheim. UA, 1941.

So Proudly We Hail!** 126m, b/w. Dir. Mark Sandrich. With Claudette Colbert, Paulette Goddard, Veronica Lake, George Reeves, Sonny Tufts, Barbara Britton, Walter Abel. Paramount, 1943.

Something for the Boys.** 87m, color. Dir. Lewis Seiler. With Perry Como, Carmen Miranda, Vivian Blaine, Michael O'Shea, Phil Silvers, Cara Williams, Sheila Ryan. Fox, 1944.

Somewhere I'll Find You.** 108m, b/w. Dir. Wesley Ruggles. With Lana Turner, Clark Gable, Robert Sterling, Reginald Owen, Lee Patrick, Rags Ragland, Patricia Dane. MGM, 1942.

Son of Lassie.** 102m, color. Dir. S. Sylvan Simon. With Peter Lawford, Donald Crisp, June Lockhart. MGM, 1945.

Song of Russia.** 107m, b/w. Dir. Gregory Ratoff. With Robert Taylor, Susan Peters, John Hodiak, Robert Benchley, Felix Bressart, Joan Lorring, Darryl Hickman, Jacqueline White. MGM, 1943.

Spy Ship.* 62m, b/w. Dir. B. Reeves Eason. With Craig Stevens, Irene Manning, Maris Wrixon, Michael Ames, Peter Whitney. WB, 1942.

Spy Train.* 61m, b/w. Dir. Harold Young. With Richard Travis, Catherine Craig, Chick Chandler, Thelma White, Evelyn Brent. Monogram, 1943.

Stage Door Canteen.** 132m, b/w. Dir. Frank Borzage. With Cheryl Walker, William Terry, Marjorie Riordan, Lon McCallister, Margaret Early, Michael Harrison. UA, 1943.

*Stand by for Action.*** 109m, b/w. Dir. Robert Z. Leonard. With Robert Taylor, Brian Donlevy, Charles Laughton, Walter Brennan, Marilyn Maxwell, Henry O'Neill. MGM, 1942.

*Standing Room Only.*** 83m, b/w. Dir. Sidney Lanfield. With Fred MacMurray, Paulette Goddard, Edward Arnold, Hillary Brooke, Roland Young, Anne Revere. Paramount, 1944.

*Star Spangled Rhythm.**** 99m, b/w. Dir. George Marshall. With Betty Hutton, Eddie Bracken, Victor Moore, Anne Revere, Walter Abel, Cass Daley, Bob Hope. Paramount, 1942.

*Storm Over Lisbon.*** 86m, b/w. Dir. George Sherman. With Vera Ralston, Richard Arlen, Erich von Stroheim, Otto Kruger, Eduardo Ciannelli, Mona Barrie. Republic, 1944.

*The Story of Dr. Wassell.*** 140m, color. Dir. Cecil B. De Mille. With Gary Cooper, Laraine Day, Signe Hasso, Dennis O'Keefe, Paul Kelly, Philip Ahn, Barbara Britton. Paramount, 1944.

*The Story of G. I. Joe.***** aka *War Correspondent.* 109m, b/w. Dir. William A. Wellman. With Burgess Meredith, Robert Mitchum, Freddie Steel, Wally Cassell, Jimmy Lloyd. UA, 1945.

   Muddy and bloody Italian campaign seen through the eyes of front-line reporter Ernie Pyle (Meredith). Mitchum is effective in his first starring role as a tired, cynical combat officer. Best scene: the officer's death has a profound impact on his men. Footnote: at its release, General Dwight Eisenhower called it the greatest war movie he'd ever seen.

*The Strange Death of Adolf Hitler.*** 72m, b/w. Dir. James Hogan. With Ludwig Donath, Fritz Kortner, Gale Sondergaard, George Dolenz, Fred Giermann, William Trenk, Merrill Rodin. Universal, 1943.

*Strange Holiday.*** aka *The Day After Tomorrow.* 61m, b/w. Dir. Arch Oboler. With Claude Rains, Bobbie Stebbins, David Bradford, Barbara Bates, Paul Hilton, Gloria Holden, Milton Kibbee, Helen Mack, Martin Kosleck. Producers Rel, 1945.

*Submarine Alert.** 67m, b/w. Dir. Frank McDonald. With Richard Arlen, Wendy Barrie, Nils Asther. Paramount, 1943.

*Submarine Base.** 65m, b/w. Dir. Albert Kelly. With John Litel, Alan Baxter, Fifi D'Orsay, Eric Blore, Iris Adrian. Producers Rel, 1943.

*Submarine Raider.** 65m, b/w. Dir. Lew Landers. With John Howard, Marguerite Chapman, Bruce Bennett, Warren Ashe. Columbia, 1942.

The Sullivans.*** aka *The Fighting Sullivans.* 111m, b/w. Dir.
Lloyd Bacon. With Anne Baxter, Thomas Mitchell, Selena
Royle, Ward Bond, Bobby Driscoll. Fox, 1944.

The Sultan's Daughter.* 64m, b/w. Dir. Arthur Dreifuss. With
Ann Corio, Charles Butterworth, Tim Ryan, Irene Ryan,
Eddie Norris. Monogram, 1943.

Sunday Dinner for a Soldier.** 86m, b/w. Dir. Lloyd Bacon. With
Anne Baxter, John Hodiak, Charles Winninger, Anne
Revere, Connie Marshall. Fox, 1944.

Sundown.** 90m, b/w. Dir. Henry Hathaway. With Gene Tierney,
Bruce Cabot, George Sanders, Harry Carey, Joseph Calleia,
Dorothy Dandridge, Reginald Gardiner. UA, 1941.

Swing Shift Maisie.* 87m, b/w. Dir. Norman Z. McLeod. With
Ann Sothern, James Craig, Jean Rogers, Connie Gilchrist,
John Qualen, Kay Medford. MGM, 1943.

Swingtime Johnny. 60m, b/w. Dir. Edward Cline. With The
Andrews Sisters, Harriet Hilliard, Peter Cookson, Tim
Ryan. Universal, 1944.

Tampico.** 75m, b/w. Dir. Lothar Mendes. With Edward G.
Robinson, Lynn Bari, Victor McLaglen, Marc Lawrence,
Mona Maris. Fox, 1944.

Tarzan Triumphs.** 78m, b/w. Dir. William Thiele. With Johnny
Weissmuller, Johnny Sheffield, Frances Gifford, Stanley
Ridges. RKO, 1943.

Tarzan's Desert Mystery.* 70m, b/w. Dir. William Thiele. With
Johnny Weissmullur, Johnny Sheffield, Nancy Kelly, Otto
Kruger, Joe Sawyer. RKO, 1943.

Television Spy.* 58m, b/w. Dir. Edward Dmytryk. With William
Henry, Judith Barrett, William Collier, Sr., Richard
Denning. Paramount, 1939.

Tender Comrade.** 102m, b/w. Dir. Edward Dmytryk. With
Ginger Rogers, Robert Ryan, Ruth Hussey, Patricia
Collinge, Mady Christians, Kim Hunter. RKO, 1943.

That Nazty Nuisance.* 50m, b/w. Dir. Glenn Tyron. With Bobby
Watson, Joe Devlin, Johnny Arthur, Jean Porter, Ian
Keith. UA, 1943.

There's Something About a Soldier.* 81m, b/w. Dir. Alfred E.
Green. With Tom Neal, Evelyn Keyes, Bruce Bennett, John
Hubbard, Jeff Donnell. Columbia, 1943.

They Came to Blow Up America.** 73m, b/w. Dir. Edward
Ludwig. With George Sanders, Anna Sten, Ward Bond,
Dennis Hoey, Sig Ruman, Ludwig Stossel. Fox, 1943.

They Dare Not Love.* 75m, b/w. Dir. James Whale. With
George Brent, Martha Scott, Paul Lukas, Egon Brecher.
Columbia, 1941.

They Got Me Covered.** 95m, b/w. Dir. David Butler. With Bob Hope, Dorothy Lamour, Lenore Aubert, Otto Preminger, Eduardo Ciannelli, Marion Martin, Donald Meek. Fox, 1943.

They Live in Fear.* 65m, b/w. Dir. Josef Berne. With Otto Kruger, Clifford Severn, Pat Parrish, Jimmy Carpenter, Erwin Kalser. Columbia, 1944.

They Met in Bombay.** 86m, b/w. Dir. Clarence Brown. With Clark Gable, Rosalind Russell, Peter Lorre, Jessie Ralph, Reginald Owen. MGM, 1941.

They Raid by Night.* 80m, b/w. Dir. Spencer Gordon Bennett. With Lyle Talbot, June Duprez, Victor Varconi, George Neise. Producers Rel, 1942.

They Were Expendable.**** 135m, b/w. Dir. John Ford, Robert Montgomery. With Robert Montgomery, John Wayne, Donna Reed, Jack Holt, Ward Bond. MGM, 1945.

    A restrained tribute to the loyal men who ran PT boats in the early unsuccessful stages of the war against Japanese vessels in the Philippines. Footnotes: Ford, a Navy captain, never was sure whether this film was good enough. Montgomery, also a naval officer, was an uncredited director for some scenes.

Thirty Seconds Over Tokyo.**** 138m, b/w. Dir. Mervyn LeRoy. With Spencer Tracy, Van Johnson, Robert Walker, Phyllis Thaxter, Scott McKay, Robert Mitchum, Stephen McNally, Louis Jean Heydt, Leon Ames, Paul Langton. MGM, 1944.

    Reenactment of Lt. Col. Jimmy Doolittle's airforce ccmmando raid on the Japanese capital in 1942. Oscar for special effects. Based on the book by participant Capt. Ted Lawson (played by Van Johnson). Best sequence: the launching of sixteen aircraft. Footnote: the "target" was actually film of the San Francisco-Oakland Bay area.

This Above All.*** 110m, b/w. Dir. Anatole Litvak. With Tyrone Power, Joan Fontaine, Thomas Mitchell, Nigel Bruce, Gladys Cooper, Sara Allgood, Philip Merivale. Fox, 1942.

This Gun's for Hire.*** 80m, b/w. Dir. Frank Tuttle. With Veronica Lake, Alan Ladd, Robert Preston, Laird Cregar, Tully Marshall, Pamela Blake. Paramount, 1942.

This Is the Army.** 120m, color. Dir. Michael Curtiz. With Irving Berlin, George Murphy, Joan Leslie, George Tobias, Alan Hale, Charles Butterworth. WB, 1943.

This Land Is Mine.** 103m, b/w. Dir. Jean Renoir. With Charles Laughton, Maureen O'Hara, George Sanders, Walter Slezak, Kent Smith, Una O'Connor. RKO, 1943.

*This Man's Navy.*** 100m, b/w. Dir. William A. Wellman. With Wallace Beery, Tom Drake, James Gleason, Jan Clayton, Selena Royle, Noah Beery, Sr. MGM, 1945.

*Thousands Cheer.**** 126m, color. Dir. George Sidney. With Mickey Rooney, Judy Garland, Gene Kelly, Red Skelton, Eleanor Powell, Ann Sothern, Lucille Ball, Virginia O'Brien, Frank Morgan, Kathryn Grayson, Lena Horne. MGM, 1943.

*Three Russian Girls.** 80m, b/w. Dir. Fedor Ozep, Henry Kesler. With Anna Sten, Kent Smith, Mimi Forsythe, Alexander Granach, Kathy Frye. UA, 1943.

*Thunder Birds.*** 78m, color. Dir. William A. Wellman. With Gene Tierney, Preston Foster, John Sutton, Dame May Whitty, Reginald Denny, Iris Adrian. Fox, 1942.

*Tiger Fangs.** 57m, b/w. Dir. Sam Newfield. With Frank Buck, June Duprez, Duncan Renaldo, Howard Banks, J. Farrel MacDonald. Producers Rel, 1943.

*Till We Meet Again.*** 88m, b/w. Dir. Frank Borzage. With Ray Milland, Barbara Britton, Walter Slezak, Lucile Watson, Mona Freeman. Paramount, 1944.

*To Be or Not To Be.**** 99m, b/w. Dir. Ernst Lubitsch. With Carole Lombard, Jack Benny, Robert Stack, Lionel Atwill, Felix Bressart, Sig Ruman, Helmut Dantine, Stanley Ridges. UA, 1942.

*To Have and Have Not.**** 100m, b/w. Dir. Howard Hawks. With Humphrey Bogart, Lauren Bacall, Walter Brennan, Dolores Moran, Hoagy Carmichael, Sheldon Leonard. WB, 1944.

*To the Shores of Tripoli.*** 86m, color. Dir. H. Bruce Humberstone. With John Payne, Maureen O'Hara, Randolph Scott, Nancy Kelly, William Tracy, Maxie Rosenbloom, Iris Adrian. Fox, 1942.

*Tokyo Rose.*** 69m, b/w. Dir. Lew Landers. With Lotus Long, Byron Barr, Osa Massen, Don Douglas, Richard Loo, Keye Luke, Grace Lem, Leslie Fong. Paramount, 1945.

*Tomorrow the World.**** 86m, b/w. Dir. Leslie Fenton. With Fredric March, Betty Field, Agnes Moorehead, Skippy Homeier, Joan Carroll, Boots Brown. UA, 1944.

*Tonight We Raid Calais.*** 70m, b/w. Dir. John Brahm. With Annabella, John Sutton, Lee J. Cobb, Beulah Bondi, Blanche Yurka, Howard da Silva, Marcel Dalio. Fox, 1943.

*Top Man.*** 83m, b/w. Dir. Charles Lamont. With Donald O'Connor, Susanna Foster, Lillian Gish. Universal, 1943.

*Torpedo Boat.** 69m, b/w. Dir. John Rawlins. With Richard Arlen, Jean Parker, Mary Carlisle, Phil Terry. Paramount, 1942.

*Tramp, Tramp, Tramp.** 68m, b/w. Dir. Charles Barton. With Jackie Gleason, Florence Rice, Jack Durant, Bruce Bennett. Columbia, 1942.

*True to the Army.*** 76m, b/w. Dir. Albert S. Rogell. With Judy Canova, Allan Jones, Ann Miller. Paramount, 1942.

*Two-Man Submarine.** 62m, b/w. Dir. Lew Landers. With Tom Neal, Ann Savage, J. Carroll Naish, Robert Williams. Columbia, 1944.

*Two Tickets to London.*** 77m, b/w. Dir. Edwin L. Marin. With Michele Morgan, Alan Curtis, Barry Fitzgerald, C. Aubrey Smith. Universal, 1943.

*Two Weeks to Live.** 76m, b/w. Dir. Malcolm St. Clair. With Chester Lauck, Norris Goff, Franklin Pangborn, Kay Linaker, Irving Bacon. RKO, 1943.

*Two Yanks in Trinidad.*** 84m, b/w. Dir. Gregory Ratoff. With Brian Donlevy, Pat O'Brien, Janet Blair. Columbia, 1942.

*U-Boat Prisoner.** 65m, b/w. Dir. Lew Landers. With Bruce Bennett, Erik Rolf, John Abbott, John Wengraf, Robert Williams. Columbia, 1944.

*Uncertain Glory.*** 102m, b/w. Dir. Raoul Walsh. With Errol Flynn, Jean Sullivan, Paul Lukas, Lucile Watson, Faye Emerson, Douglass Dumbrille, Dennis Hoey, Sheldon Leonard. WB, 1944.

*Underground.**** 95m, b/w. Dir. Vincent Sherman. With Jeffrey Lynn, Philip Dorn, Kaaren Verne, Mona Maris, Frank Reicher, Martin Kosleck. WB, 1941.

*Underground Agent.*** 70m, b/w. Dir. Michael Gordon. With Bruce Bennett, Leslie Brooks, Frank Albertson, Julian Rivero, George McKay. Columbia, 1942.

*Unseen Enemy.** 61m, b/w. Dir. John Rawlins. With Leo Carrillo, Andy Devine, Irene Hervey, Son Terry. Universal, 1942.

*Unwritten Code.** 61m, b/w. Dir. Herman Rotsten. With Anne Savage, Tom Neal, Roland Varno, Howard Freeman, Mary Currier. Columbia, 1944.

*Up In Arms.*** 106m, color. Dir. Elliott Nugent. With Danny Kaye, Constance Dowling, Dinah Shore, Dana Andrews, Louis Calhern, Lyle Talbot, Margaret Dumont. RKO, 1944.

*Voice in the Wind.**** 85m, b/w. Dir. Arthur Ripley. With Francis Lederer, Sigrid Gurie, J. Edward Bromberg, J. Carrol Naish. UA, 1944.

*Wake Island.***** 78m, b/w. Dir. John Farrow. With Brian Donlevy, Robert Preston, MacDonald Carey, Albert Dekker, Walter Abel, Barbara Britton, William Bendix. Paramount, 1942.

First WWII movie of an American unit in action. Shows how well Hollywood made inspiring propaganda out of defeat. Doomed Marines hold the island for two weeks as ammo runs low. A fine formula war movie: unflappable commander (Donlevy), feuding buddies, comic relief (Bendix, nominated for supporting actor). Footnote: Trainees cheered this movie, standard fare in WWII bootcamps.

A Walk In the Sun.**** 117m, b/w. Dir. Lewis Milestone. With Dana Andrews, Richard Conte, Sterling Holloway, George Tyne, John Ireland, Herbert Rudley, Lloyd Bridges, Huntz Hall. Fox, 1945.

One morning's march from a Salerno beachhead to a farmhouse held by entrenched Germans. A moving close-up look at ordinary soldiers who have to do a job they don't quite understand. Chatty inconsequential conversations reveal the realities of life in war. Best battle scene: the platoon uses grenades to ambush a German halftrack. Based on a novel by Harry Brown.

The War Against Mrs. Hadley.** 85m, b/w. Dir. Harold S. Bucquet. With Edward Arnold, Fay Bainter, Richard Ney, Sara Allgood, Spring Byington, Jean Rogers, Frances Rafferty, Dorothy Morris, Rags Ragland, Van Johnson. MGM, 1942.

Watch On the Rhine.*** 114m, b/w. Dir. Herman Shumlin. With Bette Davis, Paul Lukas, Geraldine Fitzgerald, Lucile Watson, Beulah Bondi, George Coulouris. WB, 1943.

Waterfront.* 65m, b/w. Dir. Steve Sekely. With John Carradine, J. Carroll Naish, Maris Wrixon, Edwin Maxwell, Terry Frost. Producers Rel, 1944.

The Way Ahead.*** aka *The Immortal Battalion.* 106m, b/w. Dir. Carol Reed. With David Niven, Raymond Huntley, Peter Ustinov, Trevor Howard. Fox, 1944.

We Dive at Dawn. 98m, b/w. Dir. Anthony Asquith. With Eric Portman, John Mills, Reginald Purdell, Niall MacGinnis, Joan Hopkins. General, 1943.

We've Never Been Licked.** aka *Fighting Command.* 103m, b/w. Dir. John Rawlins. With Richard Quine, Noah Beery, Jr., Robert Mitchum, Anne Gwynne. Universal, 1943.

What Next, Corporal Hargrove?* 95m, b/w. Dir. Richard Thorpe. With Robert Walker, Keenan Wynn, Jean Porter, Chill Wills, Cameron Mitchell. MGM, 1945.

When Johnny Comes Marching Home.* 74m, b/w. Dir. Charles Lamont. With Allan Jones, Gloria Jean, Donald O'Conner, Jane Frazee, Peggy Ryan. Universal, 1943.

When the Lights Go On Again.** 74m, b/w. Dir. William K. Howard. With James Lydon, Barbara Belden, Grant Mitchell, Dorothy Peterson, Regis Toomey, George Cleveland. Producers Rel, 1944.

The Wife Takes a Flyer.** 86m, b/w. Dir. Richard Wallace. With Joan Bennett, Franchot Tone, Allyn Joslyn, Cecil Cunningham, Chester Clute. Columbia, 1942.

Wing and a Prayer.*** 97m, b/w. Dir. Henry Hathaway. With Don Ameche, Dana Andrews, Charles Bickford, Sir Cedric Hardwicke, Richard Jaeckel, Harry Morgan. Fox, 1944.

Winged Victory.** 130m, b/w. Dir. George Cukor. With Lon McCallister, Jeanne Crain, Edmond O'Brien, Don Taylor, Judy Holliday, Lee J. Cobb, Peter Lind Hayes, Red Buttons, Barry Nelson, Gary Merrill. Fox, 1944.

Wings for the Eagle.** 85m, b/w. Dir. Lloyd Bacon. With Ann Sheridan, Dennis Morgan, Jack Carson, George Tobias, Don DeFore. WB, 1942.

Wings Over the Pacific.* 59m, b/w. Dir. Phil Rosen. With Inez Cooper, Edward Norris, Montagu Love. Monogram, 1943.

Women in Bondage.** aka *Hitler's Women.* 72m, b/w. Dir. Steve Sekely. With Gail Patrick, Nancy Kelly, Gertrude Michael, Anne Nagel, Tala Birell, Alan Baxter. Monogram, 1943.

Women in War.* 71m, b/w. Dir. John H. Auer. With Elsie Janis, Wendy Barrie, Patric Knowles, Mae Clarke, Dennie Moore. Republic, 1940.

A Yank in Libya.* 67m, b/w. Dir. Albert Herman. With H.B. Warner, Walter Woolf King, Joan Woodbury, Parkyakarkus, Duncan Renaldo. Producers Rel, 1942.

A Yank in the R.A.F.* 98m, b/w. Dir. Henry King. With Tyrone Power, Betty Grable, John Sutton, Reginald Gardiner, Donald Stuart. Fox, 1941.

Yanks Ahoy.* 60m, b/w. Dir. Kurt Neumann. With William Tracy, Joe Sawyer, Marjorie Woodworth, Minor Watson, Walter Woolf King. UA, 1943.

The Yanks Are Coming.* 65m, b/w. Dir. Alexis Thurn-Taxis. With Henry King, Mary Healy, Little Jackie Heller, Maxie Rosenbloom, William Roberts. Producers Rel, 1942.

You Came Along.** 103m, b/w. Dir. John Farrow. With Robert Cummings, Lizabeth Scott, Don DeFore, Charles Drake, Julie Bishop. Paramount, 1945.

You Can't Ration Love.* 78m, b/w. Dir. Lester Fuller. With Betty Rhodes, Johnnie Johnston, Bill Edwards, Marjorie Weaver, Marie Wilson. Paramount, 1944.

You'll Never Get Rich.*** 88m, b/w. Dir. Sidney Lanfield. With
Fred Astaire, Rita Hayworth, John Hubbard, Robert
Benchley, Osa Massen, Frieda Inescort, Guinn Williams.
Columbia, 1941.

You're In the Army Now.** 79m, b/w. Dir. Lewis Seiler. With
Jimmy Durante, Phil Silvers, Jane Wyman, Regis Toomey,
Joe Sawyer. WB, 1941.

10

World War II (Postwar Films)

CHRONOLOGY

Chapter 9, "World War II (Wartime Films)," contains the chronology of the Second World War.

COMMENTARY

Not long after the Second World War ended and the new Cold War began, war films, freed from patriotic restraints of the war years, became more searching or complex in their messages. Motivation and behavior were subjected to deeper critical investigation. By 1949 three significant films clearly reflected the new tone: *Battleground* (1949) portrayed combat in stark, realistic, if heroic, terms; *Home of the Brave* (1949) confronted the issue of racism in the army; and *Twelve O'Clock High* (1949) examined the psychological pressures of command in combat.

The Naked and the Dead (1958), a diluted adaption of Norman Mailer's novel, took the men of an archetypical platoon (the hillbilly, the wisecracking Jew, the Mexican-American and the tough sergeant) but told an original story of petty tyrannies, grim tragedy, and accidental death. Cornel Wilde's *Beach Red* (1967) carried the themes even further. War is about killing, a brutal sergeant says, "The rest is crap." *The Dirty Dozen* (1967) brought such cynical views to their logical conclusion. War, the film tells us, is best left to murderers, thieves, rapists, or other assorted criminals. *Kelly's Heroes* (1970) reduced war to utter absurdity by showing an anachronistic hippie-type driving a Sherman tank.

The years following World War II also saw Hollywood remake the image of the enemy: "We viewed the war with the Japanese as a race war and the war with the Germans as an ideological war. When we disliked Germans, it was the Nazis we meant. When we disliked the Japanese, it was all of them" (Basinger 28). Yet at the same time "It is impossible not to be impressed by the speed with which a war of seemingly irreconcilable hatred gave way to cordial relations once the fighting had ceased" (Dower 311).

This alteration in America's perception of its foes comes about in no small measure because of the onset of the Cold War. America's former friends (Russia and China) were now its enemies, and its former enemies (Germany and Japan) were now its friends. The world-turned-upside-down was reflected in the new war films. Although Germans were depicted as vicious torturers and absurd martinets, they were sometimes shown to be decent at heart, even during the war. In *Desperate Journey* (1942), members of a downed air crew are aided in their escape by a sympathetic German woman. "Tell the people in England," she states as they depart, "that there are people left in Germany still living, still hoping, still fighting." A submarine commander in *The Enemy Below* (1957) and a German infantry lieutenant in *The Young Lions* (1958) are shown to be competent but disillusioned. The commander (Curt Jurgens) is opposed to Nazism but fights well nevertheless. The lieutenant (Marlon Brando), who once supported Hitler, has become cynical and depressed. "I do not think it's possible to remake the world," he says of a Gestapo torture chamber, "from the basement of this dirty little police station."

American wartime films like *The Purple Heart* (1944) had shown Japanese to be unrelentlessly brutal and savage, but this too, would change. *Beach Red* (1967) "switches back and forth from the marines to the Japanese soldiers who, through flashbacks, are depicted as having the same thoughts of home and their families as those of the American troops" (Langman and Borg 55). *Hell in the Pacific* (1968) is a postwar allegory of one American soldier (Lee Marvin) and one Japanese soldier (Toshiro Mifune) who, abandoned by their comrades on a deserted Pacific island, are forced to cooperate to survive.

Tora! Tora! Tora! (1970) recognized that the old animosities had ended. In this joint American-Japanese film, the emphasis is on spectacle and historical reconstruction, but the message as far as the wartime issues are concerned is clearly apolitical. All motives are carefully balanced. Stephen Spielberg's *Empire of the Sun* (1987) is sympathetic to the Japanese. In one poignant scene, a British schoolboy, disillusioned by an American con-artist (John

Malkovich), joins young Japanese pilots in singing a Japanese battle hymn.

In Hollywood films, the more things change the more they remain the same. And if the movie messages about war are always mixed, it is because our attitudes toward war are always ambivalent. Perhaps *Patton* (1970) illustrates this best with its character study of soldier as hero-madman. The words and actions of Patton (George C. Scott) simultaneously appall and uplift.

Nevertheless, as with films about the First World War, it is difficult, perhaps impossible, to find any clear linear trend in the post-war attitudes held by filmmakers. *Attack!* (1956) told a story of meaningless deaths and cowardliness during the Battle of the Bulge, but in 1990 the film industry produced *Memphis Belle*, whose essentials are not far removed from the wartime cliches of *Air Force* (1943) or *Bombadier* (1943). The releasing company's promotional blurb sounds as if it came straight out of the 1940s: "These airborne marvels are joined with...a stirring story of guts and teamwork required when the flak gets so thick you can walk on it."

Basinger, Jeanine. *The World War Two Combat Film: Anatomy of a Genre*. New York: Columbia UP, 1988.

Dower, John W. *War Without Mercy: Race and Power in the Pacific War*. New York: Pantheon, 1986.

Langman, Larry, and Ed Borg. *Encyclopedia of American War Films*. New York: Garland, 1989.

FILMOGRAPHY (Postwar Films)

The following filmography lists films about the Second World War released in 1946 and after.

*About Face.** 93m, color. Dir. Roy Del Ruth. With Gordon McRae, Eddie Bracken, Dick Wesson, Phyllis Kirk, Joel Grey. WB, 1952.

*Above and Beyond.*** 122m, b/w. Dir. Melvin Frank, Norman Panama. With Robert Taylor, Eleanor Parker, James Whitmore, Larry Keating, Jim Backus. MGM, 1952.

*Act of Love.*** 108m, b/w. Dir. Anatole Litvak. With Kirk Douglas, Dany Robin, Barbara Laage. UA, 1953.

*All My Sons.*** 93m, b/w. Dir. Irving Reis. With Edward G. Robinson, Burt Lancaster, Mady Christians, Louisa Horton, Howard Duff. Universal, 1948.

Ambush Bay.** 107m, color. Dir. Ron Winston. With Hugh
      O'Brian, Mickey Rooney, James Mitchum. UA, 1966.
American Guerilla in the Philippines.** 105m, color. Dir. Fritz
      Lang. With Tyrone Power, Micheline Prelle, Tom Ewell,
      Jack Elam. Fox, 1950.
The Americanization of Emily.*** 115m, b/w. Dir. Arthur Hiller.
      With James Garner, Julie Andrews, Melvyn Douglas, James
      Coburn, Keenan Wynn, Judy Carne. MGM, 1964.
The Angry Hills.** 105m, b/w. Dir. Robert Aldrich. With Robert
      Mitchum, Elisabeth Mueller, Stanley Baker, Gia Scala,
      Theodore Bikel, Sebastian Cabot. MGM, 1959.
Anzio.** 117m, color. Dir. Edward Dmytryk. With Robert
      Mitchum, Peter Falk, Robert Ryan, Earl Holliman, Mark
      Damon, Arthur Kennedy, Patrick Magee. Columbia, 1968.
Armored Command.** 98m, b/w. Dir. Byron Haskin. With Howard
      Keel, Tina Louise, Burt Reynolds. AA, 1961.
Attack!**** 107m, b/w. Dir. Robert Aldrich. With Jack Palance,
      Eddie Albert, Lee Marvin, Robert Strauss. UA, 1956.
      An excellent anti-war movie about the Battle of the
      Bulge. Aldrich said he wanted to show "the terribly
      corrupting influence that war can have on the most
      normal, average human beings." Footnote: because the script
      showed an officer responsible for the death of his own
      men, the Department of Defense refused to offer Aldrich
      its assistance during filming.
Attack on the Iron Coast.* 90m, color. Dir. Paul Wendkos. With
      Lloyd Bridges, Andrew Kier, Sue Lloyd, Mark Eden,
      Maurice Denham. UA, 1968.
Away All Boats.** 114m, color. Dir. Joseph Pevney. With Jeff
      Chandler, George Nader, Julie Adams, Lex Barker.
      Universal, 1956.
The Bamboo Blonde.** 68m, b/w. Dir. Anthony Mann. With
      Francis Langford, Ralph Edwards, Russell Wade, Iris
      Adrian, Richard Martin. RKO, 1946.
Battle at Bloody Beach.** 83m, b/w. Dir. Herbert Coleman. With
      Audie Murphy, Gary Crosby, Dolores Michaels. Fox, 1961.
Battle Cry.*** 147m, color. Dir. Raoul Walsh. With Van Heflin,
      Tab Hunter, Dorothy Malone, Anne Francis, Raymond
      Massey, Mona Freeman, Aldo Ray. WB, 1955.
Battle of Blood Island.* 64m, b/w. Dir. Joel Rapp. With Richard
      Devon, Ron Kennedy. Filmgroup, 1960.
The Battle of Britain.** 133m, color. Dir. Guy Hamilton. With
      Michael Caine, Trevor Howard, Sir Laurence Olivier, Harry
      Andrews, Curt Jurgens, Christopher Plummer, Susannah
      York, Ralph Richardson, Michael Redgrave. UA, 1969.

Battle of the Bulge.** 167m, color. Dir. Ken Annakin. With Henry Fonda, Robert Shaw, Robert Ryan, Dana Andrews, George Montgomery, Ty Hardin, Pier Angeli. WB, 1965.

Battle of the Coral Sea.** 80m, b/w. Dir. Paul Wendkos. With Cliff Robertson, Gia Scala, Teru Shimada, Patricia Cutts, Gene Blakely, Gordon Jones. Columbia, 1959.

The Battle of the Neretva.** 175m, color. With Yul Brenner, Curt Jergens, Franco Nero, Orson Welles. AIP, 1971.

Battle Stations.* 81m, b/w. Dir. Lewis Seiler. With John Lund, William Bendix, Richard Boone. Columbia, 1956.

Battleground.**** 118m, b/w. Dir. William Wellman. With Van Johnson, John Hodiak, Ricardo Montalban, George Murphy, Marshall Thompson. MGM, 1949.

A realistic look at GI's of the 101st Airborne Division as they stand against the last major German attack. Oscars for script and photography; nomination for best picture. Best scene: as their leader (Whitmore) barks "About Face!" the knowledge that they are finally to be relieved by Patton's Third Army dawns on them. Wounded, tired, and hungry, they march back proudly in time to their own sung cadence. Footnote: producer Dore Schary used his influence to make *Battleground* when Hollywood said no one wanted another war film.

Beach Red.*** 105m, color. Dir. Cornel Wilde. With Cornel Wilde, Rip Torn, Burr De Benning, Patrick Wolfe. UA, 1967.

Beachhead.*** 89m, color. Dir. Stuart Heisler. With Tony Curtis, Frank Lovejoy, Mary Murphy, Eduard Franz. UA, 1954.

The Beginning of the End.** 110m, b/w. Dir. Norman Taurog. With Brian Donlevy, Robert Walker, Beverly Tyler, Audrey Totter, Hume Cronyn. MGM, 1947.

Behold a Pale Horse.** 118m, color. Dir. Fred Zimmermann. With Gregory Peck, Anthony Quinn, Omar Sharif. Columbia, 1964.

Berlin Express.*** 86m, b/w. Dir. Jacques Tourneur. With Merle Oberon, Robert Ryan, Charles Korvin, Paul Lukas, Robert Coote. RKO, 1948.

The Best Years of Our Lives.**** 172m, b/w. Dir. William Wyler. With Fredric March, Myrna Loy, Teresa Wright, Dana Andrews, Virginia Mayo, Cathy O'Donnell, Harold Russell, Gladys George, Steve Cochran. RKO, 1946.

A classic film about three combat veterans readjusting to civilian life. Seven Oscars including one to Harold Russell, who actually lost his hands in the war, for "bringing hope and courage to other veterans." Notable scene: when Homer (Russell) is put to bed by his father and later his fiancee, all have to deal with his prosthesis. Based on the book by MacKinley Kantor. Footnote: with inimitable logic, Samuel Goldwyn said about this movie, "I don't care if it doesn't make a nickel. I just want every man, woman and child in America to see it!"

Betrayed.** 107m, color. Dir. Gottfried Reinhardt. With Clark Gable, Lana Turner, Victor Mature. MGM, 1954.

Between Heaven and Hell.*** 94m, color. Dir. Richard Fleischer. With Robert Wagner, Terry Moore, Broderick Crawford, Buddy Ebsen, Robert Keith. Fox, 1956.

Beyond Glory.** 82m, b/w. Dir. John Farrow. With Alan Ladd, Donna Reed, George Macready. Paramount, 1948.

The Big Red One.**** 113m, color. Dir. Samuel Fuller. With Lee Marvin, Mark Hamill, Robert Carradine, Bobby DiCicco, Kelly Ward. UA, 1980.

Four buddies in the 1st Infantry Division (Big Red One) use their wits, humor and experience to survive combat in Sicily, Normandy, Belgium, and Czechoslovakia. Notable scene: after Griff (Hamill) drags TNT across a minefield, the Sergeant (Marvin) delivers a French woman's baby in a German tank using condoms for rubber gloves. Footnote: director and screenwriter Fuller was actually in the Big Red One during World War II.

Biloxi Blues.*** 107m, color. Dir. Mike Nichols. With Matthew Broderick, Christopher Walken, Matt Mulhern, Corey Parker, Markus Flanagan. Universal, 1988.

Bitter Victory.*** 97m, b/w. Dir. Nicholas Ray. With Richard Burton, Curt Jurgens, Ruth Roman, Raymond Pellegrin. Columbia, 1958.

Blood and Steel.* 62m, b/w. Dir. Bernard Kowalski. With John Lupton, James Edwards, Brett Halsey. Fox, 1959.

The Bold and the Brave.*** 87m, b/w. Dir. Lewis R. Foster. With Wendell Corey, Mickey Rooney, Don Taylor, Nicole Maurey. RKO, 1956.

The Bomb at 10:10.* 86m, color. Dir. Charles Damic. With George Montgomery, Rada Popovic, Peter Banicevic, Branko Plesa. Yugoslavia, 1966.

The Boy With the Green Hair.*** 82m, color. Dir. Joseph Losey. With Dean Stockwell, Pat O'Brien, Robert Ryan, Barbara Hale. RKO, 1949.

Brady's Escape.** 96m, color. Dir. Pal Gabor. With John Savage, Kelly Reno, Ildiko Bansagi, Lazlo Mensaros. Satori, 1984.

Breakthrough.** 91m, b/w. Dir. Lewis Seiler. With David Brian, John Agar, Frank Lovejoy, Paul Picerni. WB, 1950.

Breakthrough.** aka *Sergeant Steiner*. 115m, color. Dir. Andrew V. McLaglen. With Richard Burton, Robert Mitchum, Rod Steiger, Curt Jergens. Maverick, 1978.

The Bridge at Remagen.** 116m, color. Dir. John Guillermin. With George Segal, Robert Vaughn, Ben Gazzara, Bradford Dillman, E.G. Marshall, Peter Van Eyck. UA, 1969.

The Bridge on the River Kwai.**** 161m, color. Dir. David Lean. With William Holden, Alec Guinness, Jack Hawkins, Sessue Hayakawa, Geoffrey Horne, James Donald. Columbia, 1957.
    Wide-screen epic combines action with psychology. Seven Oscars include picture, director, actor (Guinness), cinematography, screenplay. Best scene: the British commander tries insanely to save the Japanese bridge. Based on the novel by Pierre Boule. Footnote: blacklisted Carl Foreman and Michael Wilson wrote the script under pseudonyms. In 1985, Oscars were given to their widows.

A Bridge too Far.*** 176m, color. Dir. Richard Attenborough. With Dirk Bogarde, James Caan, Michael Caine, Sean Connery, Elliott Gould, Gene Hackman. UA, 1977.

Bridge to the Sun.*** 112m, b/w. Dir. Etienne Perier. With Carroll Baker, James Shigeta, James Yagi. MGM, 1961.

Buck Privates Come Home.** 77m, b/w. Dir. Charles Barton. With Bud Abbott, Lou Costello. Universal, 1947.

The Caine Mutiny.**** 123m, color. Dir. Edward Dmytryk. With Humphrey Bogart, Jose Ferrer, Van Johnson, Robert Francis, May Wynn, Fred MacMurray, E.G. Marshall, Lee Marvin. Columbia, 1954.
    A riveting psychological drama that shifts the issue from loyalty to incompetence and back again. Best scene: under intense courtroom questioning, Queeg (Bogart) breaks down, fingers his steel ball bearings and rambles incoherently. Based on a novel by Herman Wouk; also turned into a play about the court-martial.

Captain Newman, M.D.*** 126m, color. Dir. David Miller. With Gregory Peck, Angie Dickinson, Tony Curtis, Eddie Albert, Jane Withers, Bobby Darin, Larry Storch. Universal, 1963.

Castle Keep.** 108m, color. Dir. Sydney Pollack. With Burt Lancaster, Peter Falk, Patrick O'Neal, Jean-Pierre Aumont, Scott Wilson, Al Freeman. Columbia, 1969.

Catch-22.**** 121m, color. Dir. Mike Nichols. With Alan Arkin, Martin Balsam, Richard Benjamin, Art Garfunkel, Jack Gilford, Bob Newhart, Anthony Perkins, Paula Prentiss, Martin Sheen, Jon Voight, Orson Welles. Paramount, 1970.

An anti-war black comedy based on the novel by Joseph Heller. The Air Force unit's doctor invokes "Catch-22" to deal with those who plead insanity to be relieved from duty: "No sane man would wish to fly, therefore anyone wishing to stop cannot be insane." Best scene: before a bombing mission, after all the other pilots give the thumbs-up signal, Capt Yossarian (Arkin) extends his middle finger.

*China Doll.** 99m, b/w. Dir. Frank Borzage. With Victor Mature, Li Li Hua, Ward Bond, Bob Mathias. UA, 1958.

*China Venture.*** 83m, b/w. Dir. Don Siegel. With Edmond O'Brien, Barry Sullivan, Jocelyn Brando, Richard Loo, Philip Ahn. Columbia, 1953.

*The Clay Pigeon.*** 63m, b/w. Dir. Richard O. Fleischer. With Bill Williams, Barbara Hale, Richard Quine, Richard Loo, Frank Fenton. RKO, 1949.

*Cloak and Dagger.*** 106m, b/w. Dir. Fritz Lang. With Gary Cooper, Lilli Palmer, Robert Alda, Vladimir Sokoloff, Ludwig Stossel. WB, 1946.

*Code Name: Emerald.** 93m, color. Dir. Jonathan Sanger. With Ed Harris, Max Von Sydow, Helmut Berger, Horst Buchholz. MGM, 1985.

*Colditz Story.**** 97m, b/w. Dir. Guy Hamilton. With John Mills, Eric Portman, Christopher Rhodes, Lionel Jeffries, Bryan Forbes, Ian Carmichael, Richard Wattis, Anton Diffring, Theodore Bikel. BL, 1955.

*Command Decision.**** 111m, b/w. Dir. Sam Wood. With Clark Gable, Walter Pidgeon, Van Johnson, Brian Donlevy, Charles Bickford, John Hodiak. MGM, 1948.

*Commandos.*** 89m, color. Dir. Armando Crispino. With Lee Van Cleef, Jack Kelly, Giampiero Albertini, Marino Mase, Pierre Paulo Capponi, Dulio Del Prete. Italy-Germany, 1968.

*Count Five and Die.*** 92m, b/w. Dir. Victor Vicas. With Jeffrey Hunter, Nigel Patrick, Annamarie Duringer. Fox, 1958.

*The Counterfeit Traitor.**** 140m, color. Dir. George Seaton. With William Holden, Lilli Palmer, Hugh Griffith, Erica Beer, Werner Peters, Eva Dahlbeck. Paramount, 1962.

*Counterpoint.** 105m, color. Dir. Ralph Nelson. With Charlton Heston, Maximilian Schell, Kathryn Hays, Leslie Nielsen, Anton Diffring. Universal, 1967.

*Cross of Iron.**** 133m, color. Dir. Sam Peckinpah. With James Coburn, Maximilian Schell, James Mason. Avco, 1977.

*The Cruel Sea.***** 121m, b/w. Dir. Charles Frend. With Jack Hawkins, Stanley Baker, Denholm Elliott, Donald Sinden. Ealing, 1953.

Filmed as if it were a documentary, this is an extraordinary adaption of Nicholas Monsarrat's novel about the stressful life of officers and men in the British corvettes on convoy duty in the North Atlantic. Not only an excellent film about men and machines at war, but an excellent study of men against the sea as well. Best sequence: survivors from a torpedoed ship cling to life aboard a raft.

*Cry for Happy.*** 110m, color. Dir. George Marshall. With Glenn Ford, Donald O'Connor, Miiko Taka, James Shigeta, Myoshi Umeki. Columbia, 1961.

*Cry of Battle.*** aka *To Be a Man.* 99m, b/w. Dir. Irving Lerner. With Van Heflin, Rita Moreno, James MacArthur, Leopoldo Salcedo. AA, 1963.

*D-Day, the Sixth of June.**** aka *The Sixth of June.* 106m, color. Dir. Henry Koster. With Robert Taylor, Richard Todd, Dana Wynter, Edmond O'Brien. Fox, 1956.

*The Dam Busters.**** 125m, b/w. Dir. Michael Anderson. With Michael Redgrave, Richard Todd, Ursula Jeans, Basil Sydney. WB, 1955.

*Darby's Rangers.*** 120m, b/w. Dir. William Wellman. With James Garner, Etchika Choureau, Jack Warden, Edward Byrnes, David Janssen. WB, 1958.

*Decision Before Dawn.**** 119m, b/w. Dir. Anatole Litvak. With Richard Basehart, Gary Merrill, Oskar Werner, Hildegarde Neff. Fox, 1951.

*The Deep Six.*** 105m, color. Dir. Rudolph Mate. With Alan Ladd, Dianne Foster, William Bendix, Keenan Wynn, James Whitmore, Joey Bishop. WB, 1958.

*The Desert Fox.**** 88m, b/w. Dir. Henry Hathaway. With James Mason, Sir Cedric Hardwicke, Jessica Tandy. Fox, 1951.

*The Desert Rats.**** 88m, b/w. Dir. Robert Wise. With Richard Burton, James Mason, Robert Newton. Fox, 1953.

*The Desert Song.*** 110m, color. Dir. H. Bruce Humberstone. With Kathryn Grayson, Gordon MacRae, Steve Cochran, Raymond Massey. WB, 1953.

*Destination Gobi.*** 89m, color. Dir. Robert Wise. With Richard Widmark, Darryl Hickman, Martin Milner. Fox, 1953.

*The Devil Makes Three.*** 89m, b/w. Dir. Andrew Marton. With Gene Kelly, Pier Angeli, Richard Egan. MGM, 1952.

*The Devil's Brigade.*** 131m, color. Dir. Andrew V. McLaglen. With William Holden, Cliff Robertson, Vince Edwards, Michael Rennie, Dana Andrews. UA, 1968.

The Diary of Anne Frank.*** 170m, b/w. Dir. George Stevens. With Millie Perkins, Joseph Schildkraut, Shelley Winters, Richard Beymer, Lou Jacobi, Diane Baker. Fox, 1959.

The Dirty Dozen.**** 149m, color. Dir. Robert Aldrich. With Lee Marvin, Ernest Borgnine, Jim Brown, John Cassavetes, Robert Ryan, Charles Bronson. MGM, 1967.

The archetypal film of the bad-boy unit. Recruited from prison, soldiers must raid a villa housing German officers on the eve of the Normandy landings. The message of the film is that war is brutal, obscene, and amoral. As Major Reisman (Marvin) says, "I can't think of a better way to fight a war." Best sequence: the German officers and their female companions are burned alive with gasoline in an air raid shelter. The scene expresses the tone of the film perfectly. Footnote: John Wayne turned down the lead role to make *The Green Berets*.

Don't Give Up the Ship.*** 89m, b/w. Dir. Norman Taurog. With Jerry Lewis, Dina Merrill, Diana Spencer, Mickey Shaughnessy, Robert Middleton, Gale Gordon, Claude Akins. Paramount, 1959.

Don't Go Near the Water.** 107m, color. Dir. Charles Walters. With Glenn Ford, Gia Scala, Anne Francis, Fred Clark, Eva Gabor. MGM, 1957.

The Eagle Has Landed.*** 134m, color. Dir. John Sturges. With Michael Caine, Donald Sutherland, Robert Duvall, Jenny Agutter, Donald Pleasence, Anthony Quayle, Larry Hagman. Columbia, 1976.

Eight Iron Men.** 80m, b/w. Dir. Edward Dmytryk. With Bonar Colleana, Lee Marvin, Richard Kiley, Nick Dennis, Arthur Franz, Mary Castle. Columbia, 1952.

El Alamein.** 66m, b/w. Dir. Fred F. Sears. With Scott Brady, Edward Ashley, Rita Moreno, Michael Pate. Columbia, 1954.

Empire of the Sun.*** 152m, color. Dir. Steven Spielberg. With Chistian Bale, John Malkovich, Miranda Richardson, Nigel Havers, Joe Pantoliano. WB, 1987.

The Enemy Below.*** 98m, color. Dir. Dick Powell. With Robert Mitchum, Curt Jurgens, Theodore Bikel, Doug McClure, Russell Collins, David Hedison. Fox, 1957.

The Enemy General.** 75m, b/w. Dir. George Sherman. With Van Johnson, Jean-Pierre Aumont, Dany Carrel, John Van Dreelen. Columbia, 1960.

Ensign Pulver.** 104m, color. Dir. Joshua Logan. With Robert Walker, Jr., Burl Ives, Walter Matthau, Tommy Sands, James Farentino, Diana Sands, Kay Medford, Millie Perkins. WB, 1964.

*The Eternal Sea.*** 103m, b/w. Dir. John H. Auer. With Sterling Hayden, Alexis Smith, Dean Jagger, Virginia Grey. Republic, 1955.

*The Extraordinary Seaman.** 79m, color. Dir. John Frankenheimer. With David Niven, Faye Dunaway, Alan Alda, Mickey Rooney, Jack Carter. MGM, 1969.

*A Face in the Rain.*** 81m, b/w. Dir. Irvin Kershner. With Rory Calhoun, Marina Berti, Niall McGinnis, Massimo Giuliani, Danny Ryais. Embassy, 1963.

*Farewell to the King.** 117m, color. Dir. John Milius. With Nick Nolte, Nigel Havers, Frank McRae, Gerry Lopez, Marilyn Tokuda. Vestron, 1989.

*Father Goose.**** 115m, color. Dir. Ralph Nelson. With Cary Grant, Leslie Caron, Trevor Howard, Jack Good, Nicole Felsette. Universal, 1964.

*Fifth Day of Peace.*** 100m, color. Dir. Guilliano Montaldo. With Richard Johnson, Franco Nero, Bud Spencer, Michael Goodliffe, Helmut Schneider. Italy, 1972.

*Fighter Attack.*** 80m, color. Dir. Lesley Selander. With Sterling Hayden, J. Carrol Naish, Joy Page, Paul Fierro. AA, 1953.

*Fighter Squadron.*** 96m, color. Dir. Raoul Walsh. With Edmond O'Brien, Robert Stack, John Rodney, Tom D'Andrea, Henry Hull. WB, 1948.

*Fighting Coast Guard.*** 86m, b/w. Dir. Joseph Kane. With Brian Donlevy, Forrest Tucker, Ella Raines. Republic, 1951.

*First To Fight.*** 97m, color. Dir. Christian Nyby. With Chad Everett, Marilyn Devin, Dean Jagger, Bobby Troup, Claude Akins, Gene Hackman. WB, 1967.

*5 Branded Women.*** 100m, b/w. Dir. Martin Ritt. With Barbara Bel Geedes, Van Heflin, Silvana Mangano, Jeanne Moreau, Vera Miles, Carla Gravina. Paramount, 1960.

*Five Fingers.**** aka *Operation Cicero.* 108m, b/w. Dir. Joseph L. Mankiewicz. With James Mason, Danielle Darrieux, Michael Rennie, Richard Loo. Fox, 1952.

*Five Steps to Danger.*** 80m, b/w. Dir. Henry S. Kesler. With Ruth Roman, Sterling Hayden, Werner Klemperer, Richard Gaines. UA, 1957.

*Flat Top.*** 83m, color. Dir. Lesley Selander. With Sterling Hayden, Richard Carlson, Bill Phipps, Keith Larsen. Monogram, 1952.

*Flying Leathernecks.**** 102m, color. Dir. Nicholas Ray. With John Wayne, Robert Ryan, Don Taylor, Janis Carter. RKO, 1951.

*Force of Arms.*** 100m, b/w. Dir. Michael Curtiz. With William Holden, Nancy Olson, Frank Lovejoy. WB, 1951.

*Force 10 From Navarone.** 118m, color. Dir. Guy Hamilton. With Robert Shaw, Harrison Ford, Barbara Bach, Edward Fox, Franco Nero, Carl Weathers. AIP, 1978.

*Four Horsemen of the Apocalypse.*** 153m, color. Dir. Vincente Minnelli. With Glenn Ford, Ingrid Thulin, Charles Boyer, Lee J. Cobb, Paul Henreid, Paul Lukas, Yvette Mimieux, Karl Boehm. MGM, 1962.

*Four in a Jeep.*** 100m, b/w. Dir. Leopold Lindtberg. With Viveca Lindfors, Ralph Meeker, Joseph Yadin, Michael Medwin. Praesens Film, 1951.

*Francis.*** 91m, b/w. Dir. Arthur Lubin. With Donald O'Connor, Patricia Medina, ZaSu Pitts, Ray Collins, John McIntire. Universal, 1949.

*Fraulein.*** 95m, color. Dir. Henry Koster. With Dana Wynter, Mel Ferrer, Dolores Michaels, Maggie Hayes, Theodore Bikel. Fox, 1958.

*The Frogmen.**** 96m, b/w. Dir. Lloyd Bacon. With Richard Widmark, Dana Andrews, Jeffrey Hunter. Fox, 1951.

*From Hell to Victory.*** 100m, color. Dir. Hank Milestone. With George Peppard, George Hamilton, Horst Buchholz, Capucine, Sam Wanamaker. New Film, 1979.

*From Here to Eternity.***** 118m, b/w. Dir. Fred Zinnemann. With Burt Lancaster, Montgomery Clift, Deborah Kerr, Frank Sinatra, Donna Reed, Ernest Borgnine, George Reeves. Columbia, 1953.

> Events on an Army base in Hawaii months before Pearl Harbor. Conveys a depressing view of life in the pre-World War II Army. Eight Oscars include picture, director, screenplay, and supporting actors (Sinatra and Reed). Classic romantic scene: waves break over the sergeant (Lancaster) and his captain's wife (Kerr) locked in a passionate embrace on the beach. The movie is a cleaned-up version of novel by James Jones. Footnote: this is Sinatra's comeback role.

*Gaby.** 96m, color. Dir. Curtis Bernhardt. With Leslie Caron, John Kerr, Sir Cedric Hardwicke, Taina Elg. MGM, 1956.

*The Gallant Hours.**** 115m, b/w. Dir. Robert Montgomery. With James Cagney, Dennis Weaver, Ward Costello, Richard Jaeckel. UA, 1960.

*Ghost of the China Sea.*** 73m, b/w. Dir. Fred F. Sears. With David Brian, Lynn Bernay, Jonathan Haze. Columbia, 1958.

*The Girls of Pleasure Island.** 95m, color. Dir. F. Hugh Herbert, Alvin Ganzer. With Leo Genn, Don Taylor, Gene Barry, Elsa Lanchester, Audrey Dalton. Paramount, 1953.

*Glory at Sea.** 100m, b/w. Dir. Compton Bennett. With Trevor Howard, Richard Attenborough, Sonny Tufts, James Donald. BL, 1952.

*Go For Broke.**** 92m, b/w. Dir. Robert Pirosh. With Van Johnson, Gianna Maria Canale, Warner Anderson, Lane Nakana, George Miki. MGM, 1951.

*Golden Earrings.** 95m, b/w. Dir. Mitchell Leisen. With Ray Milland, Marlene Deitrich, Murvyn Vye, Bruce Lester, Dennis Hoey. Paramount, 1947.

*The Great Battle.** aka *Battle Force.* 97m, color. With Henry Fonda, Helmut Berger, Samantha Eggar, John Huston, Stacy Keach. 1978.

*The Great Escape.**** 169m, color. Dir. John Sturges. With Steve McQueen, James Garner, Richard Attenborough, Charles Bronson, James Coburn, David McCallum. UA, 1963.

*The Guns of Navarone.**** 157m, color. Dir. J. Lee Thompson. With Gregory Peck, David Niven, Anthony Quinn, Stanley Baker, Anthony Quayle, James Darren, Irene Papas, Gia Scala, James Justice, Richard Harris. Columbia, 1961.

*Halls of Montezuma.*** 113m, color. Dir. Lewis Milestone. With Richard Widmark, Jack Palance, Robert Wagner, Jack Webb, Reginald Gardiner, Karl Malden. Fox, 1951.

*Heaven Knows, Mr. Allison.**** 107m, color. Dir. John Huston. With Deborah Kerr, Robert Mitchum. Fox, 1957.

*Hell in the Pacific.**** 103m, color. Dir. John Boorman. With Lee Marvin, Toshiro Mifune. Cinerama, 1968.

*Hell Is for Heroes.**** 90m, b/w. Dir. Don Siegel. With Steve McQueen, Bobby Darin, Fess Parker, Harry Guardino, James Coburn, Mike Kellin, Nick Adams, Bob Newhart. Paramount, 1962.

*Hell Squad.** 64m, b/w. Dir. Burt Topper. With Wally Campo, Brandon Carroll, Fred Galvin, Greg Stuart. AIP, 1958.

*Hell to Eternity.*** 132m, b/w. Dir. Phil Karlson. With Jeffrey Hunter, David Janssen, Vic Damone. AA, 1960.

*Hellcats of the Navy.*** 81m, b/w. Dir. Nathan Juran. With Ronald Reagan, Nancy Davis, Arthur Franz, Harry Lauter, Selmer Jackson. Columbia, 1957.

*Her Sister's Secret.*** 86m, b/w. Dir. Edgar G. Ulmer. With Nancy Coleman, Margaret Lindsay, Phillip Reed, Felix Bressart. Producers Rel, 1946.

*Here Come the Marines.** 66m, b/w. Dir. William Beaudine. With Leo Gorcey, Huntz Hall, Bernard Gorcey, Gil Stratton, Jr., Arthur Space, Tim Ryan. Monogram, 1952.

The Hiding Place.** 150m, color. Dir. James F. Collier. With Julie Harris, Eileen Heckart, Arthur O'Connell, Jeanette Cliff, Robert Rietty. World Wide, 1975.

High Barbaree.* 91m, b/w. Dir. Jack Conway. With Van Johnson, June Allyson, Thomas Mitchell. MGM, 1947.

Hitler.** aka *Women of Nazi Germany*. 107m, b/w. Dir. Stuart Heisler. With Richard Basehart, Cordula Trantow, Maria Emo, Martin Kosleck, John Banner. AA, 1962.

Hitler: The Last Ten Days.** 106m, color. Dir. Ennio de Concini. With Alec Guiness, Simon Ward, Adolfo Celi, Diane Cilento, Gabriele Ferzetti, Eric Porter, Doris Kunstmann. Paramount, 1973.

Home of the Brave.*** 88m, b/w. Dir. Mark Robson. With James Edwards, Douglas Dick, Steve Brodie, Jeff Corey, Lloyd Bridges. UA, 1949.

The Homecoming.*** 113m, b/w. Dir. Mervyn LeRoy. With Clark Gable, Lana Turner, Anne Baxter, John Hodiak, Ray Collins, Cameron Mitchell. MGM, 1948.

The Horizontal Lieutenant.** 90m, color. Dir. Richard Thorpe. With Jim Hutton, Paula Prentiss, Miyoshi Umeki, Jim Backus, Jack Carter, Marty Ingels. MGM, 1962.

Hornet's Nest.** 109m, color. Dir. Phil Karlson. With Rock Hudson, Sylva Koscina, Sergio Fantoni, Jacques Sernas, Giacomo Rossi Stuart, Tom Felleghi. UA, 1970.

I Deal in Danger.** 90m, color. Dir. Walter Grauman. With Robert Goulet, Christine Carere, Donald Harron, Werner Peters. Fox, 1966.

I Was an American Spy.** 84m, b/w. Dir. Lesley Selander. With Ann Dvorak, Gene Evans, Douglas Kennedy, Richard Loo, Philip Ahn. AA, 1951.

Imitation General.** 88m, b/w. Dir. George Marshall. With Glenn Ford, Red Buttons, Taina Elg, Dean Jones. MGM, 1958.

In Enemy Country.** 108m, color. Dir. Harry Keller. With Tony Franciosa, Anjanette Comer, Guy Stockwell, Paul Hubschmid, Tom Bell, Emile Genest. Universal, 1968.

In Harm's Way.** 165m, b/w. Dir. Otto Preminger. With John Wayne, Kirk Douglas, Patricia Neal, Tom Tryon, Paula Prentiss, Henry Fonda, Dana Andrews, Brandon de Wilde. Paramount, 1965.

In Love and War.** 107m, color. Dir. Philip Dunne. With Robert Wagner, Dana Wynter, Hope Lange. Fox, 1958.

Is Paris Burning?.* 173m, b/w, color. Dir. Rene Clement. With Jean-Paul Belmondo, Charles Boyer, Leslie Caron, Alain Delon, Kirk Douglas, Glenn Ford, Gert Frobe, Simone Signoret, Orson Welles, Claude Dauphin. Paramount, 1966.

*Joe Butterfly.*** 90m, color. Dir. Jesse Hibbs. With Audie Murphy, Burgess Meredith, George Nader, Keenan Wynn, Fred Clark. Universal, 1957.

*Judgment at Nuremberg.***** 190m, b/w. Dir. Stanley Kramer. With Spencer Tracy, Burt Lancaster, Richard Widmark, Marlene Dietrich, Judy Garland, Maximilian Schell, Montgomery Clift, William Shatner. UA, 1961.

A poignant courtroom drama about the Allied trial of Nazi war criminals who say they were just following orders. Oscars for Schell and screenplay. Best scene: the testimony of a woman (Garland) who had been persecuted by Nazis for polluting the Aryan race by having sex with a Jew. Footnote: the original version of this movie aired as a 1959 "Playhouse 90" TV drama.

*Jungle Patrol.*** 71m, b/w. Dir. Joseph M. Newman. With Kristine Miller, Arthur Franz, Ross Ford, Tom Noonan, Gene Reynolds, Richard Jaeckel. Fox, 1948.

*Kelly's Heroes.*** 148m, color. Dir. Brian G. Hutton. With Clint Eastwood, Telly Savalas, Don Rickles, Donald Sutherland, Carroll O'Connor, Gavin MacLeod. MGM, 1970.

*King Rat.**** 134m, b/w. Dir. Bryan Forbes. With George Segal, Tom Courtenay, James Fox, Patrick O'Neal, Denholm Elliott, James Donald, John Mills. Columbia, 1965.

*Kings Go Forth.**** 109m, b/w. Dir. Delmer Daves. With Frank Sinatra, Tony Curtis, Natalie Wood, Leora Dana. UA, 1958.

*Kiss Them for Me.*** 103m, color. Dir. Stanley Donan. With Cary Grant, Jayne Mansfield, Suzy Parker, Leif Erickson, Ray Ralston. Fox, 1957.

*The Last Blitzkrieg.*** 85m, b/w. Dir. Arthur Dreifuss. With Van Johnson, Kerwin Mathews, Dick York, Larry Storch. Columbia, 1958.

*Last Day of the War.*** 96m, color. Dir. Juan-Antonio Bardem. With George Maharis, Maria Perschy, John Clarke, James Philbrook. MGM, 1969.

*The Last Time I Saw Archie.*** 103m, b/w. Dir. Jack Webb. With Robert Mitchum, Jack Webb, Martha Hyer, France Nuyen, Joe Flynn. UA, 1961.

*The Longest Day.***** 180m, b/w. Dir. Ken Annakin, Andrew Marton, Bernhard Wicki. With John Wayne, Rod Steiger, Robert Ryan, Peter Lawford, Henry Fonda, Red Buttons, Mel Ferrer, many others. Fox, 1962.

Epic, immensely expensive and accurate docu-drama of the preparation for D-Day, the ship movement across the English channel, and the assault on Normandy. Oscars for

special effects and cinematography. Based on Cornelius
Ryan's compilation of interviews with D-Day survivors.
Notable scene: vulnerable parachutists are picked off one by
one. Footnote: British, French, and American soldiers served
as extras.

*MacArthur.*** 128m, color. Dir. Joseph Sargent. With Gregory
Peck, Ed Flanders, Dan O'Herlihy, Ivan Bonar, Ward
Costello. Universal, 1977.

*McHale's Navy.*** 93m, color. Dir. Edward J. Montagne. With
Ernest Borgnine, Joe Flynn, Tim Conway, Claudine Longet,
Jean Willes, George Kennedy. Universal, 1964.

*McHale's Navy Joins the Air Force.** 92m, color. Dir. Edward J.
Montagne. With Joe Flynn, Tim Conway, Bob Hastings,
Gary Vinson, Billy Sands, Jean Hale, Susan Silo, Edson
Stroll, John Wright, Cliff Norton. Universal, 1965.

*The McKenzie Break.*** 108m, color. Dir. Lamont Johnson. With
Brian Keith, Helmut Griem, Ian Hendry, Jack Watson,
Patrick O'Connell. UA, 1970.

*The Magic Face.*** 88m, b/w. Dir. Frank Tuttle. With Luther
Adler, Patricia Knight, William L. Shirer, Ilka Windish.
Columbia, 1951.

*Malaya.*** 98m, b/w. Dir. Richard Thorpe. With Spencer Tracy,
James Stewart, Valentina Cortese, Sydney Greenstreet.
MGM, 1950.

*A Man Called Dagger.** 86m, color. Dir. Richard Rush. With
Terry Moore, Jan Murray, Sue Ane Langdon, Paul Mantee,
Eileen O'Neill, Maureen Arthur. MGM, 1967.

*The Man Who Never Was.*** 103m, color. Dir. Ronald Neame.
With Clifton Webb, Gloria Grahame, Robert Flemyng,
Josephine Griffin, Stephen Boyd. Fox, 1956.

*Me and the Colonel.*** 109m, b/w. Dir. Peter Glenville. With
Danny Kaye, Curt Jurgens, Nicole Maurey, Francoise
Rosay. Columbia, 1958.

*Memphis Belle.*** 107m, color. Dir. Michael Canton-Jones. With
Matthew Modine, Eric Stoltz, Harry Connick, Jr. WB,
1990.

*Merrill's Marauders.*** 98m, color. Dir. Samuel Fuller. With Jeff
Chandler, Ty Hardin, Peter Brown, Andrew Duggan, Will
Hutchins. WB, 1962.

*Midway.** 132m, color. Dir. Jack Smight. With Charlton Heston,
Henry Fonda, James Coburn, Glenn Ford, Hal Holbrook.
Universal, 1976.

*Mission Batangas.** 100m, color. Dir. Keith Larsen. With Dennis
Weaver, Vera Miles, Keith Larsen, Vic Duag. Manson,
1968.

Mister Roberts.**** 123m, color. Dir. John Ford, Mervyn LeRoy.
With Henry Fonda, James Cagney, William Powell, Jack
Lemmon, Betsy Palmer, Ward Bond. WB, 1955.

Dramatizes the situation of sailors whose only combat
experience is against boredom. Movie is based on a
Broadway play by Joshua Logan and Frank S. Nugent,
also starring Fonda. Supporting Oscar for Lemmon. Best
scene: the captain (Cagney) has a fit when his prize palm
tree is thrown overboard. Footnote: Ford and Fonda came
to blows over acting interpretation; they never reconciled.

Morituri.*** aka *The Saboteur: Code Name Morituri; The
Saboteur.* 128m, b/w. Dir. Bernhard Wicki. With Marlon
Brando, Yul Brynner, Janet Margolin, Trevor Howard,
Martin Benrath, Hans Christian Blech. Fox, 1965.

The Mountain Road.*** 102m, b/w. Dir. Daniel Mann. With
James Stewart, Lisa Lu, Glenn Corbett, Henry Morgan,
Frank Silvera, James Best. Columbia, 1960.

Mystery Submarine.* 78m, b/w. Dir. Douglas Sirk. With
Macdonald Carey, Marta Toren, Carl Esmond, Ludwig
Donath. Universal, 1950.

The Naked and the Dead.*** 131m, color. Dir. Raoul Walsh.
With Aldo Ray, Cliff Robertson, Raymond Massey, Lili St.
Cyr, Barbara Nichols. WB, 1958.

The Naked Brigade.** 99m, b/w. Dir. Maury Dexter. With Shirley
Eaton, Ken Scott, Mary Chronopoulou, John Holland, Sonia
Ziodou. Universal, 1965.

Never So Few.*** 124m, color. Dir. John Sturges. With Frank
Sinatra, Gina Lollobrigida, Peter Lawford, Steve McQueen,
Richard Johnson, Paul Henreid, Brian Donlevy, Dean Jones,
Charles Bronson. MGM, 1959.

The Night of the Generals.** 148m, color. Dir. Anatole Litvak.
With Peter O'Toole, Omar Sharif, Donald Pleasence, Tom
Courtenay, Joanna Pettet. Columbia, 1967.

The Night Fighters.** 89m, b/w. Dir. Tay Garnett. With Robert
Mitchum, Anne Heywood, Dan O'Herlihy, Cyril Cusack,
Richard Harris. UA, 1960.

1941.* 118m, color. Dir. Steven Spielberg. With Dan Aykroyd, Ned
Beatty, John Belushi, Lorraine Gary, Murray Hamilton.
Universal, 1979.

No Man Is an Island.** 114m, color. Dir. John Monks, Jr.,
Richard Goldstone. With Jeffrey Hunter, Marshall
Thompson, Barbara Perez, Ronald Remy, Paul Edwards, Jr.,
Rolf Bayer, Vicente Liwanag. Universal, 1962.

None But the Brave.** 105m, color. Dir. Frank Sinatra. With Frank Sinatra, Clint Walker, Tommy Sands, Tony Bill, Brad Dexter. WB, 1965.

Notorious.*** 101m, b/w. Dir. Alfred Hitchcock. With Cary Grant, Ingrid Bergman, Claude Rains, Louis Calhern, Reinhold Schunzel, Moroni Olsen. RKO, 1946.

O.S.S.*** 107m, b/w. Dir. Irving Pichel. With Alan Ladd, Geraldine Fitzgerald, Patric Knowles, Richard Benedict, Richard Webb, Don Beddoe. Paramount, 1946.

Okinawa.** 67m, b/w. Dir. Leigh Jason. With Pat O'Brien, Cameron Mitchell, James Dobson, Richard Denning, Richard Benedict, Alvy Moore. Columbia, 1952.

On The Double.*** 92m, color. Dir. Melville Shavelson. With Danny Kaye, Dana Wynter, Wilfrid Hyde-White, Margaret Rutherford, Diana Dors. Paramount, 1961.

Once Before I Die.** 97m, color. Dir. John Derek. With Ursula Andress, John Derek, Rod Lauren, Richard Jaeckel, Ron Ely. Goldstone, 1967.

The 1,000 Plane Raid.* 94m, color. Dir. Boris Sagal. With Christopher George, Laraine Stephens, J.D. Cannon, Gary Marshall, Michael Evans. UA, 1969.

Onionhead.** 110m, b/w. Dir. Norman Taurog. With Andy Griffith, Felicia Farr, Walter Matthau, Erin O'Brien, Joey Bishop. WB, 1958.

The Only Way.** 98m, color. Dir. Bent Christensen. With Jane Seymour, Martin Porter, Ova Sprogoe. Hemisphere, 1970.

Operation Bikini.* 84m, b/w, color. Dir. Anthony Carras. With Tab Hunter, Frankie Avalon, Eva Six, Scott Brady, Gary Crosby, Jim Backus. AIP, 1963.

Operation Bottleneck.* 76m, b/w. Dir. Edward L. Cahn. With Ron Foster, Miiko Taka, Norman Alden, John Clarke. UA, 1961.

Operation Cross Eagles.* 90m, color. Dir. Richard Conte. With Richard Conte, Rory Calhoun, Aili King. Noble, 1969.

Operation Crossbow.** aka *The Great Spy Mission*. 118m, color. Dir. Michael Anderson. With Sophia Loren, George Peppard, Trevor Howard, John Mills. MGM, 1965.

Operation Daybreak.* aka *Price of Freedom*. 118m, color. Dir. Lewis Gilbert. With Timothy Bottoms, Martin Shaw, Joss Ackland, Nicola Pagett, Anthony Andrews. WB, 1976.

Operation Eichmann.** 92m, b/w. Dir. R.G. Springsteen. With Werner Klemperer, Ruta Lee, Donald Buka, Barbara Turner, John Banner. AA, 1961.

Operation Mad Ball.** 105m, b/w. Dir. Richard Quine. With Jack Lemmon, Kathryn Grant, Mickey Rooney, Ernie Kovacs, Arthur O'Connell, James Darren. Columbia, 1957.

Operation Pacific.*** 111m, b/w. Dir. George Waggner. With John Wayne, Patricia Neal, Ward Bond, Scott Forbes. WB, 1951.

Operation Petticoat.*** 124m, color. Dir. Blake Edwards. With Cary Grant, Tony Curtis, Dina Merrill, Gene Evans, Arthur O'Connell, Richard Sargent, Virginia Gregg. Universal, 1959.

Operation Secret.** 108m, b/w. Dir. Lewis Seiler. With Cornel Wilde, Steve Cochran, Phyllis Thaxter, Karl Malden, Don O'Herlihy. WB, 1952.

Out of the Depths.* 61m, b/w. Dir. D. Ross Lederman. With Jim Bannon, Ross Hunter, Ken Curtis, Loren Tindall, Robert Scott. Columbia, 1946.

Outsider.* 108m, b/w. Dir. Delbert Mann. With Tony Curtis, James Franciscus, Gregory Walcott, Bruce Bennett, Vivian Nathan. Universal, 1962.

PT 109.** 140m, b/w. Dir. Leslie H. Martinson. With Cliff Robertson, Robert Culp, Ty Hardin, James Gregory, Robert Blake. WB, 1963.

Paratroop Command.** 77m, b/w. Dir. William H. Witney. With Richard Bakalyan, Ken Lynch, Jack Hogan, Jimmy Murphy, Jeffrey Morris. AIP, 1959.

Patton.**** 170m, color. Dir. Franklin J. Schaffner. With George C. Scott, Karl Malden, Stephen Young, Michael Strong, Frank Latimore, James Edwards, Lawrence Dobkin, Michael Bates, Tim Considine. Fox, 1970.

    The tour de force investigation of a brilliant and quirky military personality. Oscars include best actor, picture, director, screenplay (Francis Ford Coppola and Edmund H. North). Great charismatic scene: Patton's opening peroration to his troops before battle in front of the American flag. Best combat scene: Patton runs out in the middle of the street to fire his revolver at two planes strafing his men. Footnote: Scott refused to pick up his Oscar.

The Pigeon That Took Rome.** 101m, b/w. Dir. Melville Shavelson. With Charlton Heston, Elsa Martinelli, Harry Guardino, Baccaloni Marietto, Gabriella Pallotta, Debbie Price, Brian Donlevy. Paramount, 1962.

The Private Navy of Sgt. O'Farrell.* 92m, color. Dir. Frank Tashlin. With Bob Hope, Phyllis Diller, Jeffrey Hunter, Gina Lollobrigida, Mylene Demongeot. UA, 1968.

The Proud and Profane.** 111m, b/w. Dir. George Seaton. With William Holden, Deborah Kerr, Thelma Ritter, Dewey Martin, William Redfield. Paramount, 1956.

Purple Heart Diary.** 73m, b/w. Dir. Richard Quine. With Frances Langford, Judd Holdren, Ben Lessy, Tony Romano, Aline Towne. Columbia, 1951.

The Quick and the Dead.* 92m, b/w. Dir. Robert Totten. With Larry D. Mann, Victor French, Jon Cedar, James Almanzar, Louis Massad. Manson, 1963.

Raid on Rommel.* 99m, color. Dir. Henry Hathaway. With Richard Burton, John Colicos, Clinton Greyn, Wolfgang Preiss. Universal, 1971.

The Raiders of Leyte Gulf.** 90m, b/w. Dir. Eddie Romero. With Michael Parsons, Leopold Salcedo, Jennings Sturgeon, Liza Moreno, Efren Reyes. Hemisphere, 1963.

Raiders of the Lost Ark.*** 115m, color. Dir. Steven Spielberg. With Harrison Ford, Karen Allen, Paul Freeman, Ronald Lacey, John Rhys-Davies, Denholm Elliott, Wolf Kahler. Paramount, 1981.

The Ravagers.* 88m, b/w. Dir. Eddie Romero. With John Saxon, Fernando Poe, Jr., Bronwyn Fitzsimmons, Michael Parsons, Kristina Scott. Hemisphere, 1965.

Red Ball Express.*** 83m, b/w. Dir. Budd Boetticher. With Jeff Chandeler, Alex Nicol, Judith Braun, Hugh O'Brian, Jack Kelly, Sidney Poitier, Jack Warden. Universal, 1952.

Rogue's Regiment.** 85m, b/w. Dir. Robert Florey. With Dick Powell, Marta Toren, Vincent Price, Stephen McNally. Universal, 1948.

The Rookie.* 86m, b/w. Dir. George O'Hanlon. With Tommy Noonan, Pete Marshall, Julie Newmar, Jerry Lester, Joe Besser, Vince Barnett, Peter Leeds. Fox, 1959.

Run Silent, Run Deep.*** 93m, b/w. Dir. Robert Wise. With Clark Gable, Burt Lancaster, Jack Warden, Brad Dexter, Don Rickles. UA, 1958.

The Safecracker.** 96m, b/w. Dir. Ray Milland. With Ray Milland, Barry Jones, Jeannette Sterke, Victor Maddern, Ernest Clark. MGM, 1958.

Sands of Iwo Jima.**** 110m, b/w. Dir. Allan Dwan. With John Wayne, John Agar, Adele Mara, Forrest Tucker, Wally Cassell, James Brown, Richard Webb, Arthur Franz, Julie Bishop, James Holden, Peter Coe, Richard Jaeckel, Bill Murphy. Republic, 1949.

The epic battle is the occasion for *the* archetypal John Wayne war movie. A hard-nosed but heroic Sgt. Stryker (Wayne) uses brutal methods to transform a loose group of individuals into a fighting unit. Best sequence: Stryker is killed ironically at the moment of victory. Footnote: the filming took place at the Marine training base at Camp Pendleton and employed thousands of actual Marines.

Screaming Eagles.*** 80m, b/w. Dir. Charles Haas. With Tom Tryon, Jan Merlin, Alvy Moore, Martin Milner, Jacqueline Beer. AA, 1956.

The Sea Chase.** 117m, color. Dir. John Farrow. With John Wayne, Lana Turner, Tab Hunter, David Farrar, Lyle Bettger, James Arness, Claude Akins. WB, 1955.

Sea Wolves.** 120m, color. Dir. Andrew V. McLaglen. With Gregory Peck, Roger Moore, David Niven, Trevor Howard, Patrick MacNee. Paramount, 1981.

Sealed Cargo.** 90m, b/w. Dir. Alfred Werker. With Dana Andrews, Carla Balenda, Claude Rains, Philip Dorn, Onslow Stevens. RKO, 1951.

Sealed Verdict.** 82m, b/w. Dir. Lewis Allen. With Ray Milland, Florence Marly, Broderick Crawford, John Hoyt, John Ridgely. Paramount, 1948.

The Search.**** 105m, b/w. Dir. Fred Zinnemann. With Montgomery Clift, Ivan Jandl, Aline MacMahon, Jarmila Novotna, Wendell Corey. MGM, 1948.

After the war, an American soldier (Clift) befriends a displaced child in Austria until the child's Czechoslovakian mother finds him. Oscars for story and outstanding juvenile performance (Jandl). Heart rending scene: the soldier must give up the child he has come to love. Footnote: this is Clift's first major adult role.

The Searching Wind.** 108m, b/w. Dir. William Dieterle. With Robert Young, Sylvia Sidney, Ann Richards, Dudley Digges, Douglas Dick, Albert Basserman. Paramount, 1946.

The Secret Door.* 72m, b/w. Dir. Gilbert L. Kay. With Robert Hutton, Sandra Dorne, Peter Illing. AA, 1964.

The Secret Invasion.*** 95m, color. Dir. Roger Corman. With Stewart Granger, Mickey Rooney, Raf Valone, Henry Silva, Edd Byrnes, Mia Massini. UA, 1964.

The Secret of Santa Vittoria.** 134m, color. Dir. Stanley Kramer. With Anthony Quinn, Anna Magnani, Virna Lisi, Hardy Kruger, Sergio Franchi, Renato Rascel. UA, 1969.

The Secret War of Harry Frigg.** 110m, color. Dir. Jack Smight. With Paul Newman, Sylva Koscina, Andrew Duggan, Tom Bosley, John Williams. Universal, 1968.

Seven Women From Hell.** *88m, b/w.* Dir. Robert D. Webb. With Patricia Owens, Denise Darcel, Cesar Romero, John Kerr, Yvonne Craig. Fox, 1961.

Situation Hopeless--But Not Serious.** 97m, b/w. Dir. Gottfried Reinhardt. With Alec Guinness, Michael Conners, Robert Redford, Anita Hoefer, Mady Rahl, Paul Dahlke. Paramount, 1965.

*633 Squadron.*** 94m, color. Dir. Walter E. Grauman. With Cliff
Robertson, George Chakiris, Harry Andrews. UA, 1964.

*Ski Troop Attack.*** 63m, b/w. Dir. Roger Corman. With Michael
Forest, Frank Wolff, Wally Campo, Richard Sinatra, Sheila
Carol. Filmgroup, 1960.

*Sky Commando.** 69m, b/w. Dir. Fred F. Sears. With Dan
Duryea, Frances Gifford, Michael Connors. Columbia, 1953.

*Slaughterhouse Five.**** 104m, color. Dir. George Roy Hill. With
Michael Sacks, Ron Leibman, Eugene Roche, Sharon Gans,
Valerie Perrine. Universal, 1972.

*Snow Treasure.** 95m, color. Dir. Irving Jacoby. With James
Franciscus, Ilona Rogers, Paul Austad. AA, 1968.

*A Soldier's Story.**** 101m, color. Dir. Norman Jewison. With
Howard E. Rollins, Jr., Adolph Caesar, Dennis Lipscomb,
Art Evans, Denzel Washington, Larry Riley, David Alan
Grier. Columbia, 1984.

*South Pacific.**** 171m, color. Dir. Joshua Logan. With Rossano
Brazzi, Mitzi Gaynor, John Kerr, Ray Walston, Juanita
Hall, France Nuyen. Fox, 1958.

*South Sea Woman.*** aka *Pearl of the South Pacific.* 99m, b/w.
Dir. Arthur Lubin. With Burt Lancaster, Virginia Mayo,
Chuck Connors, Arthur Shields, Paul Burke. WB, 1953.

*Square of Violence.**** 98m, b/w. Dir. Leonardo Bercovici. With
Broderick Crawford, Valentina Cortese, Branko Plesa, Bibi
Anderson, Anita Bjork. MGM, 1963.

*Stalag 17.***** 120m, b/w. Dir. Billy Wilder. With William Holden,
Don Taylor, Otto Preminger, Robert Strauss, Peter Graves,
Sig Ruman, Harvey Lembeck. Paramount, 1953.
    A dark comedy about the scheming, self-interested and
boring life of soldiers trying to survive in a German POW
camp. Oscar for Holden's portrayal of a wiseguy loner.
Footnote: comic relief is furnished by Strauss and Lembeck
who repeat their Broadway roles (play by Donal Bevan
and Edmund Trzcinski).

*The Steel Claw.*** 96m, color. Dir. George Montgomery. With
George Montgomery, Charito Luna, Mario Barri, Paul
Sorensen. WB, 1961.

*Step by Step.*** 62m, b/w. Dir. Phil Rosen. With Lawrence
Tierney, Anne Jeffreys, Lowell Gilmore. RKO, 1946.

*Strange Journey.** 65m, b/w. Dir. James Tinling. With Paul Kelly,
Osa Massen, Hillary Brooke, Bruce Lester. Fox, 1946.

*The Stranger.**** 95m, b/w. Dir. Orson Welles. With Orson
Welles, Loretta Young, Edward G. Robinson, Richard Long,
Martha Wentworth. RKO, 1946.

Submarine Seahawk.** 83m, b/w. Dir. Spencer G. Bennet. With
John Bentley, Brett Halsey, Wayne Heffley, Steve Mitchell,
Henry McCann. AIP, 1959.

Suicide Battalion.** 79m, b/w. Dir. Edward L. Cahn. With
Michael Connors, John Ashley, Jewell Lain. AIP, 1958.

Surrender--Hell!* *85m, b/w.* Dir. John Barnwell. With Keith
Andes, Susan Cabot, Paraluman, Nestor de Villa. AA, 1959.

Swing Shift.** 100m, color. Dir. Jonathan Demme. With Goldie
Hawn, Kurt Russell, Christine Lahti, Fred Ward, Ed
Harris. WB, 1984.

Tank Commandos.** 79m, b/w. Dir. Burt Topper. With Robert
Barron, Maggie Lawrence, Wally Campo, Donato Farretta,
Leo V. Metranga. AIP, 1959.

The Tanks Are Coming.** 90m, b/w. Dir. Lewis Seiler. With
Steve Cochran, Philip Carey, Mari Aldon, Paul Picerni,
Harry Bellaver. WB, 1951.

Tarawa Beachhead.** 77m, b/w. Dir. Paul Wendkos. With Kerwin
Mathews, Julie Adams, Ray Danton, Karen Sharpe, Onslow
Stevens. Columbia, 1958.

Target Unknown.* 90m, b/w. Dir. George Sherman. With Mark
Stevens, Alex Nicol, Robert Douglas, Don Taylor, Gig
Young. Universal, 1951.

Task Force.** 116m, color. Dir. Delmer Daves. With Gary
Cooper, Jane Wyatt, Wayne Morris, Walter Brennan, Julie
London, Bruce Bennett. WB, 1949.

A Taste of Hell.* 90m, color. Dir. Neil Yarema. With John
Garwood, Lisa Lorena, William Smith. Box Office, 1973.

The Teahouse of the August Moon.*** 123m, color. Dir. Daniel
Mann. With Marlon Brando, Glenn Ford, Machiko Kyo,
Eddie Albert, Paul Ford. MGM, 1956.

Then There Were Three.** 74m, b/w. Dir. Alex Nicol. With
Frank Latimore, Alex Nicol, Barry Cahill, Sidney Clute.
Parade, 1961.

The Thin Red Line.*** 99m, b/w. Dir. Andrew Marton. With
Keir Dullea, Jack Warden, James Philbrook. AA, 1964.

13 Rue Madeleine.** 95m, b/w. Dir. Henry Hathaway. With
James Cagney, Annabella, Richard Conte, Frank Latimore,
Walter Abel, Melville Cooper, Sam Jaffe. Fox, 1946.

36 Hours.** 115m, b/w. Dir. George Seaton. With James Garner,
Eva Marie Saint, Rod Taylor, Werner Peters, Celia Lovsky,
Alan Napier. MGM, 1965.

Three Came Home.*** 106m, b/w. Dir. Jean Negulesco. With
Claudette Colbert, Patric Knowles, Florence Desmond,
Sessue Hayakawa, Sylvia Andrew. Fox, 1950.

Thunderbirds.** 98m, b/w. Dir. John H. Auer. With John Derek, John Barrymore, Jr., Mona Freeman, Gene Evans. Republic, 1952.

Till the End of Time.*** 105m, b/w. Dir. Edward Dmytryk. With Dorothy McGuire, Guy Madison, Robert Mitchum, Bill Williams, Tom Tully, William Gargan. RKO, 1946.

A Time to Love and a Time to Die.*** 133m, color. Dir. Douglas Sirk. With John Gavin, Lilo Pulver, Jock Mahoney, Don DeFore, Keenan Wynn. Universal, 1958.   .

To Be or Not To Be.* 108m, color. Dir. Alan Johnson. With Mel Brooks, Anne Bancroft, Tim Matheson, Charles Durning, Jose Ferrer, Christopher Lloyd. Fox, 1983.

To Hell and Back.*** 106m, color. Dir. Jesse Hibbs. With Audie Murphy, Marshall Thompson, Jack Kelly, Charles Drake, Paul Picerni, Gregg Palmer. Universal, 1955.

Tobruk.** 107m, color. Dir. Arthur Hiller. With Rock Hudson, George Peppard, Nigel Green, Guy Stockwell, Jack Watson, Norman Rossington, Percy Herbert, Liam Redmond. Universal, 1966.

Tokyo Joe.** 88m, b/w. Dir. Stuart Heisler. With Humphrey Bogart, Alexander Knox, Florence Marly, Sessue Hayakawa, Jerome Courtland. Columbia, 1949.

Too Late the Hero.*** aka *Suicide Run*. 133m, color. Dir. Robert Aldrich. With Michael Caine, Cliff Robertson, Henry Fonda, Ian Bannen, Harry Andrews, Denholm Elliott, Ronald Fraser. Cinerama, 1970.

*Tora! Tora! Tora!***** 143m, color. Dir. Richard Fleischer, Toshio Masuda, Kinji Fukasaku. With Martin Balsam, Soh Yamamura, Jason Robards, Jr., Joseph Cotten, Tatsuya Mihashi, E.G. Marshall, James Whitmore. Fox, 1970.

This giant-budget docu-drama contrasts the enthusiastic, well trained, and committed Japanese with the confused pre-war Americans. Tension builds slowly but steadily to the attack. Best scene: the spectacular finale, which won an Oscar for special effects (parts of it reappear in *Midway*, 1976, and in *MacArthur*, 1977. Footnote: the movie lost so much money that, for quite some time, it frightened other studios away from making war films.

Torpedo Run.** 98m, color. Dir. Joseph Pevney. With Glenn Ford, Ernest Borgnine, Diane Brewster, Dean Jones, L.Q. Jones. MGM, 1958.

The Train.**** 140m, b/w. Dir. John Frankenheimer. With Burt Lancaster, Paul Scofield, Michael Simon, Jeanne Moreau, Albert Remy, Wolfgang Preiss. UA, 1965.

The Resistance tries to prevent Nazis from taking art treasures out of France. Great on-location cinematography. Best sequence: the movement of trains is contrasted with a chess game between a German colonel (Scofield) and French railway inspector (Lancaster). Footnote: after arguments with Lancaster and producer Jules Bricken, director Arthur Penn was replaced by Frankenheimer.

Twelve O'Clock High.**** 132m, b/w. Dir. Henry King. With Gregory Peck, Dean Jagger, Hugh Marlowe, Gary Merrill, Millard Mitchell. Fox, 1949.

A bomber-group general (Peck) cracks under the unbearable pressure of command. The experience is given effective, personal impact by being framed within the flashback of a major (Jagger). Supporting Oscar for Jagger; nomination for Peck. Notable scenes of aerial attacks. Based on the novel by Sy Bartlett and Beirne Lay. Footnote: the nervous breakdown is based on an actual incident involving Air Corps Maj. Gen. Frank A. Armstrong.

Under Fire.** 78m, b/w. Dir. James B. Clark. With Rex Reason, Steve Brodie, Jon Locke, Harry Morgan. Fox, 1957.

Under Ten Flags.** 92m, b/w. Dir. Duilio Coletti. With Van Heflin, Charles Laughton, Mylene Demongeot, John Ericson, Liam Redmond, Alex Nicol. Paramount, 1960.

Until They Sail.** 95m, b/w. Dir. Robert Wise. With Paul Newman, Joan Fontaine, Jean Simmons, Sandra Dee, Piper Laurie. MGM, 1957.

Up from the Beach.** 98m, b/w. Dir. Robert Parrish. With Cliff Robertson, Red Buttons, Irina Demick, Marius Goring, Slim Pickens, Broderick Crawford. Fox, 1965.

Up Front.** 92m, b/w. Dir. Alexander Knox. With David Wayne, Tom Ewell, Marina Berti, Jeffrey Lynn, Richard Egan. Universal, 1951.

Up Periscope.** 111m, color. Dir. Gordon Douglas. With James Garner, Edmond O'Brien, Andra Martin, Alan Hale, Jr., Carleton Carpenter, Frank Gifford. WB, 1959.

Verboten!* *93m, b/w.* Dir. Samuel Fuller. With James Best, Susan Cummings, Tom Pittman, Paul Dubov, Dick Kallman, Steven Geray. UA, 1959.

The Victors.*** 175m, b/w. Dir. Carl Foreman. With George Hamilton, George Peppard, Vincent Edwards, Eli Wallach, Melina Mercouri, Romy Schneider, Jeanne Moreau, Peter Fonda, Senta Berger, Elke Sommer, Albert Finney. Columbia, 1963.

Victory.** 117m, color. Dir. John Huston. With Michael Caine, Pele, Max Von Sydow, Sylvester Stallone, Bobby Moore. Lorimar, 1981.

Von Ryan's Express.*** 117m, color. Dir. Mark Robson. With Frank Sinatra, Trevor Howard, Raffaella Carra, Brad Dexter, Sergio Fantoni, Edward Mulhare, James Brolin, John Leyton, Vito Scotti. Fox, 1965.

The Wackiest Ship in the Army.* 99m, color. Dir. Richard Murphy. With Jack Lemmon, Ricky Nelson, John Lund, Chips Rafferty, Tom Tully, Joby Baker. Columbia, 1961.

The Walls of Hell.** 88m, b/w. Dir. Gerardo De Leon, Eddie Romero. With Jock Mahoney, Fernando Poe, Jr., Mike Parsons, Cecilia Lopez. Hemisphere, 1964.

The War Lover.** 105m, b/w. Dir. Philip Leacock. With Steve McQueen, Robert Wagner, Shirley Ann Field, Gary Cockrell. Columbia, 1962.

Warkill.** 100m, color. Dir. Ferde Grofe, Jr. With George Montgomery, Tom Drake, Conrad Parham, Eddie Infante, Henry Duval. Universal, 1968.

What Did You Do in the War, Daddy?** 116m, color. Dir. Blake Edwards. With James Coburn, Dick Shawn, Sergio Fantoni, Aldo Ray, Harry Morgan, Carroll O'Connor. UA, 1966.

When Hell Broke Loose.** 78m, b/w. Dir. Kenneth G. Crane. With Charles Bronson, Violet Rensing, Richard Jaeckel, Arvid Nelson. Paramount, 1958.

When Willie Comes Marching Home.*** 82m, b/w. Dir. John Ford. With Dan Dailey, Corinne Calvert, Colleen Townsend, William Demarest, James Lydon. Fox, 1950.

Where Eagles Dare.** 155m, color. Dir. Brian G. Hutton. With Richard Burton, Clint Eastwood, Mary Ure, Patrick Wymark, Michael Hordern. MGM, 1968.

Which Way to the Front?* 96m, color. Dir. Jerry Lewis. With Jerry Lewis, John Wood, Jan Murray, Kaye Ballard, Robert Middleton, Paul Winchell, Sidney Miller, Gary Crosby. WB, 1970.

The Wild Blue Yonder.** 98m, b/w. Dir. Allan Dwan. With Wendell Corey, Vera Ralston, Forrest Tucker, Phil Harris, Walter Brennan. Republic, 1952.

The Wings of Eagles.** 110m, color. Dir. John Ford. With John Wayne, Maureen O'Hara, Dan Dailey, Ward Bond, Ken Curtis, Edmund Lowe, Kenneth Tobey. MGM, 1957.

Women in the Night.* aka *When Men are Beasts*. 90m, b/w. Dir. William Rowland. With Tala Birell, William Henry, Virginia Christine, Richard Loo. Classics, 1948.

Yanks.** 141, color. Dir. John Schlesinger. With Richard Gere, Lisa Eichhorn, Vanessa Redgrave, William Devane, Chick Vennera. Universal, 1979.

The Young Lions.*** 167m, b/w. Dir. Edward Dmytryk. With Marlon Brando, Montgomery Clift, Dean Martin, Hope Lange, Barbara Rush, Maximilian Schell. Fox, 1958.

The Young Warriors.** 93m, color. Dir. John Peyser. With James Drury, Steve Carlson, Jonathan Daly, Robert Pine, Michael Stanwood. Universal, 1967.

You're In the Army Now.** aka *U.S.S. Teakettle.* 93m, b/w. Dir. Henry Hathaway. With Gary Cooper, Jane Greer, Millard Mitchell, Eddie Albert, John McIntire. Fox, 1951.

11

Korean War

CHRONOLOGY

The War Begins (June-September 1950):

25 June. North Korean communist forces, armed by the Soviets, unexpectedly invade South Korea across the 38th parallel.

27 June. U.S. President Harry Truman orders American forces to intervene in support of South Korea. The United Nations (U.N.) Security Council votes to oppose North Korean aggression.

June-September. American and South Korean forces retreat to the Pusan Perimeter (see *The Steel Helmet*, 1951).

8 July. U.S. General Douglas MacArthur is named commander of the unified U.N. forces.

The U.N. Offensive (September-December 1950):

15 September. MacArthur launches an amphibious landing at Inchon harbor. U.N. forces break out of Pusan and advance to the 38th parallel (see *Inchon*, 1981).

October-November. South Korean, American, and other U.N. forces advance into North Korea and move toward the Chinese border along the Yalu River.

Chinese Intervention (November 1950-January 1951):

25-26 November 1950. About 180,000 Chinese "volunteers" launch a surprise attack. U.N. forces are defeated and forced to retreat.

1-15 January 1951. A second Chinese offensive is launched. Chinese and North Korean troops cross the 38th parallel.

11 April 1951. MacArthur, who argued for an expanded effort, is relieved of command (see *MacArthur* 1977).

Stalemate and Negotiations (January 1951-July 1953):

Fighting is now a series of attacks and counterattacks. The U.N. fears an expanding war. Chinese and North Koreans suffer great casualties. Negotiations at Panmunjon drag on for two years (see *Pork Chop Hill*, 1959). Fighting continues. The treatment and behavior of American POWs become issues (see *The Rack*, 1956).

26 July 1953. An armistice is signed. South Korea is saved from communism, but few see it as a real victory.

COMMENTARY

Movies made during the Korean conflict are part of a cultural matrix of anxiety. They treat the American dread of the unknown in a variety of forms: "uncertainty about the nature or the location of...enemies; the Communist who operates behind the scenes, the delinquents who lurk around the next corner, the prehistoric monsters reactivated by the atom tests of science fiction, or the neighbors whose brains are manipulated by Martian technology" (Sayre 25). The typical Korean War film focuses on an isolated or lost platoon.

Korean War films also have a similar look. Korea is the *film noir* war. Its movies are enveloped in shadow and an atmosphere of depression. The environment of *film noir* is "murky and close, the settings vaguely oppressive...and the survival of good [is] troubled and ambiguous" (Sklar 253). The actual war was something like that. Americans have held no romantic images of the conflict as they do of the Civil War and few, if any, would call it a "good war" like that against Germany and Japan. Fought in a remote region of East Asia, it was in its origin confusing, in its course frustrating, and in its consequences unfulfilling. W. Averell Harriman called it "a sour little war" (qtd. in Goulden xv). Historian Clay Blair labeled it "The Forgotten War." As one young Texan said, in the popular slang of 1952, "Boys, there's two things we gotta avoid: Korea and gonorrhea" (qtd. in Goulden xvi). A 1990 PBS television documentary was entitled "Korea: The Unknown War." British historian Max Hastings held that the war was morally right but nevertheless a "profoundly unsatisfactory experience" (344).

The nature of the conflict is evident in four noteworthy films: *The Steel Helmet* (1951), *Fixed Bayonets* (1957), *Pork Chop Hill* (1959), and *The Rack* (1956). The first three focus on small units in combat. In Sam Fuller's melodrama *The Steel Helmet*, lost Americans cut off from their outfit form a platoon to do what they can to survive in the early days of the war. Of interest are details like tracking down an enemy sniper by his line of fire. In *Fixed Bayonets*, also by Fuller, we suffer with a squad, cut off from their lines by the enemy and the grueling Korean winter of 1951. *Pork Chop Hill*--the best actioner about the conflict--is a poignant ode to the common infantryman by Lewis Milestone who also directed great films in the same vein about previous wars--*All Quiet on the Western Front* (1930) and *A Walk in the Sun* (1945). In the film, GIs sacrifice themselves to take Pork Chop Hill, a tactically pointless objective, all the while aware that peace talks may momentarily end the war.

One additional aspect, unique to this conflict, is the issue of communist "brainwashing" of POWs. *The Rack* (1956), a courtroom drama, deals with charges of collaboration against a young soldier (Paul Newman). Other films to cover this ground include *The Manchurian Candidate* (1962), a bizarre political-psychological thriller, and *The Bamboo Prison* (1955), a film about a phony informer.

Today, the best known treatment of the Korean War is Robert Altman's black comedy *M*A*S*H* (1970), later reformed into one of television's longest running series. The film's anachronistic tone (for example, in language, anti-military attitude, social concerns, behavior, and hairstyles) derives from the Vietnam era, but its central episode--a fixed football game--may ultimately be the most appropriate symbol for what happened in Korea.

Blair, Clay. *The Forgotten War: America in Korea, 1950-1953*. New York: Times, 1987.

Goulden, Joseph C. *Korea: the Untold Story of the War*. New York: McGraw-Hill, 1983.

Hastings, Max. *The Korean War*. New York: Schuster, 1987.

Sayre, Nora. *Running Time: Films of the Cold War*. New York: Dial, 1982.

Sklar, Robert. *Movie-Made America: How the Movies Changed American Life*. New York: Random, 1975.

FILMOGRAPHY

All the Young Men.** 86m, b/w. Dir. Hall Bartlett. With Alan Ladd, Sidney Poitier, James Darren, Glenn Corbett, Mort Sahl. Columbia, 1960.

An Annapolis Story.** 81m, color. Dir. Don Siegel. With John Derek, Diana Lynn, Kevin McCarthy. AA, 1955.

Back at the Front.** 87m, b/w. Dir. George Sherman. With Tom Ewell, Harvey Lembeck, Mari Blanchard, Richard Long. Universal, 1952.

The Bamboo Prison.** 79m, b/w. Dir. Lewis Seiler. With Robert Francis, Dianne Foster, Brian Keith, Jerome Courtland, E.G. Marshall, Earle Hyman. Columbia, 1955.

Battle Circus.* 89m, b/w. Dir. Richard Brooks. With Humphrey Bogart, June Allyson, Keenan Wynn, Robert Keith, Philip Ahn. MGM, 1953.

Battle Flame.* 78m, b/w. Dir. R.G. Springsteen. With Scott Petrie, Elaine Edwards, Robert Blake, Gordon Jones, Wayne Heffley, Richard Harrison. AA, 1959.

Battle Hymn.*** 108m, color. Dir. Douglas Sirk. With Rock Hudson, Martha Hyer, Anna Kashfi, Dan Duryea, Don DeFore. Universal, 1957.

Battle Taxi.** 82m, b/w. Dir. Herbert L. Strock. With Sterling Hayden, Arthur Franz, Marshall Thompson, Joey Marston, Leo Needham. UA, 1955.

Battle Zone.** 81m, b/w. Dir. Lesley Selander. With John Hodiak, Linda Christian, Stephen McNally, Philip Ahn. AA, 1952.

The Bridges at Toko-Ri.**** 102m, color. Dir. Mark Robson. With William Holden, Grace Kelly, Frederic March, Mickey Rooney, Robert Strauss. Paramount, 1954.

Recalled to active duty, Lt. Brubaker (Holden) has to reconcile the conflicting demands of his country and his family. The movie's ending is strikingly realistic. Based on the novel by James Michener. Best scene: the strategic bombing run amid antiaircraft fire (John Fulton won an

Oscar for special effects). Footnote: the bombing runs in *Star Wars* (1977) were influenced by Fulton's use of miniatures in *Bridges at Toko-Ri*.

Combat Squad.* 72m, b/w. Dir. Cy Roth. With John Ireland, Lon McCallister, Hal March, Tris Coffin. Columbia, 1953.

Dragonfly Squadron.** 82m, b/w. Dir. Lesley Selander. With John Hodiak, Barbara Britton, Bruce Bennett. AA, 1953.

The Eternal Sea.** 103m, b/w. Dir. John H. Auer. With Sterling Hayden, Alexis Smith, Dean Jagger, Ben Cooper, Virginia Drey. Republic, 1955.

Fixed Bayonets.*** 92m, b/w. Dir. Samuel Fuller. With Richard Basehart, Gene Evans, Michael O'Shea, Richard Hylton, Craig Hill. Fox, 1951.

Flight Nurse.** 90m, b/w. Dir. Allan Dwan. With Joan Leslie, Forrest Tucker, Jeff Donnell, Arthur Franz. Republic, 1953.

The Glory Brigade.** 82m, b/w. Dir. Robert D. Webb. With Victor Mature, Alexander Scourby, Lee Marvin, Richard Egan, Alvy Moore. Fox, 1953.

Hell's Horizon.** 78m, b/w. Dir. Tom Gries. With John Ireland, Marla English, Bill Williams, Hugh Beaumont, Jerry Paris, Kenneth Duncan. Columbia, 1955.

Hold Back the Night.** 80m, b/w. Dir. Allan Dwan. With John Payne, Mona Freeman, Peter Graves, Chuck Connors, Audrey Dalton. AA, 1956.

The Hook.** 98m, b/w. Dir. George Seaton. With Kirk Douglas, Robert Walker, Nick Adams. MGM, 1962.

The Hunters.*** 108m, color. Dir. Dick Powell. With Robert Mitchum, Robert Wagner, Richard Egan. Fox, 1958.

I Want You.** 102m, b/w. Dir. Mark Robson. With Dana Andrews, Dorothy McGuire, Farley Granger, Peggy Dow, Robert Keith. Goldwyn, 1951.

Inchon.* 140m, color. Dir. Terence Young. With Laurence Olivier, Jacqueline Bisset, Ben Gazzara, Toshiro Mifune, David Janssen. MGM, 1981.

Japanese War Bride.** 91m, b/w. Dir. King Vidor. With Shirley Yamaguchi, Don Taylor, Cameron Mitchell, Marie Windsor, James Bell, Louis Lorimar. Fox, 1952.

Jet Attack.* aka *Jet Squad*. 68m, b/w. Dir. Edward L. Cahn. With John Agar, Audrey Totter, Gregory Walcott, James Dobson. AIP, 1958.

Korea Patrol.* 59m, b/w. Dir. Max Nosseck. With Richard Emory, Al Eben, Benson Fong, Li Sun. EL, 1951.

MacArthur.*** 128m, color. Dir. Joseph Sargent. With Gregory Peck, Ed Flanders, Dan O'Herlihy, Ivan Bonar, Ward Costello. Universal, 1977.

The McConnell Story.*** 107m, color. Dir. Gordon Douglas. With Alan Ladd, June Allyson, James Whitmore. WB, 1955.

The Manchurian Candidate.**** 126m, b/w. Dir. John Frankenheimer. With Frank Sinatra, Laurence Harvey, Janet Leigh, Angela Lansbury, Henry Silva, James Gregory. UA, 1962.

   Suspenseful, Cold-War paranoia. The Chinese subject American soldiers to elaborate "brainwashing" techniques. One of them is unwittingly programmed to be an assassin upon being given a subliminal signal. Based on the novel by Henry Condon. Best sequence: a Chinese psychologist demonstrates the results of his experiments on the group's behavior. Footnote: "brainwashing" was a fearful motif during the Korean War.

Marines, Let's Go.* 103m, color. Dir. Raoul Walsh. With Tom Tryon, David Hedison, Barbara Stuart. Fox, 1961.

M*A*S*H.**** 116m, color. Dir. Robert Altman. With Donald Sutherland, Elliott Gould, Tom Skerritt, Sally Kellerman, Robert Duvall, Jo Ann Pflug, Rene Auberjonois, Roger Bowen, Gary Burghoff, Fred Williamson. Fox, 1970.

   A dark, hip and sometimes mean-spirited comedy about doctors in a medical unit acting crazy to stay sane during wartime. Won an Oscar for the screenplay by Ring Lardner, Jr., based on the novel by Richard Hooker. Altman uses realistic, seemingly aimless acting with overlapping dialogue. Gruesome scene: surgeons crack jokes as blood squirts up out of their patients. Footnote: Vietnam protests determined the look and attitude of this film, which was banned from showing at Army and Air Force theaters because, it was said, the film might lower the confidence of soldiers in military medicine.

Men in War.*** 104m, b/w. Dir. Anthony Mann. With Robert Ryan, Aldo Ray, Robert Keith, Vic Morrow, James Edwards, Scott Marlowe, Victor Sen Yung. UA, 1957.

Men of the Fighting Lady.** 79m, color. Dir. Andrew Marton. With Van Johnson, Walter Pidgeon, Louis Calhern, Dewey Martin, Keenan Wynn, Frank Lovejoy, Robert Horton, Bert Freed. MGM, 1954.

Mission Over Korea.* 85m, b/w. Dir. Fred F. Sears. With John Hodiak, John Derek, Maureen O'Sullivan, Audrey Totter. Columbia, 1953.

Mr. Walkie Talkie.* 65m, b/w. Dir. Fred L. Guiol. With William Tracy, Joe Sawyer, Margia Dean, Russell Hicks, Robert Shayne. Rockingham, 1952.

*The Nun and the Sergeant.*** 73m, b/w. Dir. Franklin Adreon. With Robert Webber, Anna Sten, Leo Gordon, Hari Rhodes, Robert Easton, Dale Ishimoto. UA, 1962.

*One Minute to Zero.*** 105m, b/w. Dir. Tay Garnett. With Robert Mitchum, Ann Blyth, William Talman, Richard Egan, Charles McGraw. RKO, 1952.

*Operation Dames.** 74m, b/w. Dir. Louis Clyde Stouman. With Eve Meyer, Chuck Henderson, Don Devlin, Ed Craig, Cindy Gerard. AIP, 1959.

*Pork Chop Hill.***** 97m, b/w. Dir. Lewis Milestone. With Gregory Peck, Harry Guardino, Rip Torn, George Peppard, James Edwards, Bob Steele, Woody Strode. UA, 1959.

The best combat-action film about Korea. In the waning days of the war, a grim company fights a bloody battle to take and keep a strategically meaningless hill. Best scene: the Chinese counterattack in waves. Based on the non-fiction book by S.L.A. Marshall. Footnote: Milestone also directed superlative WWI (*All Quiet*) and WWII (*A Walk in the Sun*) tributes to the ordinary foot soldier.

*Prisoner of War.*** 80m, b/w. Dir. Andrew Marton. With Ronald Reagan, Steve Forrest, Dewey Martin, Stephen Bekassy. MGM, 1954.

*The Rack.**** 100m, b/w. Dir. Arnold Laven. With Paul Newman, Wendell Corey, Walter Pidgeon, Edmond O'Brien, Anne Francis, Lee Marvin. MGM, 1956.

*Retreat, Hell!*** 95m, b/w. Dir. Joseph H. Lewis. With Frank Lovejoy, Richard Carlson, Russ Tamblyn. WB, 1952.

*Return from the Sea.*** 79m, b/w. Dir. Lesley Selander. With Jan Sterling, Neville Brand, John Doucette, Paul Langton, John Pickard. AA, 1954.

*Sabre Jet.*** 96m, color. Dir. Louis King. With Robert Stack, Coleen Gray, Richard Arlen, Julie Bishop. UA, 1953.

*Sayonara.**** 147m, color. Dir. Joshua Logan. With Marlon Brando, Ricardo Montalban, Red Buttons, Patricia Owens, Martha Scott, James Garner, Miiko Taka. WB, 1957.

*Sergeant Ryker.*** 86m, color. Dir. Buzz Kulik. With Lee Marvin, Bradford Dillman, Vera Miles, Peter Graves, Lloyd Nolan, Murray Hamilton. Universal, 1968.

*Sniper's Ridge.*** 61m, b/w. Dir. John Bushelman. With Jack Ging, Stanley Clements, John Goddard, Douglas Henderson. Fox, 1961.

*The Steel Helmet.***** 84m b/w. Dir. Samuel Fuller. With Gene Evans, Robert Hutton, Steve Brodie, James Edwards, Richard Loo, Sid Melton. Lippert, 1951.

A hard-boiled combat movie about a lost unit made up of stragglers. One sergeant (Evans), with a bullet hole in his helmet, had survived a POW massacre by feigning death. Best scene: the sergeant locates a sniper by tracing his line of fire. Footnote: Fuller made this remarkable low-budget film without the assistance of the Department of Defense.

*Submarine Command.*** 87m, b/w. Dir. John Farrow. With William Holden, Nancy Olson, William Bendix, Don Taylor. Paramount, 1951.

*Take the High Ground.*** 101m, color. Dir. Richard Brooks. With Richard Widmark, Karl Malden, Elaine Stewart, Steve Forrest, Carleton Carpenter. MGM, 1953.

*Tank Battalion.** 80m, b/w. Dir. Sherman A. Rose. With Don Kelly, Marjorie Hellen, Edward G. Robinson, Jr., Frank Gorshin. AIP, 1958.

*Target Zero.*** 92m, b/w. Dir. Harmon Jones. With Richard Conte, Peggie Castle, Charles Bronson, Richard Stapley, Chuck Connors. WB, 1955.

*Time Limit.**** 96m, b/w. Dir. Karl Malden. With Richard Widmark, Richard Basehart, June Lockhart, Delores Michaels, Rip Torn, James Douglas. UA, 1957.

*Tokyo File 212.** 84m, b/w. Dir. Dorrell and Stuart McGowan. With Florence Marly, Robert Peyton, Katsu kaika Haida, Reiko Otani, Tatsuo Saito. RKO, 1951.

*Torpedo Alley.*** 84m, b/w. Dir. Lew Landers. With Dorothy Malone, Mark Stevens, Charles Winninger, Bill Williams. AA, 1953.

*Wake Me When It's Over.*** 126m, color. Dir. Mervyn LeRoy. With Dick Shawn, Ernie Kovacs, Margo Moore, Jack Warden. Fox, 1960.

*War Hunt.*** 81m, b/w. Dir. Denis Sanders. With John Saxon, Robert Redford, Charles Aidman, Sydney Pollack. UA, 1962.

*War is Hell.*** 81m, b/w. Dir. Burt Topper. With Tony Russell, Baynes Barron, Tony Rich, Burt Topper. AA, 1964.

*A Yank in Indo-China.** 67m, b/w. Dir. Wallace A. Grissell. With John Archer, Douglas Dick, Jean Willes, Maura Murphy. Columbia, 1952.

*A Yank in Korea.** 73m, b/w. Dir. Lew Landers. With Lon McCallister, William Phillips, Brett King, Larry Stewart. Columbia, 1951.

*The Young and the Brave.** 84m, b/w. Dir. Francis D. Lyon. With Rory Calhoun, William Bendix, Richard Jaeckel, Manuel Padilla, Richard Arlen. MGM, 1963.

12

Vietnam War

CHRONOLOGY

Prelude, French War (1945-1954):

The French attempt to reassert control over their Southeast Asia colony following World War II (see *China Gate*, 1957; *Lost Command*, 1966).

16 May 1954. French are defeated at Dien Bien Phu. Vietnam is divided into communist North and pro-Western South.

American Advisory Stage (1963-1965):

U.S. advisors begin the "Americanization" of South Vietnamese anti-communist forces (see *Go Tell the Spartans*, 1978).

3 January 1963. Battle of Ap Bac. South Vietnamese are defeated by Viet Cong (communist guerrillas).

7 February 1965. Viet Cong attack a U.S. advisory compound near Pleiku.

American War Begins (1965):

February 1965. U.S. President Lyndon Johnson orders the bombing of North Vietnam: "Operation Rolling Thunder." Bombing continues intermittently for three and one-half years (see *Flight of the Intruder*, 1991).

May 1965. The anti-war movement on U.S. university campuses begins (see *Born on the Fourth of July*, 1989).

14 November 1965. Battle of Ia Drang. The U.S. 1st Airborne (Air Cavalry Division) defeats the North Vietnamese.

Stalemate (1965-1967):

American intervention prevents an immediate communist victory. Military stalemate and war of attrition develop (see *Platoon*, 1986).

Turning Point (1968):

29 January 1968. The Tet offensive. The Viet Cong and the North Vietnamese Army launch nationwide surprise attacks. Although U.S. and South Vietnamese forces rally, the Viet Cong achieve an important political victory: the American will to continue is broken (see *Full Metal Jacket*, 1987; *Gardens of Stone*, 1987; *Platoon*, 1986).

31 March 1968. President Johnson announces he will not seek re-election.

Search for a Way Out (1969-1973):

March 1969. News of the My Lai Massacre (March 1968) surfaces (see *Casualties of War*, 1989). The "Secret Bombing" of communist bases in Cambodia begins.

8-20 May 1969. The U.S. 101st Airborne attacks Hill 937 (see *Hamburger Hill*, 1982).

25 July 1969. President Richard Nixon announces "Vietnamization" as the basis for U.S. withdrawal.

March 1972. A conventional invasion by North Vietnamese fails.

May 1972. Haiphong Harbor is mined by U.S. forces.

December 1972. "Christmas Bombing" of North Vietnam begins.

Withdrawal and Defeat (1973-1975):

29 January 1973. Hanoi agrees to a cease-fire arrangement.

August 1973. U.S. Congress prohibits further U.S. involvement. South Vietnam fights alone (see *The Killing Fields*, 1984).

30 April 1975. Communist forces parade into Saigon, renamed Ho Chi Minh City.

COMMENTARY

"Such movies as *The Green Berets* and the *The Deer Hunter* should perhaps be seen as less *about* the Vietnam war...than *part* of it--part, at least, of how it was perceived by Americans," observes Gilbert Adair (142). Indeed, our understanding of the past is always a *perception* of what happened. All that Americans have left of the Vietnam experience are certain memories--what they remember or want to remember.

Soldiers in the 1960s and 1970s "carried heroic war images [culled from World War II movies] with them to Vietnam" (Auster and Quart 1). In the 1990s soldiers in the desert of eastern Saudi Arabia were modeling their behavior on Vietnam war films. Not *The Green Berets*, but rather anti-war films like *Apocalypse Now*, *Platoon* or *Full Metal Jacket*. (For instance, during the Gulf War a story circulated about an officer who asked his young lieutenant to construct 'Nam-style latrines. The lieutenant, not old enough to have been in Vietnam, said he would construct them like in the movie *Platoon*.) Had anti-war films make Americans less eager to fight in the Persian Gulf? Apparently not, "For these guys it makes no difference that Vietnam movies are anti-war movies. The pro and anti of them means nothing. They are war, and the same way that *Sands of Iwo Jimo* was war for the men who went to Vietnam" (Allen). One young marine lance corporal who had seen *Platoon* said, "There is always glory. Nothing can compare to war. There is nothing more manly than proving yourself in war. If you can prove yourself there--everybody would like to go home, but there's that little part that will be disappointed if we do nothing" (qtd. in Allen).

Allen concludes that "the last war is like some tribal god that gets toted through the village on feast days, year after year, cracked and painted until after a while you can hardly recognize it." The allure of the old god remains as strong as ever. It was true of World War I: "The term *Lost Generation* conjures up images of sad-eyed veterans [see *In Country* (1989) for the Vietnam equivalent] denouncing war and urging peace upon future generations. The reality is more complex. Much feeling in Britain and America remained as positive about the value of war after 1914-1918 as it had been before" (Adams 113).

Why should the popular image of Vietnam be any different? What about "the lost generation" of Vietnam? Pro-war and anti-war films exist side by side or viewers simply misinterpret or ignore the message. Thus, on the eve of the Persian Gulf war, *Flight of the Intruder* (1991) appeared, which emphasized the frustrations of the Vietnam war. The film shows "two rebellious U.S Navy fighter pilots defying Washington policy and bombing the enemy capital of North Vietnam" (Sujo). If we could not win the war in Vietnam, we could get revenge in the movie theaters. "They were cheering at a screening in San Diego. We had to turn people away," said Brad Johnson, the film's lead (qtd. in Westbrook). Such films (the Rambo movies, for instance) are about revenge or fulfillment or war as adventure. We should understand that for many Americans, perhaps the majority, Vietnam was unpopular not because this particular war was cruel or horrible or stupid, but because they came to believe that America was not allowed a victory under the political rules of engagement. As a young marine said before the conflict with Iraq, "I just hope that this time they turn us loose here and let us win it" (qtd. in Allen). The slogan "No more Vietnams!" always meant different things to the anti-war and pro-war factions.

Some have thought that Vietnam had changed forever the way we see war, that America's traditional optimism had been replaced by "distrust, alienation, a loss of history, and a huddled-over sense of self-protection" (Aufderheide 111). Paul Fussell calls Vietnam a "post-modern war." By this he means that the old understanding of war no longer applies: "One characteristic of post-modern procedure in the arts is a self-consciousness bordering on contempt about the very medium or genre one is working in, amounting to disdain for the public's respect and even awe that normally attend such artifacts--the works of Andy Warhol are a well-known example" (Fussell 656). True, perhaps, for some, but for the general public Norman Rockwell has always been more popular than Andy Warhol.

Adair, Gilbert. *Hollywood's Vietnam: From "The Green Berets" to "Apocalypse Now."* New York: Proteus, 1981.

Adams, Michael C.C. *The Great Adventure: Male Desire and the Coming of World War I.* Bloomington: Indiana UP, 1990.

Allen, Henry. "Movies color soldier's view of war." *Washington Post.* Rpt. in the *Houston Chronicle* 6 Jan. 1991: A18.

Aufderheide, Pat. "Good Soldiers." *Seeing Through Movies.* Ed. Mark Crispin Miller. New York: Pantheon, 1991.

Auster, Albert, and Leonard Quart. *How the War Was Remembered: Hollywood and Vietnam.* New York: Praeger, 1988.

Fussell, Paul, ed. *The Norton Book of Modern War.* New York: Norton, 1991.

Sujo, Aly. "U.S. Films Hawking War as Clock Ticks." *Houston Chronicle* 15 Jan. 1991: D1.

Westbrook, Bruce. "Film Taught Actor Respect for Pilots." *Houston Chronicle* 18 Jan. 1991: E3.

FILMOGRAPHY

*Air America.*** 113m, color. Dir. Roger Spottiswoode. With Mel Gipson, Robert Downey, Jr. Carolco, 1990.

*Angkor: Cambodia Express.** 96m, color. Dir. Lek Kitiparaporn. With Robert Walker, Jr., Christopher George, Woody Strode, Nancy Kwan. Monarex, 1986.

*The Annihilators.** 84m, color. Dir. Charles E. Sellier. With Christopher Stone, Andy Wood. New World, 1985.

*Apocalypse Now.***** 139m, color. Dir. Francis Ford Coppola. With Marlon Brando, Martin Sheen, Robert Duvall, Frederic Forrest, Dennis Hopper, Sam Bottoms, Harrison Ford, Larry Fishburne, Albert Hall. UA, 1979.
   In a surreal hellish warzone, CIA agent (Sheen) must assassinate a psychotic American officer (Brando). Oscar for photography. Best scene: helicopters, blaring a tape recording of Wagner's "Ride of the Valkyries," destroy a Viet Cong village. The plot is influenced by Joseph Conrad's novella *Heart of Darkness*. Footnote: this weird masterpiece is fortunate to have survived Coppola's legendary cost overruns.

Born on the Fourth of July.**** 144m, color. Dir. Oliver Stone. With Tom Cruise, Raymond J. Barry, Caroline Kava, Willem Dafoe, Kara Sedgwick, Tom Berenger. Orion, 1989.

A stomach-churning experience. The war and its aftermath cause a wounded veteran (Cruise) to re-examine his notions of heroism and patriotism. Based on the memoirs of Ron Kovic. Best combat scene: in the confusion of battle, a GI accidentally kills his buddy. Footnote: the film prompted a Congressional investigation into the quality of medical attention in Veterans' hospitals.

The Boys in Company C.** 125m, color. Dir. Sidney J. Furie. With Stan Shaw, Craig Wasson, Andrew Stevens, Michael Lembeck, James Whitmore, Jr. Columbia, 1978.

Braddock: Missing in Action III.* 101m, color. Dir. Aaron Norris. With Chuck Norris, Aki Aleong. Cannon, 1988.

Casualties of War.*** 120m, color. Dir. Brian DePalma. With Michael J. Fox, Sean Penn, Thuy Thu Le. RCA, 1989.

Coming Home.*** 126m, color. Dir. Hal Ashby. With Jane Fonda, Bruce Dern, Jon Voight, Robert Carradine. UA, 1978.

The Crazy World of Julius Vrooder.* aka *Vrooder's Hooch.* 98m, color. Dir. Arthur Hiller. With Timothy Bottoms, Barbara Seagull, Lawrence Pressman, Albert Salmi, Richard A. Dysart, Dena Dietrich. Fox, 1974.

The Deer Hunter.**** 183m, color. Dir. Michael Cimino. With Robert De Niro, Christopher Walken, Meryl Streep, John Cazale, John Savage. Columbia, 1978.

A gut-wrenching allegory about the war's effect on blue-collar America. The film shifts explosively from a warm familial Ukranian community in Ohio to the insanity of war in Vietnam. Footnote: gambling on Russian roulette is a fiction. Oscars for best picture, director and supporting actor (Walken).

Don't Cry It's Only Thunder.** 108m, color. Dir. Peter Werner. With Dennis Christopher, Susan Saint James, Roger Aaron Brown, Robert Englund, James Whitmore, Jr. Sanrio, 1982.

84 Charlie Mopic.**** 95m, color. Dir. Patrick Duncan. With Jonathon Emerson, Nicholas Cascone, Jason Tomlins, Christopher Burgard, Glenn Morshower. New Cen, 1989.

A fictional six-man reconnaissance mission as seen entirely through the lens of a hand-held camera of an Army Motion Picture (MoPic) Unit cameraman. Fascinating attention to small realistic details, like GIs burying chewing gum wrappers to hide their presence from the enemy. Footnote: Duncan, a former Vietnam infantryman, shot the film near Los Angeles using Super 16mm film.

Flight of the Intruder.* color. Dir. John Milius. With Danny Glover, Brad Johnson, Willem Dafoe. Tri-Star, 1991.

Full Metal Jacket.**** 116m, color. Dir. Stanley Kubrick. With Matthew Modine, Adam Baldwin, Vincent D'Onofrio, Lee Armey, Dorian Harewood. WB, 1987.

In the first and better half of the movie, a Marine platoon trains at boot camp at Paris Island. Their training is brutal, obscene, dehumanizing, and self-defeating. In the second half, the platoon fights in the 1968 Tet Offensive. Best sequence: a unit moves across the devastated cityscape of Hue while singing the Mickey Mouse Club anthem. Footnote: Michael Herr, author of *Dispatches*, a surrealistic account of Vietnam, co-authored the script.

Gardens of Stone.** 111m, color. Dir. Francis Coppola. With James Caan, Angelica Huston, James Earl Jones, Mary Stuart Masterson, D.B. Sweeney. Tri-Star, 1987.

Go Tell the Spartans.**** 114m, color. Dir. Ted Post. With Burt Lancaster, Craig Wesson, Marc Singer, Joe Unger, Jonathan Goldsmith. Spartan, 1978.

Army brass mishandle the early days of the war after the French have left. Unsentimental yet poignant treatment. Based on the novel, *Incident at Muc Wa* by Daniel Ford (1967). Fine fire fight scene. Offers insight into why the war failed. Lancaster is impressive as a washed up major with a sense of integrity. Footnote: after the last scene, instead of "the end" we see projected "1964."

Good Morning Vietnam.*** 121m, color. Dir. Barry Levinson. With Robin Williams, Forest Whitaker. Buena Vista, 1984.

The Green Berets.**** 141m, color. Dir. John Wayne, Ray Kellogg. With John Wayne, David Janssen, Jim Hutton, Aldo Ray, Raymond St. Jacques, Bruce Cabot, Jack Soo, Patrick Wayne. WB, 1968.

Important as an attempt (which critics called inane, stupid, and absurd) to interpret Vietnam in terms of World War II. Based on the novel by Robin Moore. Best scene: tough Special Forces NCOs defend the war to dovish reporters. Footnote: a jungle encampment ("John Wayne Village") built for the film at Fort Bragg, N.C., is still used as a training site for jungle warfare.

Hail, Hero!* 97m, color. Dir. David Miller. With Michael Douglas, Arthur Kennedy, Teresa Wright, John Larch. Cinema, 1969.

Hamburger Hill.**** 110m, color. Dir. John Irvin. With Michael Dolan, Daniel O'Shea, Anthony Barille, Michael Patrick Boatman. RKO, 1987.

A unit of the 101st Airborne Division repeatedly attacks Hill 937. More realistic and less symbolic than Oliver Stone's better known *Platoon*. Haunting musical score by minimalist composer Philip Glass. Best scene: at last on top of the hill, the troops are mistakenly gunned down by machine guns from their own helicopters. Footnote: the commander of the division at the time claimed that no such battle ever took place. It was, he said, the creation of the media from a series of isolated events.

*The Hanoi Hilton.** 130m, color. Dir. Lionel Chetwynd. With Michael Moriarty, Jeffrey Jones, Paul LeMat, Lawrence Pressman. Cannon, 1987.

*In Country.*** 116m, color. Dir. Norman Jewison. With Bruce Willis, Emily Lloyd, Joan Allen. WB, 1989.

*The Iron Triangle.** 91m color. Dir. Eric Weston. With Beau Bridges, Haing S Ngor, Johnny Hallyday. Scotti Bros., 1989.

*Jacknife.*** 102m, color. Dir. David Jones. With Robert De Niro, Ed Harris, Kathy Baker, Charles Dutton, Loudon Wainwright III. 1989.

*The Killing Fields.**** 141m, color. Dir. Roland Joffe. With Sam Waterson, Haing S Ngor, John Malkovich, Julian Sands, Craig T. Nelson, Bill Paterson, Athol Fugard. WB, 1984.

Based on true story of reporter Sidney Schanberg (Waterston) and his native translator Dith Pran (Ngor) after the U.S. withdraws from Cambodia. Oscars for Ngor, cinematography, and editing. The entire movie has a suspenseful, horrific impact. Best scene: frantic scramble for the last U.S. helicopters to leave Phnom Penh.

*The Last Hunter.** aka *The Hunter of the Apocalypse*. 95m, color. Dir. Anthony M. Dawsom. With David Warbeck, Tisa Farrow, Tony King, Bobby Rhodes. Northal, 1984.

*Limbo.*** aka *Woman in Limbo, Chained to Yesterday*. 111m, color. Dir. Mark Robson. With Kate Jackson, Katherine Justice, Stuart Margolin, Hazel Medina. Universal, 1972.

*The Line.** 95m, color. Dir. Robert J. Siegel. With Russ Thacker, Lewis J. Stadlen, Brad Sullivan, Kathleen Tolan, Jacqueline Brooks, David Doyle, Erik Estrada. Enterprise, 1982.

*The Losers.** 95m, color. Dir. Jack Starrett. With William Smith, Bernie Hamilton, Adam Roarke, Houston Savage, Eugene Cornelius. Fanfare, 1970.

*Lost Command.*** 130m, color. Dir. Mark Robson. With Anthony Quinn, Alain Delon, George Segal, Claudia Cardinale. Red Lion, 1966.

Missing in Action.** Dir. Joseph Zito. With Chuck Norris, M. Emmet Walsh, Lenoire Kastorf, James Hong. Cannon, 1984.

Missing in Action 2--The Beginning.* 96m, color. Dir. Lance Hool. With Chuck Norris, Soon-Teck Oh, Steven Williams. Cannon, 1985.

Off Limits.* aka *Saigon*. 102m, color. Dir. Christopher Crowe. With Willem Defoe, Gregory Hines, Fred Ward, Amanda Pays. Fox, 1988.

Operation CIA.* aka *Last Message From Saigon*. 90m, b/w. Dir. Christian Nyby. With Burt Reynolds, Kieu Chink, Danielle Aubry, John Hoyt, Cyril Collick. AA, 1965.

Outside In.* 90m, color. Dir. Allen Baron. With Darrel Larson, Heather Menzies, Denis Olivieri, John Bill, Peggy Feury. Robbins, 1972.

Parades.* aka *Break Loose*. 95m, color. Dir. Robert J. Siegel. With Russ Thacker, Brad Sullivan, David Doyle, Lewis J Stadlen, Dorothy Chace. Cinerama, 1972.

Platoon.**** 120m, color. Dir. Oliver Stone. With Tom Berenger, Willem Dafoe, Charlie Sheen, Forest Whitaker, Francesco Quinn, John C. McGinley, Richard Edson, Kevin Dillon, Reggie Johnson, Keith David, Dale Dye. Orion, 1986.

> The definitive Vietnam film. Oscars for picture, director, editing, and sound. An innocent recruit (Sheen) is caught between evil (Berenger) and good (Dafoe) sergeants. The film's atmosphere is palpable and the details of a grunt's life are frighteningly realistic. Best scene: breathstopping exploration of a Viet Cong tunnel. Footnote: Stone, writer and director, based it on his own experiences in Vietnam.

P.O.W. The Escape.* aka *Behind Enemy Lines*. 90m, color. Dir. Gideon Amir. With David Carradine, Charles R. Floyd, Mako, Steve James, Phil Brock. Cannon, 1986.

Purple Hearts.** 115m, color. Dir. Sidney J. Furie. With Cheryl Ladd, Ken Wahl, James Whitmore, Jr. WB, 1984.

Rambo: First Blood Part II.**** 95m, color. Dir. George P. Cosmatos. With Sylvester Stallone, Richard Crenna, Charles Napier, Steven Berkoff, Julia Nickson. Tri-Star, 1985.

> An influential formula film. He-man veteran (Stallone) returns to Vietnam to rescue abandoned MIAs. He defeats the communists with explosive arrows, then wreaks havoc upon deceitful American officials. Said President Ronald Reagan: "Boy, I saw *Rambo* last night; now I know what to do next time." Best line: Rambo asks an American agent, "This time, do we get to win?" Footnote: this box-office success opened the door for serious movies about Vietnam, a subject largely considered taboo by filmmakers.

Rolling Thunder.** 99m, color. Dir. John Flynn. With William Devane, Tommy Lee Jones, Linda Haynes, Lisa Richards, Dabney Coleman. AIP, 1977.

Rumor of War.*** 200m, color. Dir. Richard T. Heffron. With Brad Davis, Keith Carradine, Michael O'Keefe, Richard Bradford, Stacy Keach. HBO, 1980.

Search and Destroy.** 93m, color. Dir. William Fruet. With Perry King, Don Stroud, Tisa Farrow, Park Jong Soo, George Kennedy. Film V, 1981.

Some Kind of Hero.*** 97m, color. Dir. Michael Pressman. With Richard Pryor, Margot Kidder, Ron Cox, Olivia Cole, Lynne Moody, Ray Sharkey. Paramount, 1982.

Southern Comfort.*** 100m, color. Dir. Walter Hill. With Keith Carradine, Powers Boothe, Fred Ward, Lewis Smith, Peter Coyote. Fox, 1981.

There Is No 13.** 91m, color. Dir. William Sachs. With Mark Damon, Margaret Markov, Harvey Lembeck, Jean Jennings, Lee Moore. Film V, 1977.

To the Shores of Hell.* 82m, color. Dir. Will Zens. With Marshall Thompson, Kiva Lawrence, Richard Jordahl, Robert Dornan, Jeff Pearl. Crown, 1966.

Tracks.** 90m, color. Dir. Henry Jaglom. With Dennis Hopper, Taryn Power, Dean Stockwell, Topo Swope. Trio, 1976.

Uncommon Valor.**** 105m, color. Dir. Ted Kotcheff. With Gene Hackman, Fred Ward, Reb Brown, Harold Sylvester, Tim Thomerson, Patrick Swayze, Robert Stack, Tex Cobb. Paramount, 1983.

   The first and best of the "return to 'Nam" movies. A retired Marine colonel (Hackman) assembles a rescue team to search for his MIA son. Best sequence: the ragtag team trains in the Texas desert. Footnote: Vietnam veteran Chuck Taylor trained the actors.

Welcome Home, Soldier Boys.* aka *Five Days Home*. 91m, color. Dir. Richard Compton. With Joe Don Baker, Paul Koslo, Alan Vint, Elliott Street, Jennifer Billingsley. Fox, 1972.

Who'll Stop the Rain?* 125m, color. Dir. Karel Reisz. With Nick Nolte, Tuesday Weld, Michael Moriarty. UA, 1978.

A Yank in Viet-Nam.** 80m, b/w. Dir. Marshall Thompson. With Marshall Thompson, Enrique Magalona, Mario Barri, Kien Chinh, Urban Drew. AA, 1964.

13

Banana Wars and Interventions

CHRONOLOGY

China:

1900-1901. The Boxer Rebellion (see *55 Days at Peking*, 1963).

1920s-1930s. American gunboats protect U.S. interests during Chinese nationalist upheavals (see *The Sand Pebbles*, 1966).

Morocco:

1904. Teddy Roosevelt orders ships and marines to a North African sultanate (see *The Wind and the Lion*, 1975).

Mexico:

1914. The U.S. Navy seizes the city of Veracruz.

1916-1917. U.S. General Pershing's expeditionary force hunts down Pancho Villa who had raided Columbus, New Mexico. Pershing fails to catch Villa but clashes with Mexican government forces in Northern Mexico.

Central America:

Guatemala: 1920.

El Salvador: 1932; 1981-present: U.S. advisors and weapons are
    sent to aid government forces fighting Marxist-led rebels
    (see *Salvador*, 1986).

Honduras: 1903; 1907; 1911; 1912; 1919; 1924-1925.

Nicaragua: 1898; 1899; 1910; 1912-1925; 1926-1933; 1981-1990:
    America aids anti-Sandinista (anti-Marxist) "Contra" rebels
    (see *Under Fire*, 1983; *Walker*, 1987).

Panama: 1903; 1908; 1912; 1918-1920; 1991.

Caribbean Islands:

Cuba: 1898-1902: Spanish-American War (see *Santiago*, 1956); 1906-
    1909; 1912; 1917-1933; 1961: U.S.-backed invasion at the
    Bay of Pigs fails; 1962: Cuban Missile Crisis results in
    nuclear standoff between the United States and the Soviet
    Union.

Haiti: 1915-1934.

Puerto Rico: 1898: Spain cedes Puerto Rico to the United States.

Grenada: 1983: The United States and its Caribbean allies invade
    Grenada (see *Heartbreak Ridge*, 1987) to protect American
    lives and prevent the establishment of a Cuban-East
    European military base.

North Africa and the Middle East:

Libya: 14 April 1986: U.S. sends planes to bomb Libyan "terrorist
    centers" (see *Top Gun*, 1985, and *Iron Eagle*, 1986, for a
    sense of international tension and high-tech warfare).

Iraq and Kuwait: 1991: The United States and its United
    Nations allies use superior technological warfare to liberate
    Kuwait from Iraqi forces in the Persian Gulf War.

COMMENTARY

American military incursions in China (during the Boxer Rebellion), Mexico, or the Caribbean and Central America (so-called "Banana Wars") have attracted slight attention from filmmakers. Designed primarily to protect American commercial and strategic interests, these interventions lack the scope and high purpose of larger conflicts. Nevertheless a few films in this category are noteworthy.

The movie *55 Days at Peking* (1963) deals approvingly with the participation of a multi-national (America, Germany, Britain, France, and Japan) intervention in China in 1904. Although the epic plotting is a bit heavy and confused, stand-in director Andrew Marton created some impressive action scenes.

Revolution and unrest in Mexico between 1900 and 1921 inspired films dealing with American mercenaries, including *Bandido* (1956), *The Professionals* (1966), and *The Five Man Army* (1970). Intervention in the poverty-stricken and unstable Central-American "banana republic" of Nicaragua is depicted in forgettable action films like *The Marines Fly High* (1940). But the best film in this genre is a comedy by Woody Allen, *Bananas* (1971), that pokes fun at revolutions and interventions. The fictional republic of San Marcos is taken over by an inept New York nebbech who is merely trying to impress his political activist girl friend.

Four recent films criticize American military policy in the region. The director of *Z* (1969), Constantin Costa-Gavras shows us in *Missing* (1982) how an ordinary American learns to his horror that the U.S. government stirred up the coup in Chile that led to the death of his own son and Salvador Allende. In *Under Fire* (1983), we identify with an American photographer trying to avoid taking sides in the Sandinista revolution in Nicaragua until he discovers the corruption created by Anastasio Somoza's rightist government. Oliver Stone's *Salvador* (1986) shows us another cynical journalist converted by the chaotic conflict in El Salvador while the United States blithely supports the war. *Walker* (1987), a surrealistic leftist film made with the cooperation of the Marxist Sandinista regime, recounts the attempt by American military adventurer William Walker to set himself up as dictator of Nicaragua in the 1850s. In heavy handed allegory that suggests the 1970s, director Alex Cox portrays the American invaders as murderers, rapists, racists, cowards and lunatics.

Clint Eastwood's *Heartbreak Ridge* (1986) gives a pro-American slant to his depiction of the 1983 invasion of Grenada. Eastwood focuses on the hard training Marines who fight to protect American lives and prevent the establishment of a Marxist base supported by Cuba. Like the *Rambo* films, *Heartbreak Ridge* seeks revenge for Vietnam (Americans "win one this time"). A spate of films that imagined little engagements won by hotshot teenagers (see *Iron Eagle*, 1986) have proved popular box office attractions.

The "Hundred-Hour War" against Iraq in February 1991 will no doubt inspire its own films. The brilliant performance and high morale of the American professional forces may put an end to the emphasis on moral confusion and defeat characteristic of most Vietnam films. A Reuters News Service story out of Los Angeles says that Hollywood is "ready to cash in on a new-found patriotism with films about the Iraqi war that recapture the glory of victory." A studio executive is quoted as saying, "It's sort of back to the World War II gung-ho war movies" ("Light, Camera, Action!"). Movies may result with hot titles like *Desert Shield*, *Human Shield*, and *Shield of Honor*.

"Lights, Camera, Action! Hollywood Eyes Gulf War." *Houston Chronicle* 13 Mar. 1991: A17.

FILMOGRAPHY

*Bananas.***** 82m, color. Dir. Woody Allen. With Woody Allen, Louise Lasser, Carlos Montalban. UA, 1971.
    Fielding Mellish (Allen), trying to make it with a political activist (Lasser), ends up as president of the imaginary Latin American republic of San Marcos. Irreverent satire is often right on target. Footnote: Sylvester Stalone has a bit part as a hoodlum.
*Bandido.**** 92m, color. Dir. Richard O. Fleischer. With Robert Mitchum, Zachary Scott, Ursula Theiss. UA, 1956.
*55 Days at Peking.**** 150m, color. Dir. Nicholas Ray. With Charlton Heston, Ava Gardner, David Niven, Flora Robson. AA, 1963.
*The Five Man Army.** 107m, color. Dir. Don Taylor. With Peter Graves, James Daly, Bud Spencer. MGM, 1970.
*Heartbreak Ridge.***** 130m, color. Dir. Clint Eastwood. With Clint Eastwood, Marsha Mason, Everett McGill. WB, 1986.
    An anachronistic gunnery sergeant Tom Highway (Eastwood) toughens up his unit, which will take part in the 1983 invasion of Grenada. Surprising depth of characterization, especially in the relationship between

Highway and his ex-wife (Mason). Best scene: when its combat radio breaks down, a Marine unit uses a long-distance credit card to patch through a public telephone call for artillery support. Footnote: Eastwood purposely delaying filming scenes unfavorable to the Marine Corps until the end of production in case the Corps might decide to withdraw its valuable technical assistance.

The In-Laws.*** 103m, color. Dir. Arthur Hiller. With Peter Falk, Alan Arkin, Richard Libertini, Arlene Golonka, Nancy Dassault, Ed Begley, Jr. WB, 1979.

Iron Eagle.* Dir. Sidney J. Furie. With Lou Gossett, Jr., Jason Gedrick, Tim Thomerson. Tri-Star, 1986.

The Marines Fly High (1940).** 60m, b/w. Dir. George Nicholls, Jr., Ben Stoloff. With Richard Dix, Chester Morris, Lucille Ball. MGM, 1940.

Missing.*** 1922m, color. Dir. Constantin Costa-Gavras. With Jack Lemmon, Sissy Spacek, John Shea. Universal, 1982.

Moon Over Parador.** 105m, color. Dir. Paul Mazursky. With Richard Dreyfuss, Raul Julia, Sonia Braga, Jonathan Winters, Charo, Sammy Davis, Jr. Universal, 1988.

The Professionals.*** 117m, color. Dir. Richard Brooks. With Burt Lancaster, Lee Marvin, Robert Ryan, Jack Palance. Columbia, 1966.

Salvador.**** 123m, color. Dir. Oliver Stone. With James Woods, James Belushi, Michael Murphy, John Savage, Elpedia Carrillo. Hemdale, 1986.

A hip, irreverent photo-journalist views the 1980-1981 situation in the corrupt, war-torn Central American state. Best sequence: the horrors of the garbage dump where the bodies of those killed by death squads periodically end up. Footnote: as a companion to the film, read Joan Didion's *Salvador* (New York: Simon and Schuster, 1983).

The Sand Pebbles.**** 195m, color. Dir. Robert Wise. With Steve McQueen, Richard Crenna, Candice Bergen, Richard Attenborough, Marayat Andrianne, Mako, Larry Gates. Fox, 1966.

Life aboard an American gunboat on the Yangtze River in 1926. Navy life is depicted as crude, somewhat corrupt, and without real purpose. One reviewer saw it as an early Vietnam allegory film. Best sequence: a crew member explains to a new transfer the role that natives play in maintaining the vessel. Footnote: this view of military life is similar to the image of the pre-war Army in *From Here to Eternity* (1953).

*Santiago.*** 93m, color. Dir. Gordon Douglas. With Alan Ladd, Lloyd Nolan, Rossana Podestsa, Chill Wills. WB, 1956.

*Top Gun.*** Dir Tony Scott. With Tom Cruise, Anthony Edwards, Kelly McGillis. Paramount, 1986.

*Under Fire.**** 127m, color. Dir. Roger Spottiswoode. With Nick Nolte, Ed Harris, Gene Hackman, Joanna Cassidy, Rene Enriquez. Lion's Gate, 1983.

*Walker.**** 95m, color. Dir. Alex Cox. With Ed Harris, Richard Masur, Peter Boyle. Universal, 1987.

*The Wind and the Lion.**** 119m, color. Dir John Milius. With Sean Connery, Candice Bergen, Brian Keith, John Huston. UA, 1975.

14

Nuclear Warfare

CHRONOLOGY

Prelude (1941-1945):

1941. The "Manhattan Project," aimed at developing atomic bombs, begins. The government, major universities, and corporations employ 120,000 scientists and workers in the "war's best kept secret" (see *Fat Man and Little Boy*, 1989).

16 July 1945. The first successful atomic-bomb testing occurs at Alamogordo, New Mexico.

Dropping of the A-Bombs (1945):

6 August 1945. Hiroshima is devastated by an atomic bomb (see *Above and Beyond*, 1953).

9 August 1945. A second atomic bomb, dropped on Nagasaki, contributes to Japan's surrender less than a month later (see also Chapters 9 and 10).

Cold War and the Arms Race (1949-1990):

1949. The Soviet Union tests its first atomic weapon.

1952. The United States successfully tests a new hydrogen super bomb.

1953. U.S. President Dwight D. Eisenhower hints that atomic weapons might be used to bring the Korean War to an end.

1954. The Eisenhower administration announces a nuclear deterrent policy of "massive retaliation" in the event of general war (see *Strategic Air Command*, 1955).

1961. The Soviet Union tests a larger hydrogen bomb.

1962. Cuban Missile Crisis precipitates a nuclear standoff between the United States and the Soviet Union. The Soviets blink.

1963. A "hot line" phone link between the U.S. and Soviet Union is set up to prevent accidental war (see *Fail-Safe*, 1964).

1964. The People's Republic of China ("Red China") tests its atomic weapon.

1977. U.S. President Jimmy Carter talks of developing new neutron bombs that will limit destruction during a nuclear exchange.

1983. U.S. President Ronald Reagan announces plans to develop the Strategic Defense Initiative weapons system, known popularly as the "Star Wars" defense (named after the science fiction film *Star Wars*, 1977). The Soviets cannot compete.

1990-1991. The Cold War comes to an end. Its economy in ruins, the Soviet empire begins to collapse. The arms race becomes less important.

COMMENTARY

Films about nuclear warfare show us little or nothing about the experience of combat or the experience of war in general. The majority of these films are cleverly summarized in the parody of lobby card advertisements on the cover of Mick Broderick's survey of 500 feature-length "nuclear" pictures:

SEE...a boy become a giant from eating the irradiated heart of Frankenstein's monster, after it is shipped to Hiroshima by Axis Fiends!

WATCH...as New York, Los Angeles, Moscow, Sydney, Paris etc., are all devastated in spectacular firestorms from mass attacks by nuclear weapons!

THRILL...to gangsters, in league with an ex-Nazi scientist, as they create a private army by sawing off human scalps and replacing brains with atomic energy!

GASP...when The Beast from 20,000 Fathoms, Godzilla, Rodan, mutant spiders, ants and crabs carve radioactive trails of destruction across the screen!

Nowhere is there an attempt to evoke what a general war resulting in a limited nuclear exchange (the most likely scenario) would really be like. Perhaps a film based on General Sir John Hackett's brilliantly conceived book *The Third World War, August 1985* could do it. Read his description of the atomic bombing of Birmingham, England.

Nevertheless, a few films honestly probe some issues. *Fail-Safe* (1964) and *The Bedford Incident* (1965) concern the possibilities of war by accident. David Greene's *World War III* (1982) deals with a Soviet invasion of Alaska and a nuclear alert. *On the Beach* (1959) and *The Day After* (1983) hauntingly describe the aftermath of nuclear warfare. Films like *Strategic Air Command* (1955), *Bombers B-52* (1957), and *A Gathering of Eagles* (1963) emphasize the competence of the military and "argue...for a strong and ever-vigilant nuclear deterrent" (Broderick 20).

Future war as teenage adventure is shown in *Red Dawn* (1984), a film for the Reagan years about a band of patriotic youngsters who defeat the Russians and their Cuban mercenaries in a ludicrously imagined post-nuclear guerrilla war fought in America's heartland. The box office also seems to love teenage heroes who bring us to and from the brink of nuclear war in fantasies like *WarGames* (1983) and *The Manhattan Project* (1986).

The best movie about nuclear warfare speaks to adult anxieties in a starkly black comedy, Stanley Kubrick's brilliant *Dr. Strangelove: Or How I Learned to Stop Worrying and Love the Bomb* (1964). The film eloquently dramatizes warfare in which strategy and tactics have become meaningless. It is an absurd world where the end is only a button-push away and the button pushers are insane enough to enjoy their work. U.S. General Buck Turgidson (George C. Scott), an opportunist who sees advantages to be gained in a nuclear first strike, accepts the accident that offers opportunity, although he admits: "I'm not saying we won't get our hair messed. But I do say no more than ten to twenty million killed, tops--depending on the breaks."

Broderick, Mick. *Nuclear Movies: A Filmography*. Northcote, Australia: Post-Modern, 1988.

Hackett, John. *The Third World War, August 1985*. New York: Macmillian, 1979.

FILMOGRAPHY

Above and Beyond.*** 122m, b/w. Dir. Melvin Frank, Norman Panama. With Robert Taylor, Eleanor Parker, Jim Backus, James Whitmore. MGM, 1953.

The Bedford Incident.*** 102m, b/w. Dir. James B. Harris. With Richard Widmark, Sidney Poitier, James MacArthur, Martin Balsom, Wally Cox. Columbia, 1965.

The Beginning or the End.** 110m, b/w. Dir. Norman Taurog. With Brian Donlevy, Robert Walker, Tom Drake, Hume Cronyn, Audrey Totter, Godfrey Tearle. MGM, 1947.

Bombers B-52.** 106m, b/w. Dir. Gordon Douglas. With Natalie Wood, Karl Malden, Efrem Zimbalist, Jr. Columbia, 1957.

The Day After.*** 126m, color. Dir. Nicholas Meyer. With Jason Robards, Jr., JoBeth Williams, John Lithgow, Steve Guttenberg. Embassy, 1983.

Dr. Strangelove: Or How I Learned to Stop Worrying and Love the Bomb.**** 102m, b/w. Dir. Stanley Kubrick. With Peter Sellers, George C. Scott, Peter Bull, Sterling Hayden, Keenan Wynn, Slim Pickens, James Earl Jones, Tracy Reed. Columbia, 1964.

One-of-a-kind satirical masterpiece pokes fun at the possibility of world conflagration. Brilliant acting and a marvelous script (written by Kubrick, Terry Southern and Peter George). Notable scene: the American President (Sellers) tries to explain to the Soviet Premier over the phone why the A-Bomb is being accidentally dropped on his country. Footnote: Kubrick uses Vera Lynn's WWII recording of "Till We Meet Again" to remarkable effect.

Fail-Safe.**** 111m, b/w. Dir. Sidney Lumet. With Henry Fonda, Dan O'Herlihy, Walter Matthau, Larry Hagman, Frank Overton, Fritz Weaver. Columbia, 1964.

A computer error sends attack orders to a flight of B-52s. Careful attention to detail with close-up camera work.

Best sequence: the president of the United States uses his translator to interpret not only the words but the nuances of speech and mood of the Soviet leader as they talk over the Washington-to-Moscow hotline. Footnote: to avoid a threatened "plagiarism" lawsuit by director Stanley Kubrick, Columbia studios agreed to release his *Dr. Strangelove*, a black comedy version with a similar theme, half a year earlier than Lumet's *Fail-Safe*.

Fat Man and Little Boy.**** 126m, color. Dir. Roland Joffe. With Paul Newman, Dwight Schultz, Bonnie Bedelia, John Cusack. Paramount, 1989.

Focuses on details of the Manhattan Project (researching, building, and testing the atomic bomb) and on the roles of its director, General Leslie Groves, and its chief scientist, J. Robert Oppenheimer. Anti-nuclear and revisionist in approach, the film takes some liberties with real events. Best sequence: a young researcher is fatally injured during an experiment. Although this never happened, the scene and its aftermath are gripping.

A Gathering of Eagles.*** 115m, color. Dir. Delbert Mann. With Rock Hudson, Rod Taylor, Mary Peach, Barry Sullivan, Kevin McCarthy, Henry Silva. Universal, 1963.

The Manhattan Project.* 117m, color. Dir. Marshall Brickman. With John Lithgow, Christopher Collet, Cynthia Nixon. Gladden, 1986.

On the Beach.*** 133m, b/w. Dir. Stanley Kramer. With Gregory Peck, Ava Gardner, Fred Astaire, Anthony Perkins, John Tate, Lola Brooks, Donna Anderson. UA, 1959.

Red Dawn.* 114m, color. Dir. John Milius. With Patrick Swayze, Charlie Sheen, Ben Johnson, Jennifer Gray. UA, 1984.

Strategic Air Command.*** 114m, color. Dir. Anthony Mann. With James Stewart, June Allyson, Frank Lovejoy, Barry Sullivan. Paramount, 1955.

WarGames.** 110m, color. Dir. John Badham. With Matthew Broderick, Dabney Coleman, John Wood. MGM-UA, 1983.

World War III.*** 200m, color. Dir. David Greene. With Rock Hudson, David Soul, Brian Keith, Cathy Lee Crosby. Zoetrope, 1982.

15

War Film Bibliography

The war film, although less studied than the western or the gangster film, has received its share of attention. Both popular and scholarly treatments have taken into account various aspects of the war film: artistic merit, historical accuracy, political influence, behind-the-scenes filmmaking, anecdotes about actors and directors, etc. Five trends in these publications are worth noting. First, more films--and studies of films--focus on World War II than on any other war: it was the object of a vast cinematic effort by a Hollywood still in its golden age and still under the strong influence of the studio system. Second, much critical attention is now being paid to films about the once ignored Vietnam War. Third, the combat film is the most often studied subgenre of the war film. Fourth, a great deal of what is written is gossip-with-photos for fans (both of war and war movies). And fifth, serious study of the war film has increased since the mid-1970s. The following bibliography includes books, essays or chapters in books, and articles that comment about the war film as a genre. It omits narrower studies that focus on only one film or one filmmaker.

Adair, Gilbert. *Hollywood's Vietnam: From* The Green Berets *to* Apocalypse Now. New York: Proteus, 1981. 192pp.

Adair examines the story tradition from films of earlier wars and recounts Hollywood's aversion to movies about Vietnam. Focuses on films in the book's subtitle plus five others: *The Boys in Company C, Coming Home, The Deer Hunter, Go Tell the Spartans.* Heavily illustrated with b/w stills. Filmography of 75 Vietnam-related films.

Aldgate, Anthony, and Jeffrey Richards. *Britain Can Take It: the British Cinema in the Second World War*. New York: Blackwell, 1986. 312pp.

Analyzes "good, popular" films (introd.) that shed light on issues at stake in the war. Although focused on British, the discussion includes American issues as well. Filmography (295-305). Supplemented by Taylor, *Britain and the Cinema in the Second World War*, 1988.

Alloway, Lawrence. *Violent America: the Movies 1946-1964*. New York: Museum of Modern Art, 1971. 95pp.

A slick museum exhibit book. In commenting on violent films in general, Alloway has some interesting things to say about how war films made during the Cold-War era reflect a cynical pragmatism about killing.

Anderegg, Michael, ed. *Inventing Vietnam: Film and Television Constructions of the U.S.-Vietnam War*. Ann Arbor: UMI, 1990. 250pp.

An anthology of essays on the various periods, modes, and genres of film and television depictions. Includes bibliography and filmography.

Aufderheide, Pat. "Good Soldiers." *Seeing Through Movies*. Ed. Mark Crispin Miller. New York: Pantheon, 1991.

Analyzes the positive military image in film.

Auster, Albert, and Leonard Quart. "Hollywood and Vietnam: the Triumph of the Will." *Cineaste* 9.3 (Spring 1979): 4-9.

The authors say films fail at giving "either a complex overview or incisive political perspective on the war" (4). Sees anti-war films as abstract, ambiguous or idiosyncratic vehicles for analyzing the postwar soul and psyche rather than the war itself. Expanded into a book.

————. *How the War Was Remembered: Hollywood and Vietnam*. Westport, CT: Praegar, 1988. 171pp.

Authors study "the social, political, and cultural meaning and value" of films from *China Gate* (1957) through *Full Metal Jacket* (1987) (introd.). After showing that films about earlier wars portrayed simplistic heroes and villains against the ambivalent backdrop of war's grandeur and horror, they claim that Vietnam soldiers went into battle with distorted heroic images from World War II films. They conclude that even the best Vietnam films lack the "broader moral and political vision" (147) to illuminate the political and social issues at the heart of the war. Bibliography and index. Worthwhile study.

Baitaille, Gretchen M., and Charles L. P. Silet. *Images of American Indians on Film*. New York: Garland, 1985. 256pp.

Essays on stereotypes, film reviews, and bibliography of how native Americans have been depicted by Hollywood. Indexed.

Baker, M. Joyce. *Images of Women in Film: the War Years, 1941-45*. Ann Arbor: UMI, 1980. 176pp.

Shows that women were especially esteemed in wartime films; later they were expected to leave the labor force for home and family. Based on 1978 thesis at U of California, Santa Barbara.

Basinger, Jeanine. *The World War Two Combat Film: Anatomy of a Genre*. New York: Columbia UP, 1988. 373pp.

Presents "a history of World War II combat films, tracing their origin and evolution and indicating important information about the system that produced them, the individuals that created them, and the technological developments that changed them" (introd.). Claims that the WWII combat movie established the pattern for all combat movies and influenced the entire concept of the war film. Especially valuable for its fully annotated 54-page chronological filmography of WWII and Korean combat films from *A Yank on the Burma Road* (1942) to *The Final Countdown* (1980). One of the better studies.

Belmans, Jacques. "Cinema and Man at War." *Film Society Review* 7.6 (February 1972): 22-37.

War films show us moral degradation, says Belman, but reflect society's view that war is a necessary "consequence of our state of civilization" (23). Dirty-faced cinematic heroes, as if in a trance, engage in the sensuality of bloodshed. A turgid but interesting discussion.

Bohn, Thomas William. *An Historical and Descriptive Analysis of the "Why We Fight" Series*. New York: Arno, 1977. 258pp.

Analyzes characteristic elements and qualities in Frank Capra's series of documentaries, some of the best military propaganda films ever produced. Commercially republished 1968 dissertation from the U of Wisconsin.

Bonoir, David E., Steven M. Champlin, and Timothy S. Kelly. *The Vietnam Veteran: a History of Neglect*. New York: Praegar, 1984.

Includes a brief overview of film--as well as television and newspaper--coverage of the Vietnam War.

Broderick, Mick. *Nuclear Movies: a Filmography*. Northcote,
    Austral.: Post-Modem, 1988. 135pp.
        International, briefly annotated filmography of 500
    feature films (1914-1988). Begins with an overview (7-29) of
    a genre "concerned with the depiction of nuclear materials
    and/or warfare" (7). Useful time lines of nuclear events.
Brownlow, Kevin. *The War, the West and the Wilderness*. New
    York: Knopf, 1979. 602pp.
        Part one "The War" (1-29) surveys "the documentary
    aspects of certain silent feature films" about WWI,
    especially *The Battle Cry of Peace, Britain Prepared, My
    Four Years in Germany, The Big Parade, Wings, Barbed
    Wire*, and *All Quiet on the Western Front*.
Butler, Ivan. *The War Film*. New York: Barnes, 1974. 191pp.
        Butler surveys chronologically by production date the
    main trends in the treatment of war by fictional cinema,
    shown in Britain and America from 1910 to 1977. Claims
    that film follows, rather than leads, pro- or anti-war
    propaganda. Offers a sketchy but helpful orientation to the
    genre. Illustrated and indexed. Contains a valuable lengthy,
    but selective, filmography arranged by individual wars. A
    solid, reliable study.
Calder, Jenni. *There Must Be a Lone Ranger: the American West
    in Film and Reality*. New York: McGraw-Hill, 1977.
        See the chapter "Taming the Natives" for a good short
    study on the treatment of Indian wars.
Campbell, Craig W. *Reel America and World War I: a
    Comprehensive Filmography and History of Motion Pictures
    in the United States, 1914-1920*. Jefferson, NC: McFarland,
    1985. 303pp.
        Impressive 120-page filmography divided into feature
    films and series, shorts, newsreels, war-related cartoons,
    Liberty Loan specials, and Bolshevik films.
Christensen, Terry. *Reel Politics: American Political Movies from
    Birth of a Nation to Platoon*. New York: Blackwell, 1987.
    244pp.
        A political scientist's selective, chronological survey of
    message-movies includes substantial commentary on war
    films of WWII, Vietnam, and Third-World interventions.
CineBooks. *War Movies*. Evanston: CineBooks, 1989. 218pp.
        An annotated viewer's guide (based on Nash and Ross,
    Motion Picture Guide, 1985) to 500+ war films on video
    cassette.

*The Civil War in Motion Pictures: a Bibliography of Films
Produced in the United States since 1897.* Compiled by
Paul C. Spehr and the Staff of the Motion Picture
Section. Washington, DC: Library of Congress, 1961. 109pp.

Filmography of 250 newsreels and a few feature films.
Indexed by subject, alternative title, and author.

Culbert, David, ed. *Film and Propaganda in America: a
Documentary History.* New York: Greenwood, 1990- . 5
vols. 6000pp.

A reference collection of documents important for
understanding the role of film propaganda during wartime.
Published so far are vol. 1 on WWI and vols. 2 and 3
on WWII. Series continues through the Vietnam conflict.

Deming, Barbara. *Running Away from Myself: a Dream Portrait of
America Drawn from the Films of the Forties.* New York:
Grossman, 1969.

Deming interprets film content psychologically as
wishful dreams. Says that 1940s films unconsciously portray
the condition from which we want to escape as more real
than any hope we have of escaping from it. See especially
these chapters on war heroes: "I'm Not Fighting for
Anything Any More--Except Myself" (8-38) and "I've Got to
Bring Him Home Where He Belongs" (39-71). Detailed
analysis of *Reunion in France* (1942), *Mr. Lucky* (1943),
China (1943), *Passage to Marseille* (1944), *The Imposter*
(1944), and *To Have and Have Not* (1944). An original, if
somewhat perverse, study. Worth a look.

Dick, Bernard. *The Star-Spangled Screen: the American World War
II Film.* Lexington, KY: UP of Kentucky, 1985. 283pp.

Dick examines WWII film "from the standpoint of the
studio system that created it and the culture that
embraced it" (introduction). Good 7-page bibliographical
essay includes archival material and dissertations.

Dittmar, Linda, and Gene Michaud, eds. *From Hanoi to
Hollywood: the Vietnam War in American Film.* New
Brunswick: Rutgers UP, 1990. 387pp.

Anthology of 19 essays on topics like remaking history,
detailed representation, subtext, and documentary. Includes
lengthy chronology (299-349) and filmography (350-75).

Dolan, Edward F., Jr. *Hollywood Goes to War.* New York: Smith,
1985. 192pp.

Coffee-table picture book with text. Focuses especially
on WWI, WWII. Alphabetical filmography and index.
Interesting feature is the list of major awards and
nominations for war films.

Dowling, John. "Nuclear War and Disarmament." *Sightlines* 15.3 (1982): 19-21.

>A useful, selective list of films and videos on the nuclear theme.

_____. *War-Peace Film Guide*. 3rd ed. Chicago: World Without War Council, 1980. 188pp.

>Contains an annotated list of some 300 films, primarily documentaries, about war. Definite anti-war perspective. Valuable for detailed suggestions for using films in study groups and public programs.

Dworkin, Martin S. "Clean Germans and Dirty Politics." *Film Comment* 3.1 (Winter 1965): 36-41.

>Dworkin examines the trend in some American and British WWII films (e.g., *The Desert Fox, The Young Lions, The Enemy Below*, and *I Aim at the Stars*) to depict civilized, apolitical Germans.

Eiserman, Frederick A. *War on Film: Military History Education*. Historical Bibliography No. 6. Fort Leavenworth, KS: U.S. Army Command and General Staff College, 1987. 274pp.

>Intended as a guide for teachers of American military history. Useful primarily for its listing and annotation (somewhat rudimentary) of documentaries, arranged by subjects like general military history, commanders, unit histories, and specific wars.

Evans, Gary. *John Grierson and the National Film Board: the Politics of Wartime Propaganda*. Toronto: U of Toronto P, 1984. 329pp.

>Canadian film propaganda, chronicled in the book, may be compared to the similar U.S. approach.

Farber, Manny. "Movies in Wartime." *New Republic*, 3 January 1944, pp. 16-20.

>A perceptive reviewer calls war film a "slight" genre with four subjects: praising one branch of service, dramatizing actual battles, recounting the resistance of occupied nations, and showing life on the home front; "the first and second produced the best pictures, the fourth the worst and the third the most" (18). Claims that war films borrowed images from westerns and avoided controversial issues. An influential, early study.

Farmer, James H. *Celluloid Wings: the Impact of the Movies on Aviation*. Blue Ridge Summit, PA: Tab, 1984. 369pp.

>Discussed aviation in movies and television from 1908 to 1950. Includes 300+ annotated "air film" titles; lists screen appearances by specific aircraft types.

Furhammer, Leif, and Folke Isaksson. *Politics and Film*. New
York: Praeger, 1971. 257pp.
Analyzes the political content of war films. Discusses
propaganda; images of heroes, allies, and enemies.
Bibliography and index.

Fyne, Robert. "The Unsung Heroes of World War II."
Literature/Film Quarterly 7.2 (1979): 148-54.
Nostalgic, superficial overview of B-production
propaganda films by Monogram, Republic, etc. Useful for
neglected actors and film titles.

Garland, Brock. *War Movies: the Complete Viewer's Guide*. New
York: Facts on File, 1987. 240pp.
A viewer's guide to some 450 films, arranged
alphabetically; entries include date of release, studio,
director, b/w or color designation, actors, trenchant
comments, and a 4-star rating system. Superb index (215-
30) by war and type, contains useful overlapping
subdivisions like "WWII, combat," "WWII, air action," and
"WWII, biography." Good introduction (1-13) argues for a
broad definition of the genre that can include non-combat
and science fiction films. Popular treatment.

Gehring, Wes D., ed. *Handbook of American Film Genres*.
Westport, CT: Greenwood, 1985. 405pp.
Chapter 6, "The World War II Combat Film" (85-102)
by Kathryn Kane, argues persuasively for the combat film--
depicting uniformed military engagement--as the central
genre of war films. Convenient and suggestive discussion of
the genre's dualities, themes, setting, characterization, and
plots. See Kane, *Visions of War* (1982) for a more detailed
treatment along the same lines.

Gillett, John. "Westfront 1957." *Sight and Sound* 27.3 (Winter
1957-1958): 122-27.
Contrasts British and American post-war films and
their treatment of soldiers and war. Americans focus on
neurotic soldiers in a conflagration; British stress the stiff
upper lip of ordinary heroes doing their job.

Gilman, Owen W. Jr., and Lorrie Smith, eds. *America
Rediscovered: Critical Essays on Literature and Film of the
Vietnam War*. New York: Garland, 1990. 386pp.
Collection of essays includes discussion of war films.

Grant, Barry Keith, ed. *Film Genre Reader*. Austin: U of Texas
P, 1986. 425pp.
Twenty-four essays on genre theory and criticism;
amplification of 1977 Scarecrow edition. Maurice Yacowar's

"The Bug in the Rug" that treats carnage-and-destruction war films as part of the genre of disaster films. Includes a 3-page unannotated bibliography of books and articles on war films.

Grossman, Edward. "Bloody Popcorn." *Harper's*, December 1970, pp. 32-40.

A psycho-social discussion of *M*A*S*H*, *Patton*, and *Catch 22* as "a new generation of war movie that became necessary for this peculiar time" (32). Says that war films attempt to satisfy unconscious guilt feelings by letting civilians experience the horrors of war. Insightful.

Hilger, Michael. *The American Indian in Film*. Metuchen, NJ: Scarecrow, 1986. 196pp.

Chronological, briefly annotated filmography reveals that Indians have usually been stereotyped as either "too good or too bad" (introd. 1). Remarkably detailed index allows one to find films that show attacks on U.S. soldiers, cavalry, or forts; films that portray historical events or figures; films that focus on a particular tribe, etc.

Hughes, Robert, ed. *Film, Book 2: Films of Peace and War*. New York: Grove, 1962. 255pp.

Anthology of international scope with a pacifist bent. Contains shooting scripts of censored documentaries: John Huston's *Let There Be Light* and Jean Resnais' *Night and Fog*. Includes the transcript of a roundtable discussion of eminent film professionals on the problems of making effective films about war. Impressive contributors.

Hutton, Paul Andrew. "'Correct in Every Detail': General Custer and Hollywood." *Montana: the Magazine of Western History* 41.1 (Winter 1991): 29-57.

The most complete study of portrayals of Custer on film. Illustrated with lobby cards and stills.

Isaacs, Hermine Rich. "Shadows of War on the Silver Screen." *Theatre Arts* 26.11 (November 1942): 689-96.

A chatty, wartime perspective of films released and under production. Comments on training films of the Signal Corps, information shorts of the Office of War Information, and seized Nazi propaganda films.

Isenberg, Michael T. "An Ambiguous Pacifism: a Retrospective on World War I Films, 1930-38." *Journal of Popular Film* 4 (1975): 98-115.

Material later expanded into the book *War on Film*.

_____. *War on Film: the American Cinema and World War I, 1914-1941*. East Brunswick, NJ: Assoc. UP, 1981. 273pp.

Isenberg uses film as historical evidence about commonly held ideas, attitudes, and values regarding WWI-- a corrective to standard intellectual histories, based on the views of the social elite. Focuses on the history of ideas *in* film rather than the history *of* film (aesthetic judgment). Has chapters on images of the enemy, the ally, and the homefront; anti-war film; women; and comic attitude toward authority. Generously documented; contains filmography and brief bibliography of scripts, manuscripts, special collections, and dissertations. A scholarly treatment, especially useful for historians.

Jackson, Kathy Merlock. *Images of Children in American Film.* Metuchen, NJ: Scarecrow, 1986. 223pp.

Survey of films with significant roles for children; see especially the discussion of wartime films (72-81). Jacksonsays that in post-WWII films, children were portrayed as less innocent.

Jacobs, Lewis. "World War II and the American Film." *Cinema Journal* 7 (Winter 1967-1968): 1-21.

Discusses films that went beyond propaganda and entertainment in their examination of the horrors of fascism and war. Reprinted in Arthur F. McClure, *The Movies: An American Idiom* (Rutherford, NJ: Fairleigh Dickinson UP, 1971).

Jacobson, Herbert L. "Cowboy, Pioneer and American Soldier." *Sight and Sound* 22 (1953): 189-90.

Claims that the screen cowboy's heroic image--self-confidence, inventiveness, and marksmanship--has influenced the expectations and behavior of American soldiers in two world wars.

Jacoby, Monica E., and Frederick C. Fulfer. *Reel Wars: a Facts Quiz Book about War Films.* Middletown, CT: Southfarm, 1986. 78pp.

Collection of 325 trivia questions, indexed by filmmakers and films. Pleasant fluff.

Jeavons, Clyde. *A Pictorial History of War Films.* Secaucus, NJ: Citadel, 1974.

A rambling, chronological essay of films depicting armed conflict in the 20th century. A coffee-table book.

Johnston, Winifred. *Memo on the Movies: War Propaganda, 1914-1939.* Norman, OK: U of Oklahoma P, 1939.

Johnston's is the first booklength treatment of war films published by a university press, but it is lamentably undocumented. Argues that pro-war propaganda in film is controlled by financial and political interests; predicts that U.S. will fight in Europe.

Jones, Ken D., and Arthur F. McClure. *Hollywood at War: the American Motion Picture and World War II*. New York: A.S. Barnes, 1973. 320pp.

A photo book with film credits: identifies actors and their roles, distributor, and director for some 450 influential films, listed in order of *exact* release date, from *Blockade* (17 June 1938) to *A Walk in the Sun* (3 December 1945). One black and white still from each movie. Includes no discussion or analysis. For a more selective and informative treatment, See Morella et al., *The Films of World War II*.

Jowett, Garth. *Film: the Democratic Art*. Boston: Little, 1976. 518pp.

Chapter 3 mentions WWI films, and chapter 12 treats the social history of WWII films thoroughly: politics, propaganda, and entertainment. Argues that film has helped replace small-town values with a national consciousness.

Kane, Kathryn. *Visions of War: Hollywood Combat Films of World War II*. Ann Arbor: U of Michigan P, 1982.

Uses the techniques usually applied to westerns and gangster films to analyze conventions of the WWII combat film: she identifies recurring motifs and formulas of theme, character, setting, and plot. Focuses on *Bataan, Objective, Burma!, Air Force, Guadalcanal Diary, The Story of G.I. Joe*, and *They Were Expendable*. Very suggestive categories.

Kagan, Norman. *The War Film: a Pyramid Illustrated History of the Movies*. New York: Pyramid, 1974. 160pp.

Sketchy treatment of 59 key films, from 1915 to 1970, indicates major trends. Illustrated. Useful quick overview.

King, Larry. "The Battle of Popcorn Bay." *Harper's*, May 1967, pp. 50-54.

A nostalgic and witty account of teenaged moviegoers during WWII. Depicts the audience's total emotional involvement with admittedly simplistic renderings of combat. Notes recurrent film themes and change from blood-and-thunder to fluff films as the war was ending.

Koppes, Clayton R., and Gregory D. Black. *Hollywood Goes to War: How Politics, Profits and Propaganda Shaped World War II Movies*. New York: Free, 1987. 374pp.

The authors deal "with the enduring question of the appropriateness of governmental coercion and censorship of private media, the ways in which American society was mobilized for war, and the consequences of these methods for peace" (pref.). Says that the Office of War Information and box-office receipts influenced the content of Hollywood movies. Claims that if movies reflect society, those "reflections are refracted through multiple mirrors, each of which distorts and sometimes obliterates certain images" (pref.). Bibliography (359-63). Worthwhile.

Kozloff, Max, William Johnson, and Richard Corliss. "Shooting at Wars: Three Views." *Film Quarterly* 21.2 (Winter 1967-68): 27-36.

Analyzes *Battle of Algiers, Far from Vietnam, Les Carabiniers,* and *How I Won the War.*

Kracauer, Siegfried. *From Caligari to Hitler: a Psychological History of the German Film.* Princeton: Princeton UP, 1947. 361pp.

Analysis of how German films 1918-1933 show "deep psychological dispositions" (preface v). Interesting supplement "Propaganda and the Nazi War Film" (273-331) may be compared to the American effort.

Kuiper, John B. "Civil War Films: a Quantitative Description of a Genre." *Journal of the Society of Cinematologists* 5 (1965): 81-89.

A statistical study of 495 Civil War films (1897-1961) shows that the plurality favored the South; 1910-19 was the peak decade (359 released); 1913, the peak year. Contains only tables and classifications.

Landrum, Larry M., and Christine Eynon. "World War II in the Movies: a Selected Bibliography of Sources." *Journal of Popular Film* 1.2 (Spring 1972): 147-53.

Lists 58 annotated sources for further study.

Langman, Larry, and Ed Borg. *Encyclopedia of American War Films.* New York: Garland, 1989. 696pp.

Alphabetically arranged brief entries on 2,000 American-made war films (fiction and documentary) and American military history. Includes mostly plot summaries plus overviews of filmed wars, battles, famous soldiers, and odd topics (e.g., spy films, sea warfare, doctors in war, service comedies), but no entries on key film topics such as filmmakers, studios, and actors. See Appendix C (682-96) for a list of wars and their related films. An excellent companion for scholars and history buffs.

Lewis, Leon, and William David Sherman. "War Movies." In *The Landscape of Contemporary Cinema.* Buffalo: Buffalo Spectrum, 1967. 49-55.

Uses *The Train, The Great Escape,* and *Dr. Strangelove* to show the cycle of post-WWII war movies.

Lingeman, Richard R. *Don't You Know There's a War On? The American Home Front, 1941-1945.* New York: Putnam, 1970.

Shows the social and cultural effect of war on the media. See especially chapter 6 "Will This Picture Help Win the War?" (168-223).

Look Magazine, ed. *Movie Lot to Beachhead: the Motion Picture Goes to War and Prepares for the Future.* Salem, NH: Ayer, 1980; rpt. of 1945 ed.

Generously illustrated study by a popular wartime magazine. Preface by Robert St. John.

McClure, Arthur F. "Hollywood at War: the American Motion Picture and World War II, 1939-1945." *Journal of Popular Film* 1.2 (Spring 1972): 123-35.

Says that films tried to give unity of purpose to the war effort and strength of purpose to the homefront. Reprinted as introduction to Ken D. Jones and Arthur F. McClure. *Hollywood at War: the American Motion Picture and World War II* (New York: A.S. Barnes, 1973).

Madsen, Alex. "Vietnam and the Movies." *Cinema* (U.S.) 4.1 (Spring 1968): 10-13.

The first scholarly article on the films of the Vietnam war. Comments on why Hollywood filmmakers--except for John Wayne--avoided the war.

Manchel, Frank. "A Representative Genre of the Film." Chap 2. in *Film Study: a Resource Guide.* Rutherford, NJ: Fairleigh Dickinson UP, 1973. 55-83.

Defines war films in terms of the Beograd (Belgrade) Film Institute's definition of genre. Manchel says that the treatment and the emphasis of war films from 1914-1970 respond to prevailing public attitudes.

Manvell, Roger. *Films and the Second World War.* New York: A.S. Barnes, 1974. 388pp.

Discusses a cross section of international films, both fictional and factual, to show the popular image of WWII and its motivation. Says that allies and enemies became more psychologically complex in later films. Illustrated. Impressive for its detailed analysis.

Mariani, John. "Let's Not Be Beastly to the Nazis." *Film Comment* 15.1 (January-February 1979): 49-53.

Despite its flippant tone, a revealing survey of the evolution of the Nazi screen image: pre-war films' foreign-accented spies; wartime films' despicable madmen; post-war films' distinction between bad war criminals and good apolitical Germans. Comments briefly on about 12 films.

Mast, Gerald. "The War Abroad, a War at Home (1941-1952)." Part 6 in *The Movies in Our Midst: Documents in the Cultural History of Film in America*. Chicago: U of Chicago P, 1982.

Anthology includes key contemporary essays on wartime film. Frederick C. Othman's "War in the World of Make Believe" (1942) tells how Hollywood dealt with shortages of materials and male actors. Bosley Crowther's "The Movies" (1946) summarizes wartime movie activities. James Agee's "So Proudly We Fail" criticizes the banality of Hollywood's war films. Dorothy B. Jones' "Is Hollywood Growing Up?" (1945) defends Hollywood's achievement in bringing about needed social and political change. Worth reading.

Morella, Joe, Edward Z. Epstein, and John Griggs. *The Films of World War II*. Secaucus, NJ: Citadel, 1973. 249pp.

Identifies studio, producer, director, screenplay writer, and cast for the most significant 100 films, from the pre-war propaganda of *The Last Train from Madrid* (1937) to the post-war adjustment of *The Best Years of Our Lives* (1946). Includes excerpts from two or three contemporary reviews and the authors' brief comments for each film. Eloquent introduction by Judith Crist. One of the better coffee-table books.

Mould, David H. *American Newsfilm, 1914-1919: the Underexposed War*. Dissertations on Film Series. New York: Garland, 1983. 320pp.

Examines how newsreel film was shot and used for propaganda. Discusses the newsreel business, camera equipment, faked war films, and the Committee on Public Information. (M.A. thesis at U of Kansas.)

O'Connor, John E., and Martin A. Jackson, eds. *American History/American Film: Interpreting the Hollywood Image*. New York: Ungar, 1988. 306pp.

Six of the 15 scholarly essays are about war films: *The Big Parade* (1925), *Drums Along the Mohawk* (1939), *Mission to Moscow* (1943), *The Best Years of Our Lives* (1946), *Dr. Strangelove* (1964), and *Platoon* (1986). Introduction by Arthur M. Schlesinger, Jr. Fine anthology.

Olson, James S., and Randy Roberts. "Distorted Images, Missed Opportunities, 1975-1990." Chap. 11 in *Where the Domino Fell: America and Vietnam, 1945-1990*. New York: St. Martin's, 1991. 264-80.

Surveys the popular image of the Vietnam war and American veteran in television and film.

Parish, James Robert. *The Great Combat Pictures: Twentieth-Century Warfare on the Screen*. Metuchen, NJ: Scarecrow, 1990. 476pp.

Discussion of key films. Includes filmography (463-72).

Pendo, Stephen. *Aviation in the Cinema*. Metuchen, NJ: Scarecrow, 1985. 402pp.

An annotated filmography of feature and television films that highlight some aspect of aviation. The index can be used to locate aviation films about particular wars. Bibliography of film reviews and articles (312-70).

Perlmutter, Tom. *War Movies*. Secaucus, NJ: Castle, 1974. 160pp.

A lavishly illustrated book of stills, frame enlargements, posters, one-sheets, double-page foldouts, etc. mostly in black and white. Spiral bound so it lies flat open. Discusses the history and criticism of war films.

Pickard, Roy. *A Companion to the Movies: From 1903 to the Present Day*. London: Lutterworth, 1972. 286pp.

Chapter on "War" (173-92) identifies production facts and comments briefly about ten "milestone" films: *All Quiet on the Western Front* (1930), *Twelve O'Clock High* (1949), *The Wooden Horse* (1950), *The Cruel Sea* (1953), *A Time Out of War* (1954), *The Bridge on the River Kwai* (1957), *Paths of Glory* (1957), *Battle of Britain* (1969), *M*A*S*H* (1970), and *Patton* (1970). Useful Who's Who of filmmakers. British emphasis.

Pitts, Michael R. *Hollywood and American History: a Filmography of Over 250 Motion Pictures Depicting U.S. History*. Jefferson, NC: McFarland, 1984. 333pp.

A generously annotated filmography of feature films (plus some shorts and series). The index contains cross references to specific wars.

Polan, Dana. *Power and Paranoia: History, Narrative, and the American Cinema, 1940-1950*. New York: Columbia UP, 1986. 336pp.

Chapters 2 & 3 deal with war: "Wartime Unity: the Representation of Institutions and the Institutions of Representations" (45-99) and "Narrative Limits: the Fiction of War and the War of Fictions" (101-57).

Ray, Robert B. *A Certain Tendency of the Hollywood Cinema, 1930-1980*. Princeton: Princeton UP, 1985.

Chapter 4, "Classic Hollywood's Holding Pattern: the Combat Films of World War II" (113-25), says combat films made during the war merely recast old melodramas in new settings. Ray shows that wartime films adhered to the morale-boosting, good-teamwork formula established by Howard Hawks' *Only Angels Have Wings* (1939).

Reeves, Nicholas. *Official British Film Propaganda During the First World War*. London: Croom Helm, 1986. 288pp.

Analyzes the "achievements of those film-makers who worked under official sponsorship" (introd. 6). Bibliography (261-78). Useful for comparison with American system.

Renov, Michael. *Hollywood's Wartime Woman: Representation and Ideology*. Ann Arbor: UMI, 1988. 275pp.

See especially chapter 2, "(Her)story: Women at War" (33-47), for the classification of the war-film woman as job stealer, glamour girl, and excess labor.

Rollins, Peter C., ed. *Hollywood as Historian: American Film in a Cultural Context*. Lexington: UP of Kentucky, 1983. 276pp.

Anthology contains scholarly essays on *The Birth of a Nation*, *The Negro Soldier*, *Dr. Strangelove*, and *Apocalypse Now*. Focus is on how American culture influences and is influenced by film.

————. "The Vietnam War: Perceptions Through Literature, Film, and Television." *American Quarterly* 36 (1984): 419-32.

Discusses impact of visual images.

Rubin, Steven Jay. *Combat Films: American Realism, 1945-1970*. Jefferson, NC: McFarland, 1981. 233pp.

Behind-the-scene information about eight films that "present the story of warfare without the glory or the manufactured heroics": history is aim of *A Walk in the Sun* (1945), *Battleground* (1949), *The Longest Day* (1962), *The Great Escape* (1963); psychological motivation of fighting men is the aim of *Twelve O'Clock High* (1949), *The Bridge on the River Kwai* (1957), and *Hell is for Heroes* (1962); *Patton* (1970) is the synthesis. Emphasizes filmmakers' painstaking attempts at accurate, historical detail. Indexed. Great for anecdotal material about script, actors, directors, producers, and shooting. Informative.

Sayre, Nora. *Running Time: Films of the Cold War*. New York: Dial, 1982. 243pp.

A cultural study that notes the recurrent theme of fear and "uncertainty about the nature or the location of our enemies" (25).

Searle, William J. ed. *Search and Clear: Critical Response to Selected Literature and Films of the Vietnam War*. Bowling Green: Bowling Green State UP, 1988. 215pp.

Includes scholarly essays on Vietnam War films. See
Toby C. Herzog, "John Wayne in a Modern *Heart of
Darkness*: the American Soldier in Vietnam" (16-25), and
Louis J. Kern, "MIAs, Myths, and Macho Magic: Post-
Apocalyptic Visions of Vietnam" (37-54).

Shaheen, Jack G., ed. *Nuclear War Films.* Carbondale: Southern
Illinois UP, 1978. 193pp.

An anthology of essays on 12 feature films, from *The
Beginning or the End* (1946) to *Dr. Strangelove* (1964).
Also deals with documentaries and educational shorts about
nuclear threats.

Shain, Russell Earl. *An Analysis of Motion Pictures About War
Released by the American Film Industry, 1930-1970.* New
York: Arno, 1976. 448pp.

Commercially republished 1971 dissertation. Despite the
title, coverage actually begins with 1939. Claims that the
screen image is more influenced by the era of production
(WWII, Cold War-Korea, or Vietnam) than the war
depicted. Includes 9-page review of literature; a filmography
(387-405) of 815 films with notations about which received
assistance from the Department of Defense; and numerous
statistical and informational tables based on the results of
a questionnaire. Suggestive survey is sometimes
overwhelmed by trivial statistics. Bibliography (363-69).

Shindler, Colin. *Hollywood Goes to War: Films and American
Society, 1939-1952.* Boston: Routledge, 1979. 152pp.

A British television producer describes films that
responded to and intensified social, political and ideological
stimuli. Says that studios made what the public wanted.
Interesting discussion from the practitioner's perspective.

Short, K.R.M., ed. *Film & Radio Propaganda in World War II.*
Knoxville: U of Tennessee P, 1983. 341pp.

Essays from a 1982 conference take a global view of
Allied, fascist Europe, and Japanese propaganda.

Shull, Michael S., and David E. Wilt. *Doing Their Bit: Wartime
American Animated Short Films, 1939-1945.* Jefferson, NC:
McFarland, 1987.

Analyzes propaganda in cartoons. Bibliography (172-77).
Filmography (178-80).

Sklar, Robert. *Movie-Made America: a Cultural History of
American Movies.* New York: Random, 1975. 340pp.

Chapter 15, "Hollywood at War for America and at
War With Itself" (249-68), discusses Hollywood's activities in
war service and under suspicion by HUAC. Well written
and carefully documented.

Skogsberg, Bertil. *Wings on the Screen: a Pictorial History of Air Movies*. Trans. George Bisset. San Diego: A.S. Barnes, 1981. 210pp.

Technically knowledgeable and readable text (mostly plot summaries), generously illustrated, discusses films about flying both in peace and war. Includes profile of William Wellman. Indexed by film title, country of origin, filmmaker, and--an unusual feature--by aircraft type.

Smith, Julian. *Looking Away: Hollywood and Vietnam*. New York: Scribner's, 1975. 228pp.

A chatty account of 30 years of moviegoing, peppered with reviews, overheard conversations, awards, earning records. Claims that, although Hollywood ignored the ongoing Vietnam War, the Vietnam experience affected the way film saw previous wars (especially WWI and the Indian wars). Lists movies (1949-68) receiving Department of Defense assistance and quotes from the DoD guidelines. Regardless of its title, this study looks at war film from WWII to imagined nuclear wars. Quirky and fascinating.

Smith, Myron J. *Air War, Southeast Asia, 1961-1973: an Annotated Bibliography and 16mm Film Guide*. Metuchen, NJ: Scarecrow, 1979. 298pp.

Includes a filmography of 77 16mm-films, most made by the military.

Soderbergh, Peter A. "*Aux Armes!* The Rise of the Hollywood War Film, 1916-1930." *South Atlantic Quarterly* 65.4 (Autumn 1966): 509-22.

The rise and development of plot conventions in combat films, illustrating especially the contributions of D.W. Griffith and King Vidor.

Solomon, Stanley J. *Beyond Formula: American Film Genres*. New York: Harcourt, 1976. 310pp.

Chapter 6, "Wars: Hot and Cold" (241-95), analyzes *Hell's Angels* (1930), *Gone With the Wind* (1939), *To Be or Not To Be* (1942), *Casablanca* (1942), *Paths of Glory* (1957), *North by Northwest* (1959), *Dr. Strangelove* (1964), and *Patton* (1970). Claims the genre is relatively formless. Discusses topics like propaganda, war in the air, war as background, victims of war, exiles and isolated heroes.

Spears, Jack. "*The Civil War on the Screen*" *and Other Essays*. South Brunswick, NJ: Barnes, 1972.

Spears surveys (11-116) the Civil War films from *Birth of a Nation* to *Gone With the Wind*; comments on screen images of Lincoln, Lee, Grant, and the common soldier;

includes illustrations and an annotated filmography of 100
films. He also examines (191-213) the career of pug-faced
actor Louis Wolheim, the old soldier in *All Quiet* (1930).

_____. "World War I on the Screen." 2 pts. *Films in Review*
17.5 (May 1966): 274-92; no. 6 (June-July 1966): 347-65.

Spears' analysis of WWI films from 1914 to 1939
shows that pacifism and neutrality gave way to militancy
and disillusion.

Studlar, Gaylyn, and David Desser. "Never Having to Say You're
Sorry: *Rambo*'s Rewriting of the Vietnam War." *Film
Quarterly* 42.1 (Fall 1988): 9-16.

A Freudian explanation of films evoking sympathy for
the American soldier in Vietnam. Claims that their heroic
myth-making follows a well established pattern for
confronting the repressed cultural and psychological trauma
caused by bad wars.

Suid, Lawrence H. *Guts & Glory: Great American War Movies*.
Reading, MA: Addison, 1978. 357pp.

A revised dissertation from Case Western Reserve. Suid
focuses on the creation of the American military image in
72 Hollywood feature films from 1915 to 1978. Analyzes in
detail the relationship between the Hollywood establishment
and the American defense establishment. Based on more
than 300 interviews with people in the film industry
(actors, producers, directors), the media, and the military.
See the chapter on the Marines and John Wayne. Includes
photos and an index. A reliable scholarly book.

_____. "Hollywood and Vietnam." *Film Comment* 15.5
(September-October 1979): 20-25.

Surveys the background of ten films from *The Green
Berets* to *The Deer Hunter*. Says that Vietnam films
cannot glorify the American war effort but can depict
individual bravery and capture the essence of combat.

Taylor, Philip M., ed. *Britain and the Cinema in the Second
World War*. New York: St. Martin's, 1988. 210pp.

Collects essays from a 1985 conference of historians
interested in film. Supplements Aldgate and Richards,
Britain Can Take It, 1986.

Taylor, Richard. *Film Propaganda: Nazi Germany and Soviet
Russia*. New York: Barnes, 1979. 265pp.

Analyzes 8 propaganda films, 4 each from Russia and
Germany. Filmography (234-37), Bibliography (238-57).

Thomas, Tony. *The Cinema of the Sea: a Critical Survey and
Filmography, 1925-1986*. Jefferson, NC: McFarland, 1988.
248pp.

Chapter 6, "War on Water" (96-123) surveys sea-warfare films from *Convoy* (1940) to *The Final Countdown* (1980) with brief commentary, mostly plot summary.

Thorpe, Frances, and Nicholas Pronay, with Clive Coultass. *British Official Films in the Second World War: a Descriptive Catalogue*. Oxford: Clio, 1980. 321pp.

Annotated chronology of about 2,000 Government-sponsored propaganda films. Indexed by titles and credits.

Tyler, Parker. *Magic and Myth in the Movies*. New York: Simon, 1947. 283pp.

See chapter 7 "The Waxworks of War" (132-47). Tyler's Freudian interpretation sees war films as unintentionally emphasizing America's neuroses and psychopathic traits. Fascinating and original study.

Valleau, Marjorie A. *The Spanish Civil War in American and European Films*. Studies in Cinema, No. 18. Ann Arbor: UMI, 1982. 222pp.

Says American treatments of the Spanish Civil War were less political and innovative than their European counterparts. Discusses *The Last Train from Madrid* (1937), *Blockade* (1938), *For Whom the Bell Tolls* (1943), *The Confidential Agent* (1945), *The Angel Wore Red* (1960), and *Behold a Pale Horse* (1964).

VideoHounds. *VideoHounds Golden Movie Retriever, 1991*. Detroit: Visible Ink, 1991.

Useful catalog of 20,000 films available on Beta, VHS, and laserdisc. Annotations are often tongue in cheek. Index includes war-film topics (e.g., anti-war movies, big battles, Central America, military comedy, Nazis, World War I).

Virilio, Paul. *War and Cinema: the Logics of Perception*. Trans. Patrick Camiller. New York: Routledge, 1988. 200pp.

Virilio is concerned "not with film history but with the osmosis between industrialized warfare and cinema" (58). Philosophical discussion says war is life-size cinema; cinema is war. Challenging but unnecessarily turgid text.

Ward, Larry Wayne. *The Motion Picture Goes to War: the U.S. Government Film Effort During World War I*. Ann Arbor: UMI, 1985. 176pp.

Analyzes the activities of the Committee on Public Information (CPI), the U.S. propaganda agency, in creating a Division of Films under George Creel. Ward says that, even with the cooperation of the private film industry, CPI did little to change public opinion.

Wilson, James C. *Vietnam in Prose and Film*. Jefferson, NC: McFarland, 1982. 130pp.

Chapter 10, "Derealizing Vietnam: Hollywood" (79-96), contrasts Vietnam films (like *Coming Home* and *The Deer Hunter*) that distort and sentimentalize with those (like *Apocalypse Now* and *Hearts and Minds*) that reveal complexities of the war.

Winter, J.M. *The Experience of World War I*. New York: Oxford UP, 1988. 256pp.

Contains a brief, insightful survey (238-47) of WWI films (1918 to 1982) in six categories: mythologies, landscapes, camaraderie, romantic themes, noble warriors, pacifism, and pity of war.

Woll, Allen L. *The Hollywood Musical Goes to War*. Chicago: Nelson, 1982. 186pp.

A scholarly essay claims that the most successful musicals, "the dominant genre of wartime Hollywood" (introduction ix), dealt with serious war and economic issues; they were not pure escapism. Filmography (171-74). Bibliography (175-78).

Zinsser, William. *Seen Any Good Movies Lately?* New York: Doubleday, 1958. 239pp.

"She Made Him Forget He Was a Soldier" (183-95), takes a witty look at Hollywood's exaggerated image of the WWII soldier. Pleasant, light reading.

16

General Reference to Film

BOOKS

Film Bibliographies

The bibliographic guides in this section list books about film; they also point to sources for further information about war films and related topics. For exhaustive research, also consult more general bibliographic guides: like *Books in Print* and *Forthcoming Books in Print* (see "War films" in the subject guide), *Bibliographic Index* (see "Moving pictures," "Actors," etc.), *Biography Index* (see "Actors," "Actresses," "Motion picture directors," etc.), and *Essay and General Literature Index* (see "Moving-pictures"). The most selective and convenient bibliography for a specialized topic is often at the end of an individual book or article about war films (see items cited in our chapter "War Film Bibliography"). Most libraries use the subject heading "War films" in their card catalogs (see also: specific wars, e.g., "World War, 1939-1945--Motion pictures and the war"; "Nuclear warfare in motion pictures"; and "Moving-pictures--Plots, themes, etc.").

Armour, Robert A. *Film: A Reference Guide*. Westport, CT: Greenwood, 1980. 251pp.
     Literate bibliographic essays on the history of film, film production, film criticism, film genres, film and related arts, film and society, major actors, directors and producers, major films, international influence on American film, and reference works and periodicals. Includes a brief section on war movies. Contains a chronology of American films and

events; lists research collections. A readable and easy-to-use guide both for the serious student and the beginner.

Cochran, Blake. *Films on War and American Policy*. Washington, DC: American Council on Education, 1940.

The Motion Picture Project of the American Council on Education compiled this bibliography as a guide for teaching about the issues that underlie war and the nation's response to it.

Dyment, Alan R., ed. *The Literature of the Film: A Bibliographical Guide to the Film as Art and Entertainment, 1936-1970*. London: White Lion, 1975. 398pp.

Annotates about 1,300 books, indexed by names and title. Its coverage begins at the cutoff date of the Writers' Program *Film Index*. See also Ellis et al., *Film Book Bibliography* for a fuller treatment of the same subject.

Ellis, Jack C., Charles Derry, and Sharon Kern, eds. *Film Book Bibliography, 1940-1975*. Metuchen, NJ: Scarecrow, 1979. 752pp.

Lists 5,400 books and dissertations on "various aspects of the motion picture." Arranged by subject and then chronology, with annotations for many items; indexed by title, name, and subject. It brings up to date the Writers' Program *Film Index*. More comprehensive than Dyment, *Literature of Film*.

Fielding, Raymond. *A Bibliography of Theses and Dissertations on the Subject of Film, 1916-1979*. Houston, TX: U Film Assoc., U of Houston, 1979. 72pp.

Lists by author, about 1,420 master's theses and doctoral dissertations. Contains a subject index.

Rehrauer, George, ed. *Cinema Booklist*. Metuchen, NJ: Scarecrow, 1972. 473pp. Supplement 1 (1974), 405pp. Supplement 2 (1977), 470pp.

Contains 4,000 annotated items: biographies, autobiographies, and other books, arranged alphabetically by title. Use the most recent supplement's cumulative index by filmscript, subject (see "War"), filmmaker, and author. The annotations are lengthy and informative. Updated by Rehrauer, *Macmillan Film Bibliography*.

———. *The Macmillan Film Bibliography: A Critical Guide to the Literature of the Motion Picture*. New York: Macmillan, 1982. 2 vols. 1501pp.

Contains 7,000 citations, generously annotated. Index in vol. 2 by film, performer, author and subject. Together with the *Cinema Booklist*, the most comprehensive bibliography available.

Writers' Program. *The Film Index: A Bibliography.* Vol. 1. New
    York: Wilson, 1941; rpt. Arno, 1966. 723pp.
        Contains an annotated listing, up to 1936, of books,
    articles, and film titles on the subject of the film as art,
    its history and techniques. See "War Films" (542-58). A
    beautiful job, with helpful cross-references and an
    impressive index. Only vol. 1: *Film as Art* was completed
    by the WPA group; vol. 2: *Film as Industry* (1984) and
    vol. 3: *Film in Society* (1985) have now been published
    (Kraus International) from the group's original index cards
    in the Museum of Modern Art. Brought up to date by
    Ellis et al., *Film Book Bibliography.*

Film Reviews and Criticism

Reviews indicate how favorably a film was first received by the
public; criticism shows how well a film has withstood the test of
time. The library tools in our section "Indexes to Periodical
Literature About Film" are keyed to the periodicals in which a
specific review or piece of criticism originally appeared. However
the best reviews and criticism are often reprinted in convenient
anthologies, available in many libraries. (Note: many film critics
have published collections of their reviews; use bibliographies, card
catalogs or Heinzkill, *Film Criticism: An Index to Critics'
Anthologies,* to find them.) The following anthologies of reviews
and criticism are especially useful for the study of war film.

Agee, James. *Agee on Film: Reviews and Comments by James
    Agee.* New York: Grosset, 1969. 433pp.
        Anthology of reviews by one of the best critics ever,
    originally published in the *Nation* and other periodicals
    (1941-50). (Almost as good are the WWII-year reviews by
    Manny Farber in the *New Republic.*) Includes Agee's
    perceptive comments on WWII films like *Bataan, The Story
    of G.I. Joe,* and *A Guy Named Joe.*
Brownstone, David M., and Irene M. Franck, ed. *Film Review
    Digest Annual.* Millwood, NY: KTO, 1976- . Annual.
        Each volume contains excerpts from about 1,500
    reviews, selected from American, British, and Canadian
    publications. Good for quick overview about a film's
    reception.
Film Review Annual. Englewood Cliffs, NJ: Ozer, 1982- .
    Annual.

Reprints newspaper and magazine reviews of "full-length films released in major markets in the United States" (pref.). Alphabetically listed by film title; indexed by names of critics, actors, directors, etc. Notably absent are any reviews from the *New York Times* and *New Yorker*.

Magill, Frank N., ed. *Magill's Survey of Cinema: Silent Films*. Englewood Cliffs, NJ: Salem, 1982. 3 vols.

_____. *Magill's Survey of Cinema: English Language Films*. Englewood Cliffs, NJ: Salem. First series, 4 vols., 1980. Second series, 6 vols., 1981.

_____. *Magill's Cinema Annual*. Englewood Cliffs, NJ: Salem, 1982- . Annual.

All of the books in the Magill's series contain lengthy, reliable plot summaries (arranged alphabetically by title) and signed summaries of mainstream critical commentary about each film. Indexed by directors, screenwriters, cinematographers, editors, and performers. Useful for its selective list of the most important films. Available in most libraries.

New York Times Film Reviews, 1913-1978. New York: Arno, 1970- . 6 vols. 4961pp.

Reprints facsimiles of about 16,000 reviews from the *New York Times*. Also includes special articles about "best" and award-winning films, and photographs of performers. Indexed by titles, persons, and corporations. Supplemented biennially. Convenient source for reviews of all noteworthy films.

Slide, Anthony, ed. *Selected Film Criticism*. Metuchen, NJ: Scarecrow, 1982- . In progress. 5 vols., ea. 325pp.

Reprints important reviews first published 1896-1950.

Film Handbooks, Histories, and Encyclopedias

Handbooks, histories, and encyclopedias give brief answers to identification problems. For instance, a reader can use these books to find quickly and easily the background of a director, the films in which a certain actress appeared, the historical context of a film, or the meaning of a cinematic term.

American Film Institute Catalog of Motion Pictures produced in the United States. New York: Bowker, 1971-76. In progress.

Lists feature films alphabetically by title, with descriptions, credits, and plot summary. Also indexed by credits and subject headings. When completed in 19 vols. (about 2000pp. each), it will be the definitive source of facts on pictures made between 1893 and 1970.

Bawden, Liz-Anne. *Oxford Companion to Film*. New York: Oxford UP, 1976. 767pp.

Reliable source of information "to answer any query which may occur to the amateur of film" (preface). Widely available.

Halliwell, Leslie. *The Filmgoer's Companion*. 8th ed. New York: Scribner's, 1984. 704pp.

A popular compendium frequently revised. Alphabetical entries on directors, producers, photographers, technical terms and other items.

_____. *Halliwell's Film Guide*. 4th ed. New York: Scribner's, 1983. 936pp.

A frequently revised guide to films by title. Includes facts, synopses, and comments on about 10,000 films.

Jacobs, Lewis. *The Rise of the American Film: A Critical History*. New York: Teachers Coll. P, 1968. 631pp.

Called the "best general (though badly outdated) history of the American film" to 1939 (Isenberg, *War on Film*). Covers WWI in chapter 14, "Movies in the World War" (248-63). Includes footnotes and bibliography.

_____. *The Emergence of Film Art: the Evolution and Development of the Motion Picture as Art, from 1900 to the Present*. Hopkinson, 1979.

Surveys cinema selectively in well organized and informative prose. A fine general introduction.

Katz, Ephraim. *The Film Encyclopedia*. New York: Crowell, 1979. 1266pp.

Offers worldwide coverage, country by country. Includes entries on filmmakers and filmmaking; inventions, organizations, and technical terms; biographies of performers and production staff (but no entries on film titles). The most authoritative film encyclopedia available.

Koningsberg, Ira. *The Complete Film Dictionary*. New York: NAL, 1987. 420pp.

Alphabetical listing of more than 3,500 entries "for the individual who finds pleasure in casually examining literature on the art of the cinema" (preface). Includes brief, readable entries (see "genre" and "war film").

Nash, Jay Robert, and Stanley Ralph Ross. *The Motion Picture Guide, 1927-1983*. Chicago: CineBooks, 1985. 12 vols.

This massive encyclopedia with annual updates is *the* indispensable guide to "English-speaking (and notable foreign) films released theatrically and on video cassette" (foreword). Individual film-title entries summarize plot, relate anecdotes, and comment on significance. Vol. 10 covers silent films. Vols. 11-12 provide an index to proper names, alternate titles, series, and major award nominees. An on-line version is planned.

Sadoul, Georges. *Dictionary of Films*. Trans. and updated by Peter Morris. Berkeley: U of California P, 1972. 432pp.

A selective annotated list by title of some 1,200 of the most influential films; international in scope. Originally published as *Dictionnaire des Films* (1965).

Videolog. San Diego: Trade Service Corp., 1991.

A continually updated encyclopedic list (in looseleaf format) of films on video. Includes bulletins on the video industry and new releases. Cross-indexed by filmmakers and genre. Available for reference at major home video dealers.

Filmmaker Biographies and Individual Films

Book-length studies have been devoted to one director, actor, or film; bibliographies (see our section "Film Bibliographies") and card catalogs are the best ways to find them. The annually updated *Reader's Advisor* (see vol. 3, "Film") lists, with some annotations, the best available books by and about film artists. *Biography Index*, the standard guide to biographies appearing in books and articles, is particularly useful for individuals who have not been the subject of books (see the individual's name or occupation, e.g., "Actors," "Actresses," "Motion picture directors"). A number of series are worth noting for their reliability.

Film Directors and Genre Series. Boston: Hall, 1977- . In progress.

Each volume (about 200pp. ea.) focuses on a director like Charles Chaplin, Stanley Kubrick, and Robert Aldrich. Includes biography, survey of themes and techniques, chronology of films, annotated bibliography.

Filmguide Series. Ed. Harry M. Geduld and Ronald Gottesman. Bloomington: Indiana UP, 1973-77.

A reliable paperback series; each volume is devoted to a single film.

Twayne's Filmmakers Series. Boston: Twayne, 1978- . In
  progress.
    Each volume focuses on a single figure--like Frank
  Capra, Francis Ford Coppola, Laurence Olivier, Samuel
  Goldwyn--involved in the making of film. Supersedes
  Twayne's Theatrical Arts Series.

PERIODICALS

Indexes to Periodical Literature About Film

The indexes in this section help students find film articles
published in periodicals. For exhaustive research, consult more
general (non-film) indexes like *Arts and Humanities Citation Index*,
Index to Book Reviews in the Humanities, *Book Review Index*,
Current Book Review Citations, *Humanities Index*, *Readers' Guide*
(see "Motion pictures--War films," especially for reviews by film
title), *Art Index* (see "Moving pictures"), *British Humanities Index*,
New York Times Index (see "Motion pictures," for recent reviews),
and on-line indexes like *InfoTrac* (see "War films"). The most
selective and valuable listing of articles is often found in a
bibliography included in a pertinent book or article (see our
section "War Film Bibliography").

Batty, Linda, ed. *Retrospective Index to Film Periodicals, 1930-
  1971*. New York: Bowker, 1975. 425pp.
    Indexes retrospectively 14 journals that are currently
  indexed by the *International Index to Film Periodicals*.
  Arranged by film titles, subjects, and book reviews. Only 2
  of the journals go back past 1950.
Bowles, Stephen E., ed. *Index to Critical Film Reviews in British
  and American Film Periodicals, together with: Index to
  Critical Reviews of Books About Film*. New York: Burt
  Franklin, 1975. 3 vols. in 2.
    Film section indexes about 30 periodicals (coverage
  primarily in 1950s and 1960s), arranged by film title, with
  director and reviewer indexes. Book section is arranged by
  title, with author, reviewer and subject indexes.
Brady, Anna et al., eds. *Union List of Film Periodicals: Holdings
  of Selected American Collections*. Westport, CT: Greenwood,
  1984. 316pp.

A list, by subject and title, of the periodical holdings of 35 libraries. Useful for interlibrary loans.

Film Literature Index: A Quarterly Author-Subject Index to International Periodical Literature of Film with Expanded Coverage of Television Periodical Literature. Albany, NY: Filmdex, 1973- . Quarterly, with annual cumulation.

Indexes about 300 film periodicals and 125 general periodicals for articles about film. Also indexes pertinent book reviews. Contains entries for film titles, personal names, and subject (see "War Films"). The best periodical index for film. Updates MacCann and Perry, *New Film Index*. Easier to use than *International Index to Film Periodicals*, 1972- .

Hanson, Patricia King, and Stephen L. Hanson, eds. *Film Review Index. Vol. 1: 1882-1949* (1986), 397pp. *Vol 2: 1950-1985* (1987), 416pp.

A "retrospective bibliography of articles about specific films which have, over the years, established themselves as being of the highest interest to researchers and students" (introd.). Covers some 7,000 feature films in two volumes, each with its separate alphabetical list by film title. Vol. 2 includes cumulative indexes by director, year of film production, and country of film production. Selectively cites the more significant reviews from widely available periodicals (also lists some chapters and book citations). A useful new index.

Heinzkill, Richard, ed. *Film Criticism: An Index to Critics' Anthologies* Metuchen, NJ: Scarecrow, 1975. 151pp.

A guide to essays and reviews that have been published in single-author anthologies. Criticism is indexed by the title of the film it discusses. An easy-to-use index for a limited purpose.

International Index to Film Periodicals, 1972- . New York: Bowker, 1973- . Annual.

Covers 60-85 journals "likely to be of lasting interest from an aesthetic or critical point of view" (preface, 1972). Includes brief abstracts. More selective and stronger in foreign languages than *Film Literature Index*. Arranged by film title, with director, author and subject indexes. Unfortunately, many of the journals indexed are not widely available.

MacCann, Richard Dyer and Edward S. Perry. *New Film Index: A Bibliography of Magazine Articles in English, 1930-1970.* New York: Dutton, 1975. 522pp.

Indexes about 12,000 articles, arranged by subject (see "Films about War and Peace" and "Special Effects"). Also has an author index. Useful for articles (not books) published before the period covered by the *Film Literature Index*. Easy to use.

Periodicals About Film

Each film index (see our section "Indexes to Periodical Literature About Film") lists the titles of periodicals whose contents it indexes; only the more important periodicals are indexed. Another indication of importance is how often articles in a journal are cited by scholars. Here are some of the best sources for articles on war films.

American Film: Journal of the Film and Television Arts.
     Washington, DC: American Film Institute, 1975- . 10/yr.
          Articles by well-known critics and filmmakers; also news on film festivals and the activities of the institute. Popular treatment.
Cineaste. New York, Cineaste. 1967- . Quarterly.
          Specializes in independent, politically oriented commentary about the cinema. Covers foreign film, documentaries, and independent releases.
Film & History. Newark, NJ: New Jersey Institute of Technology, 1972- . Quarterly.
          Interdisciplinary emphasis on historical themes and teaching methods. Articles and 500-word book and film reviews, written by teachers and graduate students. Supersedes "Historians Film Committee Newsletter."
Film Comment. Brookline, MA: Film Comment, 1962- . Quarterly.
          Stylish journal, written from the perspective of the student of culture and history. Features interviews. Lavish illustrations. For scholars and general audience. Available in most libraries.
Film Culture. New York: Box 1499, 1955- . Irregular.
          An intellectual magazine specializing in experimental filmmaking. Speaks with an assertive, independent voice.
Film Quarterly. Berkeley: U of California P, 1945- . Quarterly.
          Contains long, scholarly articles. Includes a useful annual survey of international scholarship. Authoritative and lively. Widely available.

Filmfacts. Los Angeles: U of Southern California, 1938-   .
    Biweekly.
        Contains long plot summaries and excerpts from
    published reviews. Lists film award winners.
Historical Journal of Film, Radio and Television. Abington,
    England: International Association for Audio-Visual Media in
    Historical Research and Education, 1980-   . 3/yr.
        More specialized than *Film & History*. Emphasizes
    elements of mass media as primary sources of evidence for
    historians and social scientists.
Journal of Popular Film and Television. Washington, DC: Heldref,
    1978-   . Quarterly.
        Broad, scholarly journal with lively voice. Great for
    filmographies and bibliographies on topics like war films.
Literature/Film Quarterly. Salisbury, MD: Salisbury State College,
    1973-   . Quarterly.
        Scholarly journal, written especially for students of
    literature. Specializes in screen adaptations of printed
    works. Often devotes issues to a single theme.
Sight and Sound: The International Film Quarterly. London:
    British Film Institute, 1932-   . Quarterly.
        The best journal for British film. Also covers American
    and international film. Authoritative and often cited;
    handsomely printed and widely read.
War, Literature, and the Arts. USAF Academy, CO: U.S. Air
    Force Academy, 1989-   . Biannual.
        A promising, new scholarly journal on war as depicted
    in film and in other art forms like fiction and painting.
    Specialized focus.

Appendix A

Top Ten War Films

A personal list of the best American war films of all time:

Rank	Film
1	*All Quiet on the Western Front* (1930)
2	*The Birth of A Nation* (1915)
3	*The Best Years of Our Lives* (1946)
4	*Platoon* (1986)
5	*Dr. Strangelove* (1964)
6	*Patton* (1970)
7	*Wings* (1927)
8	*A Walk in the Sun* (1945)
9	*The Longest Day* (1962)
10	*She Wore a Yellow Ribbon* (1957)

Appendix B

Best Film for Each War

A personal list of the best film about each American war:

Wars	Film
Early American	*Drums Along the Mohawk* (1939)
Mexican	*The Alamo* (1960)
Civil	*The Birth of A Nation* (1915)
Indian	*She Wore a Yellow Ribbon* (1949)
New Imperial	*The Real Glory* (1939)
World War I	*All Quiet on the Western Front* (1930)
World War II	*Patton* (1970)
Korean	*Pork Chop Hill* (1959)
Vietnam	*Platoon* (1986)
Interventions	*Bananas* (1971)
Nuclear	*Dr. Strangelove* (1964)

Appendix C

Releasing Companies

AA--Allied Artists
AFN--Associated First National Pictures
AIP--American International Pictures
All Star--All Star Features
Anchor--Anchor Film Distributors
AP--Associated Producers
ARC--American Releasing Companies
Argosy--Argosy Productions
Arrow--Arrow Films
Art--Artcraft
Astor--Astor
Astra--Astra Films
Avco--Avco Embassy

BD--British and Dominions
BI--British Instructional
BIP--British International Pictures
BL--British Lion
Box Office--Box Office International
Butterfly--Butterfly
BV--Buena Vista (Walt Disney)

Cannon--Cannon
Cappagariff--Cappagariff
Cavalcade--Cavalcade

Chatham--Chatham
Chester--Chesterfield
Cinema--Cinema Center
Cinemation--Cinemation
Cinerama--Cinerama
Classics--Film Classics
Colony--Colony Pictures
Columbia--Columbia
Cosmo--Cosmopolitan (Hearst)
Crest--Crest
Crown--Crown International

DeMille--DeMille Productions
Disney--Walt Disney Productions

EL--Eagle-Lion
Embassy--Embassy Pictures Corporation
Enterprise--Enterprise Pictures
Excellent--Excellent
Exhibitors--Associated Exhibitors

Famous--Famous Players (and Famous Players Lasky)
Fanfare--Fanfare
FD--First Division
Film V--Film Ventures International
Filmgroup--Filmgroup
Fine--Fine Arts
FN--First National
Fox--20th Century Fox (and Fox Productions)
FP--Forrester-Parant

Gaumont--Gaumont (British)
General--General Film Distributors
GN--Grand National
Goldwyn--Samuel Goldwyn Productions
Gotham--Gotham

Heritage--Heritage

Jewel--Jewel

Key--Key International

Lasky--Lasky Productions (Jesse L. Lasky)

Life Photo--Life Photo
Lippert--Lippert

Mascot--Mascot Films
Maverick--Maverick Pictures International
Metro--Metro
MG--Metro-Goldwyn
MGM--Metro-Goldwyn-Mayer
Monarex--Monarex
Monogram--Monogram
Mutual--Mutual

National--National General
New Cen--New Century
New Era--New Era
Northal--World Northal

Orion--Orion Productions
Oxford--Oxford Exchange

Pathe--Pathe Films (France)
Pioneer--Pioneer Film Corporation
Preferred--Preferred
Producers Distr--Producers Distributing Corporation
Producers Rel--Producers Releasing Corporation
Paramount--Paramount

Radio--Radio Pictures
Real--Real Art
Republic--Republic
Resco--Rescofilm
RKO--RKO Radio Pictures
Roach--Hal Roach
Robbins--Robbins
Rockingham--Rockingham

Sanders--Sanders Brothers Productions
Sanrio--Sanrio Communications
Satori--Satori
Sono--Sonofilms
South Cal--Southern California Pictures
Spartan--Spartan
Syndicate--Syndicate Releasing Company

Temple--Temple
Tiffany--Tiffany
Triangle--Triangle
Tri-Star--Tri-Star

UA--United Artists
Universal--Universal (and Universal International)
UP--United Players
UPTA--United Picture Theatres of America

Venture--Venture Distributors
Vitagraph--Vitagraph

Wardour--Wardour
WB--Warner Brothers (and Warner Brothers Seven Arts)
World--World

Main Index

The main index records pertinent information contained within the body of the text and of the annotations to the filmographies.

Director Index

The director index is a comprehensive guide to directors of films listed in all the filmographies.

Title Index

The title index is a comprehensive guide to film titles listed in all the filmographies.

About the Authors

FRANK J. WETTA, Professor of History and Assistant Dean of Instruction for the Humanities and Social Sciences, Galveston College, has written on military and Civil War history.

STEPHEN J. CURLEY, Associate Professor of English and Department Head of General Academics, Texas A&M University at Galveston, has written articles on literature, popular culture, and film matters.

Recent Titles in
Research Guides in Military Studies

The Peacetime Army, 1900-1941: A Research Guide
Marvin Fletcher

Special Operations and Elite Units, 1939-1988: A Research Guide
Roger Beaumont

The Late 19th Century U.S. Army, 1865-1898: A Research Guide
Joseph G. Dawson III

U.S. Military Logistics, 1607-1991: A Research Guide
Charles R. Shrader